LOVE FOR THE FUTURE

LOVE FOR THE FUTURE

A journey

David Osborne

First published 2013 by
Wild Goose Publications,
Fourth Floor, Savoy House,
140 Sauchiehall Street, Glasgow G2 3DH, UK,
the publishing division of the Iona Community.
Scottish Charity No. SC003794.
Limited Company Reg. No. SC096243.
www.ionabooks.com

ISBN 978-1-84952-263-2

Cover image: Rural Landscape © Liliia Rudchenko/123rf Stock photo.com

Overseas distribution
Australia: Willow Connection Pty Ltd, Unit 4A, 3–9 Kenneth Road, Manly Vale, NSW 2093
New Zealand: Pleroma, Higginson Street, Otane 4170, Central Hawkes Bay
Canada: Bayard Distribution, 10 Lower Spadina Ave., Suite 400, Toronto, Ontario M5V 2Z

Printed by Bell & Bain, Thornliebank, Glasgow

For

Susan Green

Acknowledgements

Numerous people have contributed to this book, many of whose names I don't know. They were people with whom I had a chance conversation, who took part in one of many discussions, or who encouraged and helped me on one of my journeys. But for the long walk that I describe here I particularly wish to thank Bishop John Davies who made it possible, Rob Bianchi who took great interest in the project and joined me for a short way, and the staff at Scargill House, Stanley and Kathleen Hope, Peter Norton, the community at Samye Ling, my sister Margaret Robertson, and the Resident Group at the MacLeod Centre who all provided great hospitality.

The ideas developed in many discussions within the Diocese of Bath and Wells, especially in the Environment Group, and I am particularly indebted to Jane Eastell, Michael Perry, Bernard Joy, Cathy Horder, David Maggs, Melvyn Matthews, Lydia Avery, Adrian Armstrong, Brian Kellock and Nick Denison, the Diocesan Secretary, who was fully behind the development of a diocesan environment policy. Also to Professor Tim Gorringe of Exeter University for his consideration with me of the fundamental ideas in the book.

For help in writing it I wish to thank Sue Dorricott for typing up my original journey notes, Brendan Walsh for suggestions regarding the structure, Bishop Peter Maurice for a short sabbatical that gave me time to think, Elizabeth Thomson for applying her language and literary skills to one of my drafts, Sandra Kramer at Wild Goose Publications for her interest and superb editorial work, and to Susan Green, my colleague, without whose commitment to parish work I would not have had the time to do it.

And for all of it I owe great thanks to Madron who is happy to let her husband go wandering off through Britain and mainland Europe, then hide himself away for hours of writing, and who contributes her own wisdom to my thinking about faith and the environment.

Contents

Introduction

The storm

I was walking along low cliffs and below me the sea was swirling and churning against the rocks. Inland there was rough grass and heather, rising up to a low hill. Above was a big sky, blue and bright with a few racing clouds. I was on Papa Westray in the north of Orkney and walking around the north end of the island. It is a nature reserve, a nesting site for terns and skuas.

There were plenty of skuas. An arctic skua with its pointed tail followed me for some way, coming in close at times and eyeing me as if to make it clear that this was his patch, not mine. I knew not to cut across the heather where the birds nested but to keep to the coast. But as I walked the coastal path I often looked inland as well as out to sea, and I saw very few terns. None on nests. This was not what I was expecting.

As I turned the headland to face west I could see that the clouds that way were bigger and darker. Some were very dark and to the south-west the neighbouring island of Westray was disappearing from sight into falling rain. I increased my pace. I had a waterproof coat with me but would have liked some shelter. This could be fierce. I knew from experience that waterproofs do not always stand up to driving rain. The wind was strong and the clouds were moving fast.

In the centre of the reserve I could see a small building which I took to be a bird observatory. It was probably an old coastguard station, taken over by the RSPB. But to get to it I would have to walk across the nesting grounds and I was not going to do that. Ahead of me, near the shore, I could see what looked like a short wall so I sped up a bit more and headed for that instead.

It was further than I had thought and the rain was beginning to wash across the island as I reached it. And it was, it seemed, simply a single wall of rough stones: a cairn built not into a tower but as a wall, presumably as a shelter. There was no roof, but with the strong wind from the west it was still helpful, and I squatted down and watched the rain, and then hail, rush past me on either side and the heather and grass ahead of me disappear into greyness.

I watched the grey deepen. Small streams formed and flowed through the grass and heather. Around my shelter small pools formed. Then slowly the view ahead cleared and colour returned to the land.

Fifteen minutes later the storm had passed and only the bottoms of my legs were soaked. By the time I had continued along the coast path and then back to the road down the spine of the island they were dry and I could see the rain falling on North Ronaldsay to the east.

Later that afternoon I was at the island's youth hostel and talking to another guest. I commented that although I had seen a number of arctic and great skuas I had seen very few terns. She said that in recent years there had been fewer terns nesting and a possible reason was climate change. The seas were getting warmer so the plankton were moving deeper into the water. This meant that the small fish that eat the plankton were also deeper and that is a problem for terns and some other birds. Terns do not go deep into the water to catch their food; they pluck it from the near the surface. Now that the small fish are no longer there, the terns cannot catch the food they need for their young.

It made sense as an explanation. Detailed research had yet to be done to check whether this was the case, but it was certainly true that there were fewer terns nesting at North Hill on Papa Westray than there had been a few years before. It is also true that the earth's climate is changing, the seas around the British Isles are currently getting warmer, and no one knows how this change will develop.

The north of Papa Westray is rough and wild, but most of the island is fertile farmland. Hoy, in the south of Orkney, has large expanses of moorland but most of Orkney is green and used for raising dairy and beef cattle as it has been for hundreds of years. The islands have been inhabited for thousands of years. That evening I visited the Knap of Howar, an ancient farmstead on the west side of Papa Westray dating from 3800 BC. The island is exposed to the winds and the oceans but the temperature is modified by the Gulf Stream, the ocean current that flows up from the Gulf of Mexico making the north-west coast of Europe considerably warmer than the east coast of North America at the same latitude. But as the climate changes the Gulf Stream could move north or south and Britain could end up with a climate like that of Nova Scotia. No one knows if it will. No one knows what the long-term effects of climate change will be in Orkney, or anywhere else.

I had come to Orkney for a break. I had been interested in wildlife for as long as I could remember and concerned about environmental issues since the '60s, but in the last few years I had been very involved in trying to help my Anglican diocese operate in a more environmentally friendly way. This had involved not only catching the news when it came my way but deliberately finding out what was going on in terms of climate change, greenhouse gases, renewable energy, wildlife conservation, sustainable building methods, and other such issues. It had involved a lot of meetings and discussions, and sometimes arguments. I had also been very involved in developing a 'green group' within my immediate locality. Now I was away on my own for a break.

But there is no getting away from what is happening. Apart from the lack of terns I was aware of the plastic and nylon washed up on the beaches. There has always been flotsam and jetsam, and one of the pleasures of seaside holidays as a child was walking along the shore to see what we could find: bits of rope, whitened wood, a bottle perhaps. But plastic is more insidious. Much of it takes decades to break down, and in the process it forms small granules which cause damage to fish and other sea creatures.

On the boat to Papa Westray I had a conversation with one of the ferrymen. He had worked for years as a fisherman out of Fraserburgh, but there was little work there now. The fish stocks were so depleted that only a few boats went out. I had been to Fraserburgh a few years before and seen the idle trawlers in the docks. And at Wick I had seen pictures of the fishermen and fishwives working to process the millions of herring which were landed each year, but which are now fished out.

There is no getting away from what is happening. On my way to the Knap of Howar I stood for a few minutes and looked around at a peaceful scene. A tractor was ploughing, followed by gulls. The sea was glistening in the sun. Waves were breaking on the shore. A small fishing boat moved slowly southwards. I could feel a fresh wind against my skin. It was very different from the squall a few hours earlier. The squalls come and they go. But it is as if we have a storm coming which is not going to pass by.

Standing there, I ran through in my mind part of the catalogue of problems we face. The climate is changing and it is also clear that the amount of arable land on the earth is reducing year by year. Deserts are increasing in size and in some places soil is being eroded by storms and floods which will become more frequent as the earth's atmosphere warms up. Industrial processes continue to pollute the air and watercourses. Species are disappearing at a fast rate and ecosystems are changing rapidly. The economies of the world depend on manufacturing and, while there is plenty of iron and aluminium in the earth, many metals – particularly the rare earths used in the electronics industry – are in short supply. And oil, on which our agriculture, transport systems and chemical industries depend, is going to run out at some point. The world's human population is getting bigger, although in some places, like Britain, the average age is increasing and that will lead to other problems in the national economies.

Like watching clouds and rain approaching across the sea, we do not know how the storm will hit us but it is on its way. The small changes in sea temperature, the unused fishing boats in the harbours, the litter of plastic on the beaches, the reduced numbers of sea birds, the greater extremes of weather: these are like the first spots of water from an incoming storm.

Which is not what you want to be thinking about on your holidays. Real storms are bad enough. They can spoil your day out. This is stuff that can spoil a life, and not just your own.

The journey

I did not want to be thinking about all this on my holiday in Orkney. I wanted a break. But there it was. There it is. It is the world we live in and the world we are part of. There is no getting away from it. The question is: what do we do?

We can, of course, pretend it is not happening. We can numb our senses with drugs or escape into fantasy worlds and there are plenty of opportunities and encouragements to do so. The pharmaceutical companies, drug barons and entertainment industries are thriving. But if we resist these temptations and keep our eyes and our minds open, what do we do?

We may dream of finding a place where we and a few other people can hold out. A patch of ground somewhere, or an island, where we can grow our food, live in peace and let the storm blow over us while the rest of the world is devastated. But it will not work. We can draw our lines on the ground and put up fences but the rest of the world will ignore them. Food production needs pollinating insects and suitable weather and they take no notice of fences and notices. Wind- and waterborne pollution and nuclear fallout are not stopped by passport control. A billion people on the move, desperate for food and land, are not going to be stopped for ever by border guards. We are part of the world and the world's problems are our problems.

There is in fact no shortage of papers putting forward possible technical solutions to practical problems. For example, there are rapid developments in the field of renewable energy which can reduce our consumption of fossil fuels and so cut down the amount of carbon dioxide we put into the atmosphere. Alterations can be made to cattle feed which mean that the cattle produce less methane: another significant greenhouse gas. Advances in organic agriculture lead towards improvements in soil quality and reductions in the pollutants in the soil and watercourses.

But there are also questions of economics and politics, about how these developments will be paid for and how to balance the desires and needs of individuals with those of society and the world as a whole. And, of course, there are vested interests, ranging from oil and nuclear power companies to individuals who want green energy but do not want to see wind turbines from their bedroom windows or a dam and tidal generators across their local estuary.

There are practical answers to the question of what we should do, and there are political and philosophical debates. There are also plenty of books and magazines which put forward and promote alternative visions of how we could organise ourselves and live more harmoniously with each other and with the other life on this planet. Any bookshop will have some. And there are plenty of people to tell us, one way or another, what is going wrong and how we could do things better: journalists, film-makers, preachers and campaigners. All this is helpful and encouraging. But it seems to me that we also need to come at the question from another angle.

In his book *Why We Disagree About Climate Change*[1] Mike Hulme reckons that there are four myths which shape our different responses to climate change. He is using the term 'myth' in the technical sense, as a story that shapes how we feel and think about things. One is the myth of the Garden of Eden. This is the idea that there was a time in the past when all was lovely but we have messed it up and are now having to live with the consequences. Another is the myth of the Tower of Babel: our human pride has led us to overreach ourselves and the result is chaos and confusion. A third is Apocalypse: that we are facing a catastrophe. And the fourth is Jubilee: that the nature of the crisis means we can think radically about the way we live and do things very differently, for the good of all.

In the Hebrew and Christian scriptures there is a fifth storyline which I think can be helpful. It is that of the Journey. The myth of the Journey is not, of course, restricted to the Jewish and Christian Bibles. It is universal. From Australian Aboriginal songs to Hollywood road movies it emerges time and again in different cultures.

It is the theme of children's songs and adverts for banks. And presumably it arises from the simple fact that we experience life as if we are moving from one place to another. We can look back on where we have been but we cannot be sure where we are going. I suggest that this image is useful in thinking about the ecological crisis we face.

Our future is going to be very different from how life is for us now. This may be because we will be devastated by a storm of environmental disasters and social crises. It may be because we manage to alter our ways of living so that the approaching storm is not so severe. And it may be that we will change our ways and still suffer severe problems as societies and in the world as a whole. They just will not be as bad as if we had simply carried on as before. But one way or another we are moving into a different and challenging future. It is like being on a journey. Where we get to will depend to some extent on the decisions we make. And we do not have a clear idea of where we are heading.

As well as providing an image of our situation, journeys are part of our experience, and we can learn from them. I had travelled to Papa Westray during a four-week break from my normal work. I had known for over a year that I could take this break and had planned on making a long journey. On several occasions in the past I had made a number of long journeys on foot and by bike. During a couple of months twenty years before this I had walked from a village in Shropshire to Iona, making a point of travelling through several places that had been significant in my life so far. Then, ten years later, I had set off determined to walk from Paris to northern Italy. But on that walk I had hit a mental block at Dijon and been unable to face walking any further. After taking a week out at Taizé I had then continued my walk through the Jura mountains and the Alps to Italy, thinking that at any moment I might catch a bus, but never doing so. I had later linked that route up with the Mediterranean at Marseille, and since then, in several stages, had cycled between the Danube and the Atlantic. I could look back on quite a number of long and satisfying journeys.

For this holiday, after weighing up a lot of possibilities, I had planned to cycle through Britain. I had the equipment. I had bought the maps I would need. I had almost booked a bed for the first night but when I dialled the hostel the line was engaged and for some reason I put it off. But then, a few weeks before I was due to go, I dropped that idea and decided to travel by train and boat to the north of Britain, catching up with some old friends, meeting new people and visiting some places I'd been before and others that were new to me, like Papa Westray.

When I was weighing up the possibilities for this journey I had been in two minds. I thought over the long walks and rides I had done before and knew that I had enjoyed them. A part of me wanted to do another one. But I also kept thinking of the discomfort and occasional pain involved, and the anxiety of approaching the end of a day not knowing where I was going to stay for the night, and of sitting in my hostel room in Dijon unable to face the thought of picking up my rucksack for another day's slog through a strange countryside. I knew, though I could not think it through clearly, that making a long journey is not just a matter of skills, equipment and physical stamina. It is a matter of attitude. It is a mental and spiritual endeavour. And eventually I realised that I did not at that time have the attitude and resources I would need to spend six weeks in the saddle or walking trackways.

Sports people and trainers know about mental attitude. Winning matches and races, climbing mountains and sailing round the world are not just a matter of skill. Attitude and emotional and spiritual resources are just as important, if not more so. The confidence of footballers before a big match may seem tedious or unrealistic to sceptical viewers who do not really reckon their chances very highly, but it is important for the team. If they think they are likely to lose, their chances of doing so are higher. Anyone who speaks or writes about an epic journey will describe the times when they were stretched to the limit, and how they somehow found the resources to continue, to overcome their tiredness, or their loneliness and fear.

So it is for the journey into the future. To respond as a society and as individuals to the ecological crisis, we need an understanding of what is happening and we need technological innovation. These are crucially important. We need the skills, the energy and the equipment. But we also need suitable attitudes. We need to be able to face up to what is happening. And having done so, we need to be able to deal with the fears, frustration and sadness we feel. We need to be able to assess possibilities, and make changes, to avoid being paralysed or debilitated by what we know is happening or the fear of what might happen. Our survival and the health of life on the earth depend not just on ideas and technological changes but also on our attitudes, and on finding the mental and spiritual resources to be able to deal with what is happening.

That is what this book is about.

The book

It seems to me that if we can think of life as being like a journey we can possibly draw from our experience of real journeys lessons that are helpful for life as a whole. And that is what I will aim to do in this book. My basic question is: what can we do that will help us be people who respond in the best way to the ecological crisis that we are in? And to try to answer that I will draw on two particular sources.

First, I will reflect on my own experience of long journeys, and on one in particular: the walk I did from my home in England to the Scottish island of Iona. At the same time I will draw to some extent on insights of the Hebrew and Christian faiths as they are found in the Bible and in the history of the church. The two are closely linked. My walk to Iona was a pilgrimage which I made as a Christian who was concerned about environmental issues, while the image of the journey is very strong in many of the books in the Bible.

The stories of journeys in the Hebrew and Christian scriptures operate on two levels. Journeys often provide the big story, but then episodes within the big story are also significant. The Hebrews at a harvest festival would recite a prayer which began, 'A wandering Aramean was my father'. They would recognise that their roots were among herders who travelled from place to place. But also the individual stories of these Patriarchs – Abraham, Isaac and Jacob – form moral or theological tales. The journey of the Israelites from Egypt is one of the formative narratives of the Hebrew people, but also many of the details of the story – the complaining, the idolatry, the lack of faith – are timeless images of how the people of God sometimes behave whether or not they are on an actual journey.

The gospels also take the form of travel narratives, of Jesus walking round Palestine and finally going up to Jerusalem, to his death. But within those overall narratives are smaller stories of people Jesus meets, of challenges and questions, and of how Jesus responded in different situations. Each one is told because in itself it is thought to provide valuable insight for life as a whole.

Then, within both the Christian church and the Jewish faith, pilgrimage has at times been a common practice, as it has in other religions. Millions of people make journeys to well known pilgrimage sites: Compostela, Rome, Jerusalem, Mecca, Benares. Others make smaller journeys to places important for them, their family or their religious group. Traditionally, the point of a pilgrimage in many religions is not simply to get to the end. The journey itself is hopefully a source of insight and a means to personal or spiritual growth. The hope is that pilgrims return wiser and able to live better the lives that remain ahead of them. So, drawing on the experience of a pilgrimage to try to learn how we might be able to respond to the crisis of our time has a long pedigree, even though our crisis is not one that has been faced by people before.

The journey I made from Shropshire to Iona was the first of several long journeys I have made. Compared to the epic walks of some people – Nick Crane walking from Compostela to Istanbul along the mountains[2], William Dalrymple following on foot the route of crusader Robert Cuthose from Rouen to Jerusalem[3], Hamish Brown climbing all the Munros in one journey without the use of a motor[4] – this walk was a very modest affair. I do not offer the story as a tale of a great achievement but simply as a journey worth thinking about, although it was both interesting and demanding at the time.

More important than the walk was what came out of it for me and possibly for other people: not simply ideas but things that we can do, whether or not we are on an actual journey, which will help us on the metaphorical journey that is our life. This book therefore includes some suggestions that you, if you continue to read it, might wish to take up. After each chapter of the story there is a short section of resources. Some of these are practical: exercises if you like. There will also be details of several books which are, in one way or another, relevant to what I am talking about and may be of interest or help to anyone who is either wanting to read more or is looking for practical ideas. Some of these books are theoretical and others are workbooks.

There will also be references to several relevant passages from the Bible. These don't simply relate to isolated verses that I have quoted, but to longer passages to which I may have referred or alluded and which some readers might want to look at for themselves. Each reference has a few notes to give it some kind of context or background. The Bible is a collection of books of different kinds and from different periods spanning over a thousand years. I do not believe it is fair or helpful simply to pull a sentence from here and another from there and expect them to clinch an argument or answer a question. The Bible needs to be treated with more respect than that. I have occasionally quoted single sentences from the Bible. I cannot resist it. The Bible is full of good lines. But the Bible passages mentioned after each chapter are there so you can, if you wish, check out for yourself how what I am saying relates to the Bible.

But you do not need to do that. You can simply read the story and, I hope, enjoy it. Or you can read the narrative through and then go back to some of the other material if there is something you want to take further. You might find that each chapter makes a good story on its own. You can use the book in a number of ways.

I made my long walk and I was glad I had. You do not have to do that. But you are on a kind of journey whether you like it or not. I hope that what I learnt from my journey will be helpful for yours.

Caught in the storm of Papa Westray I found shelter behind a cairn. I was fairly confident that the storm would pass quite quickly. But I have been walking on days when the rain has been relentless and I have had no expectation that it would stop at all. I have also walked under clear blue skies and a burning sun. In both cases, from time to time you have to stop and find shelter for a while if you can. It is a way of recharging and often an opportunity for planning out the next bit of the journey.

Pilgrimages as a whole are like that. They are time out from the normal pattern of life. They provide an opportunity to reflect on the life you normally live and to which you will probably return, hopefully with new energy and imagination.

Perhaps this book can be like that too. The questions and debates about the environment sometimes seem like a storm in themselves – a mass of interconnected problems, all needing attention. This book is not intended to be an escape, but a shelter. It might enable you to sit out of the storm for a short while and discover how you can find new energy for the next stages of the journey. Like a pilgrimage, it might help you to see normal life in a new way, and to live differently.

References

1. Mike Hulme, *Why We Disagree About Climate Change* (Cambridge: Cambridge University Press, 2009)
2. Nicholas Crane, *Clear Waters Rising: A mountain walk across Europe* (London: Penguin, 1997)
3. Preamble to William Dalrymple, *In Xanadu: A quest* (London: Collins, 1981)
4. Hamish Brown, *Hamish's Mountain Walk: The first traverse of all the Scottish Munros in one journey* (London: Paladin, 1980)

One

Opening Wonder

My walk from Shropshire to Iona began at the edge of the Cheshire Plain. I had spent a lot of time looking at Cheshire. By 1992 I had lived for eight years in a vicarage in a village called Wrockwardine, perched on the top of a Shropshire hill. It was not one of those big rambling Victorian vicarages with a wine cellar and separate stairs for the servants. That one had been sold off some years before to a jeweller from Birmingham. This was a 1960s' vicarage, built on a plot of land at the corner of the village. The architects who had designed it had been given a fairly free rein and they had chosen to build it with long corridors on both floors and large windows which faced east and north. On the south-west corner, the part which would catch the warmest of the sun, they had put the pantry and coal house. So it was not the most environmentally friendly of houses and it cost a small fortune to keep above freezing in the winter. But it did mean that my study had a view northwards for many miles.

I never managed to work out how many miles because there were few landmarks in the far distance. The land simply stretched away, field after field, trees and hedges, till it all became a green haze. There were a few low hills, some of which I tried to identify on a map from time to time, but I was never confident about where they were, except for Clive, with its church spire at the east end of the long hill. And in the far distance, on a very clear day, I could see a white structure which I thought might be Jodrell Bank radio telescope, but I was not sure. My view was across the north of Shropshire and into Cheshire, over the Cheshire Plain.

Beyond it, I knew, were Manchester and Liverpool, and beyond them the Pennines and the Lake District. And then the hills of Southern Scotland. I could imagine the land stretching away. I had travelled it many times, by car and by train. I had lived and worked in Edinburgh at one time. I had then studied in Birmingham and had travelled the M6 north and south since the days when it started in Walsall and ended in Carnforth. Then it was the old A6 up over Shap Fell, where there had been a transport cafe which sold amazing bread pudding. I had memories of Carlisle as both a friendly haven and a source of traffic holdups. I had travelled the main road through the borders in many weathers, including following a snowplough for twenty miles in a mini with two other students and a term's worth of luggage.

More recently I had travelled north not so much to Edinburgh but to Iona, the island in the West of Scotland where St Columba had founded his monastery in the sixth century and George MacLeod had begun rebuilding the abbey in the 1930s. The island, the abbey, the play of light on the water, the prayers and songs in the church and the attitudes and faith style of the Iona Community had deeply impressed me the first time I went there. And the second.

The first journey to Iona had been with my wife and two children. We had travelled by car to Edinburgh, making it a pilgrimage through significant Christian sites: Lichfield, Durham and Lindisfarne. Then from Edinburgh we had gone by train and boat to Iona. A year or so later we had taken a few friends, travelling through the night by train. Now I wanted to go back again, and I had the idea that I might do it on foot. I knew that I might be able to get three months as a sabbatical away from my work and this might appeal to my bishop as a suitable project for that time. And it did. So, after an exchange of letters, I was committed to giving it a go.

It took a lot of preparation – looking at maps, finding out about accommodation, saving money, working out what I would need to take, and making arrangements for my work to be done while I was away. I did some fitness training, but training for a long walk is hard. You can run and do weight exercises but when you are walking you do not need your muscles to be geared for speed, like running, or for strength, like when you are lifting weights. You need your muscles to be geared for, well, walking. And the only way to prepare for that is to walk, and that takes time.

With my normal job I didn't have much time to walk. Most of the time I needed to drive, or ride a bike. But I did what I could. When I had time I walked or ran down the lanes, and several times I walked from my house, down the valley to the south and up and over the much bigger hill beyond, known as the Wrekin. From the top the view northwards stretched much further, but still it always disappeared across the plain into a green haze. I expected that the first part of the way north would not be the most exciting landscape.

Eventually, early one morning just after Easter, I headed northwards with boots and rucksack. I saw Bill Boyd bringing his cows in for milking. There were a few cars on the roads as people set off early for work in Birmingham. The *Today* programme had already begun on Radio 4. Five Los Angeles policemen were on trial for beating a suspect after a car chase. An oil tug off New Jersey had spilt 60,000 barrels of oil in an area severely damaged by an oil leak two years earlier. And across the world government officers and non-governmental organisations were preparing for the first Earth Summit in Rio.

In Shropshire it was cloudy with a look of rain. Down by the river I heard a curlew and noticed four Canada geese grazing. Three miles on I saw my first swallow of the year. I followed footpaths and small roads. Hedges and trees were coming into leaf. There were daffodils and primroses. And slowly, very slowly, the Wrekin behind me got smaller as I inched my way northwards. I would spend that first day walking in Shropshire. The next day I would cross into Cheshire, then it would be several days till I got to Manchester. And that would be the start. I reckoned that I would feel I was getting somewhere when I was in the Pennines. Before that I would have to plod across the Cheshire Plain.

To someone who does not know Britain, crossing the Cheshire Plain might sound dramatic, like crossing the Kalahari or the Appalachians. But it is not. The most remarkable thing about the Cheshire Plain is how unremarkable it is. It is flat, but not dramatically flat like the Fens or the Somerset Levels with their peaty ditches and big skies. There are trees, but no forests, and there are hills, but none that you would noticeably climb or that would give you a good view from the top. The whole area, stretching from Wrockwardine to the Dee, is like the bottom of a great drained pond – which is what it is.

Before the last ice age water from the Cambrian Mountains flowed northwards into the sea at what is now the Dee estuary. But then, some fifteen thousand years ago, an ice sheet blocked the flow of water and it built up into a great lake. Finally the water forced a way out to the south, through what is now the Ironbridge Gorge, and ever since then the waters of the River Severn have flowed from Wales down to the sea in the south at the Bristol Channel. The ice sheet retreated, the lake drained and the Cheshire Basin was formed. To the west there are drumlins, where water from the melting ice washed the debris into rounded hillocks. There is a low ridge in the centre of the plain, but mostly the land is fairly level and, after generations of farming, it is mile after mile of fields, hedges, farms, villages and small towns. Crossing this was not going to be physically hard. It was, I feared, going to be a bit boring. It was simply land I had to cross in order to make it to the more interesting hills of Lancashire.

For those who live there, no doubt there are unusual landmarks that remind them they are approaching home, but to someone passing through, that part of the journey north or south is simply something that needs to be done. When I travelled it regularly in the late '60s, either as a hitchhiker in trucks or driving my own old van, there were mileage signs at regular intervals. Just when you were forgetting how uninteresting the journey was and had stopped calculating how much longer it might take to get to the end, a board reminded you of how far you still had to travel. The distance markers encouraged you to reduce your journey to counting off the miles.

I was tempted to do that as I left that morning. I did not know how far I had to go altogether. Five hundred miles or so, perhaps. I hadn't worked it out. I had three months off, which ought to be plenty of time. I knew it was about eighty miles to the Pennines beyond Manchester, and it was tempting to start counting down.

But I didn't.

Several things helped me pay attention to my immediate surroundings. One was the bird life. Apart from the curlew and what I thought was perhaps a shelduck, there was nothing unusual for that kind of country, but there was plenty of it. There were thrushes, and finches of various kinds. Moorhens and mallards. And having seen one swallow I kept alert for other returning migrants: swallows, martins, swifts. The sound of a cuckoo. Elusive warblers in the bushes.

It was spring. In places the hawthorn buds were opening, but in others they were still tightly closed. There was more than a hint of green in some trees, as leaves were slowly opening. The oaks were a mustard colour, beeches almost yellow in their freshness. Cow parsley was turning the roadsides white. There were washes of yellow and blue in the more sheltered banks, and occasionally violets. Walking beside a hedgerow I noticed the variety of plants: as well as hawthorn there was elder, blackthorn, elm and oak. The variety gave a clue to the age of the hedge. Even where the hedges had an initial appearance of being planted at one time there were stretches of much older hedgerow, and in places the lanes had all the signs of being once significant roads, with wide verges.

In the hedges there were also signs of human activity long passed, and long forgotten. A short stretch of wall. A tumbledown shed. Old posts. A now-redundant bridge over a ditch. And the farm buildings and the houses were of a range of ages: some with hardly a straight wall and small windows; others large and speaking of nineteenth-century wealth; new homes with large '60s' windows and '80s' double garages. All reminders that this landscape had not just happened but had been shaped by people over many centuries, and was continuing to be shaped and altered.

The sky also helped me pay attention to where I was. The cloud was a continually changing display of light and movement. Much of the time it looked like it might rain, and it did occasionally, but only in showers. And reading the road signs I came to relish the place names: Child's Ercall, Waters Upton, Great Bolas,

Hungryhatton.

I was also helped to resist mile-crunching by the fact that after three hours on the road I lost my map. I deliberately did not want to keep it in my hand. I have seen other walkers do that, and had read John Merrill saying how he always held his map so he would not waste a moment when he came to a junction and had to decide his way. To me that made sense for someone orienteering, and racing against the clock, but I was on a long walk. I did not want to be thinking of myself as creeping slowly up a map. I wanted to be where I was, and take notice of what I could see and hear and feel. I was on a pilgrimage on foot, and my map would help me find my way when necessary. But then I lost it anyway.

I don't know how. At one junction I had it, and stuffed it into my belt. A bit later on I didn't. And when I walked back I couldn't see it anywhere. So that was it. No map and five hundred miles to go.

I knew I was heading for Market Drayton, which was more or less to the north, and if I kept walking northwards it would appear on signposts. Then when I had walked far enough I would walk onto my next map. I was surprised to find how relaxed I was about it. In my normal working mode this would have been a stress. It would have been holding me up. It would have been a foolish error on my part. Now, it was OK. I would just walk on, and see what happened.

As it was, what happened was that I met a couple out looking for a dog. 'Had I seen a black Labrador?' No sorry. But had they seen a map? I ended up with a cup of coffee and an Ordnance Survey map which I promised to post back when I had walked off it. Then five miles later, while I was sitting in a bus shelter eating a chocolate egg, a man came past with a dog asking if I had any idea who the owner of this wandering black Labrador was. I did, and I told him. As I set off my map-lenders arrived and were reunited with their pet.

All this helped me stay aware that I was not five hundred miles short of my destination, but I was where I was. Interesting things were happening. There were good things to be seen. Presumably there would be more to follow. North Shropshire and Cheshire were not boring green miles to be trudged across but were full of interesting and enjoyable sights.

Some months before this I had signed up for an in-service training course which was billed as a 'contemplative walk'. There was a lot of open countryside in the region but this course took place in Bilston – not the first place I would have thought of for a contemplative walk. Bilston is located in the middle of the conurbation between Wolverhampton and Birmingham and at that time it was particularly depressed. Much of the heavy industry of the Midlands was collapsing as a result of a major recession. There was high unemployment, a lot of poverty and not a lot of open space.

The course began in a church hall. There was some talk and discussion about how our minds tend to drift off into planning for the future or turning over past events. We then thought about how we can use our senses to help keep ourselves in the present moment. We spent a period sitting in silence simply listening to the sounds coming into or from within the room. Then we were to go out and walk around the area alone or in pairs and without speaking. We could stop a while if we wanted to, but the suggestion was that we simply keep walking at a steady and gentle pace. We had no purpose or instruction other than to look and listen and feel the place.

It was a hot day and I remember finding myself after a short while walking down the main street. Trucks rumbled past, stirring up dust and pumping out fumes. Then I wove my way back through a housing estate to the hall where we were to meet up again. I was out for perhaps three-quarters of an hour. It was not long but Bilston was never the same for me after that walk.

Two things particularly stayed in my mind. One was a plant breaking through the rubble on a derelict piece of land. The plant was nothing special as far as I knew. I don't know what it was. But it was life amidst the dust, brick and concrete. The sight stayed in my mind.

The other was a young woman with a pram. She was obviously not well off and her clothes were cheap. The pram was not new but it was brilliantly clean and her baby inside was covered with a smooth white shawl. What I saw was the love of a mother for her baby and her determination to care for it well in a bad environment and with few resources.

I knew that if I had been rushing for a bus, or planning a talk, or talking to a companion, I would have missed them both. Instead I was walking contemplatively, and was open to what Bilston had to offer. Now I was walking through North Shropshire and in contemplative mode again.

Contemplation has been described as 'a long, loving look at what is real'. It is not specifically religious in the sense of requiring a particular religious doctrine or organisation. Many teachers who have specialised in contemplation, like Thomas Merton or Richard Rohr, while being religious themselves, are clear that by contemplation they are not talking about what many people would describe as a 'religious' activity. It is not something that takes place only in churches and shrines or necessarily involves thoughts of God. It is a way of being in a particular place and time, and of relating to what is around. It is a way of being present in which you are not concerned to change or analyse or understand what you see, but to observe it as it is, and to respect and appreciate it.

Some years after this walk I was in Burgundy with Madron, my wife. We went to a wine co-operative to stock up with a few bottles to take home with us. This was not a fancy place with a name known to the wine cognoscenti. It was fairly basic. Locals were filling up plastic cans from two hoses like drivers at a garage. There were also plenty of bottles to choose from and the opportunity to taste before buying.

I had never been to a wine-tasting. Coming from a family that had one bottle of wine a year, at Christmas, I had grown up thinking of beer as the basic drink. But I had developed a taste for wine and we always took some home from a holiday in France. Presented with an array of different wines, but all from the same area, we decided to do some tasting and make some comparisons. So I had a sample and the man serving suggested how I might first smell it, then drink it so as to explore the blend of flavours. Which I did.

I had never tasted wine like it. It was fantastic. The flavour was full on, and rich. Wonderful stuff. Yes please: a couple of cases. I discovered later that it was indeed good wine, but not that good. Now that I have come to drink other wines in the same way, focusing on the smell and the flavour, I have realised that it was not so much the wine but the way that I was drinking it. Paying attention to what I was doing. To the taste of the present moment.

I have never heard of contemplative drinking, or contemplative eating, but why not? I remember a letter by a Frenchman in a newspaper correspondence about binge drinking. He suggested that the problem was principally that the drinkers had never learnt how to savour the taste of what they were drinking so they just poured it down. Similarly a psychotherapist friend of mine reckons that one of the causes of obesity is that people have grown up rushing their food so they do not taste it. Eating has become something people do to fill their stomachs, not something they deliberately set out to enjoy. It is certainly interesting that in a culture like that of France, in which traditionally great attention is paid to the flavour of food and wine, there are far fewer problems of binge drinking and less obesity.

What the man wrote was directly about binge drinking but I suspect the principle might also apply to other aspects of our culture. Our way of life is based on consuming more and more. News reports will tell us whether the last month was a good or a bad one for the High Street. We suffer a continual onslaught of adverts trying to induce us to buy more. We have grasped only a fraction of what our latest electronic gadget can do and a new model is on the market which will do even more, more quickly. Landfill sites are filling up, recycling centres work at a furious pace. Much of the traffic on the roads is vehicles carrying goods from one place to another. Scattered around Britain now are lockups where people can keep things which they don't have room for in their houses. We are like binge drinkers, not appreciating what we have but continually reaching out for more.

I don't know who the man was who served the wine in the cave in Burgundy but I know the name of one man who helped me to see in a new and contemplative way. That was J.M.W. Turner. A couple of years before I set off on my walk to Iona I was persuaded to go on a coach trip to the Tate Gallery in London to see a Turner exhibition. The journey involved travelling down the M1 which, in my opinion, could claim the prize for the most boring stretch of motorway in Britain. Fortunately I was able to pass the time in an interesting conversation with the homoeopath sitting next to me. And the exhibition was well worth the journey.

I had been to few exhibitions at that time and was struck by how different the real paintings were from what you see in a book of prints. One or two, which I had not thought twice about when I had seen them as book illustrations, really grabbed my attention. But I was also struck by Turner's skies in many of his less famous paintings. They glowed. They were glorious. The interplay of light and shadow and their depth held my attention, and I simply stood or sat and looked for minutes at a time.

On the way home I spoke to no one. I sat on the coach looking out and simply enjoying the skies above Bedfordshire as the light slowly changed into evening and early night. And now as I walked across North Shropshire and Cheshire I enjoyed the changing skies and the land below them.

For me walking can be a contemplative activity, and one I take to easily. For others walking might not be anything of the sort. Two weeks on from Cheshire I was sitting on a hillside in Yorkshire, listening to the wind and the birds, and watching the play of light on the land below. Slowly another sound came into my consciousness and gradually increased. Two people were walking along the path above me and talking continuously. As soon as one stopped the other began. Sometimes they both spoke together. They passed above me and the sound faded as they continued on their way.

It may be that their animated conversation was doing great things for them both. Perhaps they were solving a political or scientific problem and thereby doing something significant for the world. As a result of their walk their relationship with each other, or with other people in their circles, may well have been stronger. I do not want to criticise what they were doing. Maybe they could not have talked that well if they had been sitting over a cup of tea or a beer. But their walk was not contemplative.

I suspect that a contemplative walk needs to be taken alone or in silence. On this journey to Iona I was alone almost all the time. There was no question of my passing the time in animated conversation with someone else. However, I could have spent my time solving problems in my head, or rehearsing imaginary conversations, or weighing up the pros and cons of various courses of action, or of routes. And some of the time I did. There are various other ways I could have spent my time as well – many of them creative. Contemplation is just one way of engaging with one's surroundings when walking. But one outcome of it is that you come to appreciate the place where you are.

There are many other ways of contemplating which also give that sense of appreciation. As a young man Peter Scott was both a wildfowler and an artist. He hunted birds and he painted them. In his autobiography, *The Eye of the Wind*, he tells of an occasion when he was hunting with a friend and came to two birds he had shot and wounded.[1] What he found was that he now wanted to keep them alive. He succeeded in doing so and began a new course in his life which was concerned with preserving the lives of birds rather than killing them. It involved a lot of scientific work and the organisation that he founded, now the Wildfowl and Wetlands Trust, has always been at the forefront of research on wild birds. Scott stopped hunting and devoted his life to helping birds survive and helping other people appreciate them.

It is worth wondering whether, if Scott had not been a painter as well as a hunter, his life would have changed as it did. There is no way of knowing, but he clearly developed a great appreciation of birds as they were in themselves, and not simply as potential meals. And as he worked in conservation, doing work that required a great deal of focused attention, of debate and argument, of study and presentation, he also continued painting. He carried on with the contemplative activity which strengthened his appreciation of the birds he was working for, and perhaps energised him for the work he was doing.

Painting, sketching, perhaps photography, birdwatching, skywatching, listening to the wind or the sea, feeling the texture of sand or soil beneath one's feet – or the water when you are swimming – eating, drinking, these can all be contemplative, as well as simply sitting and looking at what is there. And I think the effect is fourfold.

Contemplation can help bring us into the present and away from the endless possibilities and memories that buzz around in our heads. I suspect that my calm acceptance of losing my map was partly a result of the fact that I had spent a couple of hours walking contemplatively rather than purposefully travelling to a schedule or plan.

Often contemplation will give a deeper appreciation of what we see or feel, as it did for me walking the streets of Bilston and the lanes of Shropshire. Apart from any other consequences, that in itself can be pleasurable.

But contemplation also affects what we do. Appreciation leads on to a respect for things in themselves. In the corner of the garden next to where I live now there was a scarlet hawthorn tree. Each May it produced red blossom which I enjoyed as I walked out the gate, and I would sometimes look at as I sat outside in the morning eating my cereal. I had never engaged in a deliberate act of contemplating the tree but I had come to appreciate it through seeing it often and in various seasons. But the garden was sold and the new owner immediately cut it down to build a garage. I often wonder whether, if he had lived in his house for some time and seen his tree through the seasons, he would perhaps have found some other place to site his garage.

Fourthly, contemplation sometimes opens us to a pleasure that is beyond appreciation. On that first morning, seeing wild geese in the meadows beside the river, and being passed by my first swallow of the year, and seeing the hawthorn buds poised ready to open into blossom, and the intricate tangled mass of growth beneath the hedges, my feeling was of more than appreciation. It can be described as a sense of wonder. When I met up with the man looking for the owner of a dog, an hour or so after leaving the people who had lost it, I had a sense of deep pleasure. I knew that what I was seeing were all the normal signs of spring in rural England, and that hedges and banks are always green and tangled, and that in April the pace of growth is quickening. I might calculate the probability of meeting up with the lost dog, but whether it was high or low would be irrelevant. In all this I had a sense of joy, like a slow surprise. It was all very ordinary, but it was still a source of wonder.

Early on my second day after setting off from Wrockwardine I came to the Shropshire Union Canal. A few years earlier I had been birdwatching at Belvide, a small reservoir that feeds this canal twenty miles to the south. At certain times of the year a large number of waders would stop by and the West Midland Bird Club had built a hide there. On this particular occasion there were a lot of birds and I spent some time trying to distinguish one medium-sized brown bird from another. Unfortunately I hadn't brought a book with me so was having to make do with a few pictures pinned to the hide wall and I was doing sketches to refresh my memory later.

What particularly caught my attention was a pair of geese, just down below the hide. One was white, with a bit of black on it, and the other was a grey. They were not particularly large geese, and they were not doing anything except rest, but I had not seen geese like them before and was intrigued.

Another birdwatcher came into the hide for a while. I took him to be more knowledgeable than me, which would not have been difficult. On and off I had watched birds for most of my life but never taken birdwatching particularly seriously. I was an occasional birder. I knew the common garden birds, but not many geese and I always had difficulty with waders. This man obviously knew a redshank from a knot and I asked him about these geese. What did he reckon they were?

He looked at them for a bit and then said, 'I reckon they've just escaped from someone's farmyard,' and left it at that. He then left the hide and I stayed on. After a short while the geese decided to move on, and they took off. I knew immediately they had not just escaped from a farmyard. They were birds built for flying. Their movement was strong and majestic, and they were beautiful.

The white one had black wingtips, the other was a blue-grey colour, and they flew together up over the water and above the trees at the edge of the reservoir. In a few moments they were gone, but the image stayed with me: one of powerful flight, off and away out of my sight, on what I imagined was a long journey. It was an experience of awe.

The excitement remained with me as I drove home. I thought I knew what they were, but I couldn't be sure till I had consulted my books and it turned out as I suspected: they were snow geese, North American birds and rare visitors to Britain. They spend their summers in the Arctic tundra and then migrate south for the winter. Occasionally they go off course and cross the Atlantic. It was possible that these birds had done that.

It was also possible that they had simply escaped from a park somewhere. Maybe they had come up the Severn from Slimbridge. I had no way of knowing. But I can still recall the sight of these birds taking off and flying over the water. The sense I had is hard to describe. 'Awe' is the best word I can find.

Contemplation can lead to appreciation of what is around us.

Sometimes this is tinged with wonder – a sense of amazement at the colour, shape, movement, diversity and sheer existence of it all. And sometimes beyond the wonder is awe. As I walked across the Cheshire Plain I experienced no sense of awe, but such things are not to be expected, simply received, like gifts, when they come. Nevertheless this whole area, which I had expected to be so very ordinary, simply a necessary prelude to the exciting walk later, was indeed a place of wonder. Small things. Common things. Ordinary things, but a source of pleasure. And that was the beginning of the journey. It was tiring, walking all day each day, but the times of wonder seemed to give me energy.

Of course, I was not walking in a contemplative mode all or even most of the time. Much of the time I was thinking about which path or road to take at a junction, where I could buy food or get water, where I would stay for the night or where there might be a toilet. I would wonder how my family at home were, or how some people who I knew were in difficulties were getting on. I would speak occasionally with people I passed, usually just exchanging greetings but occasionally discussing the weather or the path. And at times discomfort or pain in my legs and shoulders would draw my attention.

Later, when pain in my feet or legs became particularly bad, I found that deliberately focusing my attention on what I could see or hear around me helped me to keep going. There was a time in Scotland when one of my feet had swollen badly and I was almost having to walk sideways so as not to bend my ankle. I turned over in my mind whether or not I should stop and hitch a lift or whether I could hobble on to the next town and find a bed and breakfast. I decided on one more stretch of hobbling and looking at what I could see. There were flowers in the bank, and a fascinating signpost that told the distance to a village to the nearest furlong. Then there was a letterbox with a sign stuck on it saying it should not be used as it was occupied by a family of blue tits. I smiled, and the thought that the local people would make a point of posting their letters elsewhere until the nest was empty stayed with me till I walked into the next town.

I believe this sense of wonder is essential as we make the journey into the future, for two reasons. Firstly, it means we engage with the world we are a part of with a proper sense of its inherent worth. The earth is not just a great ball of natural resources – minerals, plants and animals – existing for our benefit alone. These things have a value in themselves. As we open ourselves to a sense of wonder at the world we sense that value. That means that as we make decisions affecting the world, which we do all the time, we do not do so lightly.

It is possible to become romantically attached to the living world, so that every turn of the soil, every tree felled, every watercourse altered, is felt to be the desecration of a work of art. I am not suggesting that. The soil must be turned so that people can eat. Felled trees make homes, and musical instruments, and beautiful sculptures and furniture, and the space created gives light for other plants. Sometimes if rivers are not diverted people and animals die in floods. I am not suggesting that we humans should somehow try to avoid altering the world we are part of. All I am suggesting is that when we make changes, whether they are in altering a garden layout or building a dam, we weigh up the consequences not just for people but for other life as well, and that a sense of wonder can help us do that not just as an ethical demand but as a matter of course.

Secondly, we need this sense of wonder for ourselves. In 2008 the RSPB began a recruitment and fundraising campaign in which they got people to describe what they called 'RSPB moments'. People wrote in, and were then quoted in the organisation's publicity, describing times they had seen a bird or wild animal and known that they had to do something to protect wildlife. It may have been a darting kingfisher, or some deer in the morning mist, or geese flying overhead. Whatever it was there was something wonderful about it, and that wonder led them to act for wildlife or wild places.

It was a powerful and effective campaign which I believe tapped into something important. It helped people identify this sense of wonder and realise that they were not alone or strange in having it. It was a common experience. But the RSPB also encouraged people to do something for wildlife, not on the basis that something dreadful or sad would happen if they did not but as a natural extension of the good experience they had had. Fear or guilt can drive us into action but they also debilitate us. Pleasure, wonder and awe give us energy.

We need this sense of wonder not only for the sake of the world in crisis, but also for ourselves, because we need the energy generated by this combination of joy and surprise. In 1950 Dag Hammarskjöld wrote, 'God does not die on the day when we cease to believe in a personal deity, but we die on the day when our lives cease to be illumined by the steady radiance, renewed daily, of a wonder, the source of which is beyond all reason.'[2]

In the face of what we now know is happening to the world I wonder whether Hammarskjöld was saying more than he knew: that a lack of wonder not only diminishes and stifles our own life but leads us to live in ways that fatally damage the whole life of earth.

Developing a sense of wonder requires no gadgets and is free. It simply requires time. It means giving ourselves the time to see, feel, taste, hear and smell the world we are part of. To take a long loving look at what really is, and open ourselves to the glory of its colours and textures, its sounds, its scents and its tastes and the marvel of its very existence.

References

1. Peter Scott, *The Eye of the Wind* (London: Hodder & Stoughton, 1977)
2. Dag Hammarskjöld, *Markings* (London: Faber, 1966) p64

Resources 1: Wonder

Columba

'Don't think, just look.' According to Richard Rohr that was Wittgenstein's maxim.[1] It is an interesting suggestion, coming as it does from one of the twentieth century's greatest thinkers.

'Just looking' is what contemplation is about. Looking, or feeling, or listening. And it has a long history in Christianity.

There certainly have been times when looking at the world was not encouraged. Many Christian children have been taught, and sometimes still are, to close their eyes when they pray. It is certainly good sometimes. It is helpful if you are trying to imagine something that is not there. Or if you are listening to music, or perhaps feeling the texture of something.

But there have been plenty of Christians who have wanted people to open their eyes and see. To appreciate the world they are part of. And to wonder at it.

In the seventeenth century, Thomas Traherne asked, 'Can you take too much joy in your Father's works? He is himself in every thing.'[2]

Earlier, John Calvin had said that Nature was a theatre of God's glory, 'crammed with innumerable miracles'. A visible image of the invisible God.[3]

In the sixth century, Columba is reputed to have spent time simply watching the sea, and to have written:

Delightful would it be to me
to be on the pinnacle of a rock,
that I might often see the face of the ocean;
that I might see its heaving waves
over the wide ocean,
when they chant music to their Father
upon the world's course.[4]

References

1. Richard Rohr, *Simplicity*, (New York: Crossroad Publishing, 2003) p90
2. Thomas Traherne, *Centuries* (London: The Clarendon Press, 1960) I.25
3. Christopher Elwood, *Calvin for Armchair Theologians* (Louisville KY: Westminster John Knox Press, 2002) p42
4. Murray Watts, *The Wisdom of Saint Columba of Iona* (Oxford: Lion, 1997) p16

For reflection or group discussion

1. Think of an occasion when you have had a sense of wonder. Remember it and enjoy the memory, or if you are in a group, tell each other about any such occasions.

2. Do you have contemplative activities which you enjoy and find helpful? Perhaps sitting in a park or a square and 'watching the world go by', or birdwatching, painting or sketching, photography, walking. Try to identify ones that really suit you as a person. If you are in a group, tell each other about these, and what you gain from them.

3. What makes it hard to make time for contemplation? It may be your circumstances. It may be thoughts in your head or remembering things you were told when you were young about doing something useful or not wasting time. If you want to give some time to contemplation, what might be helpful ways of dealing with this problem?

Some Bible passages relevant to the theme

Psalm 104
The ancient Hebrew idea of the structure of the universe was, of course, very different from that of present-day science, but this is not science, it is poetry. This is a poem of appreciation of the

world, created by God, in which humanity has a place among the animals and plants.

Psalm 8
The writer, reflecting on the magnificence and magnitude of the universe is struck also by the power of humanity within it.

Genesis 1:1-2:3
In this poem God calls the universe into being, appreciates its goodness and ordains a time for rest and contemplation.

Job 38:1-40:5
At the climax of a dramatic debate Job is overawed by the power of God that the universe displays.

Matthew 13:24-35
The stories that Jesus told show that he was clearly someone who had spent time looking at the world and society he was part of.

Action

1. Find a place to sit where you can see something of the living world and the sky: in a park, on a hillside, beside a window, beside a river or the sea. Give yourself a period of time in which to do this: say, ten or fifteen minutes. Do not talk or listen to music. First listen to what you can hear, perhaps with your eyes closed. Then open your eyes and pay attention to what you can see. Then what you can feel on your skin. Then what you can smell. When you find yourself thinking about other things (and you will) gently bring your mind back to what you have set out to do: hearing, seeing, feeling and smelling, and carry on where you left off before your mind went off elsewhere.

2. Go for a short slow walk. Go alone or agree with the person you are walking with to walk in silence, at least for a while. Pay attention to what you can see, looking in turn at different kinds

of things: plants, birds, people, the colours and textures of building materials, clouds and the light in the sky. Do not be concerned to identify or name each thing you see; just notice it as it is. When you return spend a few minutes running through in your memory what you recall seeing.

3. Take up an activity which involves regularly spending time looking at the world – say, birdwatching, identifying flowers or trees, skywatching, looking for insects. Or if hearing is your strongest sense, regularly listening to music, not as a background but as the focus of your attention. And then look out for these things at other times, or deliberately when you are out and about listen to the 'music' of the world around you: the babble of voices, traffic, birdsong, other people's music.

Further reading

Annie Dillard, *Pilgrim at Tinker Creek* (New York: Harper & Row, 1974)
A beautiful telling of a year of engagement and contemplation.

Simon Barnes, *How to Be a Bad Birdwatcher: To the greater glory of life* (London: Short, 2004)
A book to get you started.

Colin Tudge, *The Secret Life of Trees: How they live and why they matter* (London: Penguin, 2006)
For those who like detail and entertainment at the same time.

Bill Bryson, *A Short History of Nearly Everything* (London: Doubleday, 2005)
A book for anyone who is afraid that understanding how the world works will detract from its 'wow' factor.

Richard Mabey, *The Unofficial Countryside* (1973 republished 2010, Wimborne Minster: Little Toller Books)

A classic. Mabey explores the wildlife of the cities and their often unappealing margins and corners. Since he wrote, the ecology of the cities has changed, and there are now even more exciting things to discover.

Books of photos, paintings or sketches which you can browse and which will help you see things you may not otherwise notice.

Two

Touching the Earth

It is sometimes said that the world is much smaller now. It only seems smaller because we miss most of it out.

On the fourth day of my walk to Iona I set off early. I had camped for the night and woken as it began to get light. After a quick breakfast I packed up and followed a lane away from the campsite. Then it was a mixture of roads and footpaths.

A few early starters were setting off to work by car. There were a couple of tractors. No one else was walking. I slowly became aware of a sound that was getting gradually louder. It began as a deep whisper on the edge of my hearing and then developed into a roar. I knew what it was.

For some reason I remembered reading when I was young of David Livingstone and his companions walking through the bush towards an increasing roaring noise. What they came upon took their breath away. They had never seen anything like it before. It was a great waterfall on the river Zambesi, which the locals called Mosi-oa-Tunya: The Smoke that Thunders. The British, with imperial arrogance, renamed it the Victoria Falls.

I was not in the African bush but the English countryside, and this was no river. It was something I had seen many times before. A motorway. I knew from my map it was coming but I would have recognised that sound anywhere. For four years I had lived with a view of the M6 further south in Staffordshire. We were half a mile away and except on the rare days when there was an east wind we could hear it all the time. Sometimes, I had to close the window before I answered the phone or I could not hear what the caller was saying.

At times when I found it particularly wearing I would try to pretend it was a river. That would be restful. I thought maybe I could imagine water rushing over rocks, and then running down to gentle lowlands where it would flow through quiet meadows. But I could never do it. It was not the same sound. There was nothing musical about this roar of engines and tyres on concrete. It was abrasive and continuous. And now I could hear it again.

So eventually I came through a small wood and beheld the

motorway. It was very strange. I had lived with motorways most of my life. I had driven up this very one more times than I could remember. But I had never before seen a motorway in quite this way.

I had only spent three days walking along lanes and footpaths. It was not even as if I had been crossing a deserted moorland. I had met people and spoken with a few. I had been passed by cars, tractors and the occasional lorry. I had walked through several small towns. But the motorway seemed to me now like a very strange thing.

What I saw was people in metal canisters shooting along at high speeds, sealed off from the world around them in every way except by vision, and looking only ahead, focused on the road and the other vehicles. Beside me were trees, and a grass verge with some small flowers. The coolness of the morning was lifting now and I could feel the warmth of the sun on my skin, and a slight breeze. They could neither feel nor see any of that. And if they could hear it they would not notice the roar that was pressing on my ears.

Above the motorway there was a plane climbing into the sky. It had obviously just taken off from Manchester airport, and by the time I stopped for lunch it would perhaps be in Italy or Majorca, or half way across the Atlantic. The passengers who had boarded the plane that morning in Manchester would step out in a very different place, with no sense at all of what they had passed over. They would move from one world to another.

For the people in the cars it would be similar. They would have seen the land passing by, but they would have had no sense of continuity between the place they had left and the place where they arrived. They would have used their car, as they might have said, to get from one place to another. Which is what I would also normally do much of the time. But now I was not trying to get from one place to another. I was doing something else.

It may be that the motorway seemed particularly strange to me that morning because I had spent several days travelling slowly, outdoors, vulnerable to the elements and sensitive to what I could see, hear and feel. I was already losing track of how long I had been travelling. I only knew it was the fourth day by thinking back over the journey. But it is also possible that the motorway seemed so strange because of what I was trying to do on my walk.

Some months before I thought of walking to Iona I had gone out for a walk and made my way four miles or so to another village. It was a place I knew well. I was the vicar and went there several times most weeks, usually by car but occasionally on a bike. This time I walked and my arriving was strangely different. This was partly because I had come by another route, using paths and a footbridge across the small river Tern, but it was also, I was sure, because I had walked. I now felt that this village was not another place separate from where I lived but part of the same place. The walking had given me a sense of continuity between one area and the other.

I reckoned this was because I had felt the slope of the land and the wind on my face. I had seen the sky changing and noticed the flowers and the detail of the hedges. I had been moving at a human speed – the speed at which our senses can take in information and assimilate it.

For hundreds of thousands of years we humans have moved around the world. From our origins in Africa we have spread to inhabit most of the world's land, and once settled in an area, people have moved to trade, to meet up, to hunt and to farm. But always at about three miles an hour. Only since the 1850s have many people moved much faster than that. Before the railways even those who rode horses still moved at little more than walking pace most of the time. But with the railways speeds of twenty, thirty, then fifty miles an hour were achieved. And so on to the roads and motorways of the late twentieth century.

A hundred and fifty years is the blink of an eye in human development. Our brains are geared to moving at three miles an hour. Most of the time when we travel we feel that we leave one place and arrive in another. The rest is a blur, even if we have paid attention to what we are passing through. And most of the time we have not even done that.

When we travel by train we read, or talk, or work on our laptops. When we drive we are focused on the road immediately in front of us, and the other traffic. Our lives depend on it. We cannot afford to be enjoying the view or watching the wildlife. And because the only effort we have expended has been pressing pedals and turning the wheel we have little sense of when we have gone up or down. We travel in the shade so have little sense of the position of the sun. And our heaters and air conditioners mean that we would have no idea what the air temperature was outside if we did not have a thermometer on our control panel. On this particular day's walk I had been moving slowly, and without thinking about what was happening I had developed a sense of the place I was moving through. I felt I had not gone from one place to another but had moved through one place.

I had not set out to try to discover something. I had had no particular purpose that day except to have a relaxing walk on my own, but my sense of where I was had changed. Now I realised for myself what I had come across before as an idea but which had until then remained simply an idea. I remembered, once I started thinking about it, that Ivan Illich had written about how increased speed meant a decrease in the efficiency of our other ways of functioning.[1] I remembered too Kosuke Koyama, a south-east Asian theologian, writing about how for many people talk about God needed to be related to their lives, and particularly to the speed of their lives.[2] And I recalled an old story of nineteenth-century Western missionaries pressing on through the African bush and finally having their porters refuse to go any further. It was not that they were tired but that they needed to wait for their souls to catch up.

A question in my mind was whether the sense of continuity I had experienced in a short walk of a few miles would persist if I walked further. So, when I had the chance, I set off on a whole day's walk, and found that it did. A short while later I spent a week walking across Wales and found as I sat on the beach at Aberystwyth that I could think back over the route through the hills, back to my home in Shropshire. I read John Hillaby's 1960s' book *Journey Through Britain* and found that one of the reasons he set off to walk on his own from Land's End to John O'Groats was because he wanted to get a sense of Britain as a whole.[3]

There was another book that got me thinking further about this. Bruce Chatwin's *On the Black Hill* is a novel about two brothers living on the Herefordshire-Wales border. Some of what he described rang true with my experience of life in Shropshire.[4] Then I came across another novel of his, this time set in Australia, *The Songlines.*[5] In it he sets out some of his reflections about travel and describes the Australian Aborigine concept of the songline. These songlines tell of the creation of the land and its life in the dreamtime, but they also describe the landscape. So an Aborigine who knew his song could walk alone across hundreds of miles of bush that he had never travelled before. The landscape would be familiar from the song. And the land, as told in the song, gave a sense of identity to the tribe and the individual.

It was a fascinating concept, and added another dimension to my thoughts about slow journeys. I was now aware that a slow journey could give a sense of continuity between places. Here was an additional idea: that a journey could also give a sense of identity to the traveller. I read and thought more about why people sometimes chose to make journeys: Americans who would visit villages in Britain or Ireland that their ancestors had come from; Catholics who travel to Rome; Protestants who cross the world to visit the Sea of Galilee where Jesus taught; Nigerian Muslims I had known who travelled to Mecca and returned now to be addressed as 'Alhaji': one who had made the pilgrimage. All this came together with an idea for myself.

Looking out across North Shropshire and Cheshire I could imagine the land stretching beyond my sight to places that I not only knew but which were for various reasons significant for me: Edinburgh where I had lived for several years in my late teens and where Madron had grown up; Scargill House in Wharfedale where we had first gone at a time of grief after the death of our third child, and been welcomed and helped; Carlisle where I had stopped many times on journeys from the Midlands to Scotland and had found the people friendly and the chip shops excellent; Ben Lomond that I had seen in the west many times from my parents' home in Queensferry, many miles away but somehow enticing; and Iona, beginning to feel like the home I had hardly visited. So there was the idea. I would walk my own songline, linking these places.

Now I was on that walk and standing at the edge of a motorway. What I was doing was something that could not be done by car. Of course, many of the car drivers were doing things that could not be done on foot. I could not have got to Liverpool for a meeting in an hour's time, or delivered urgent medicines to a Leeds hospital, or visited friends in Burnley for lunch. We were a few feet apart and on very different journeys.

Since that time I have driven many times up and down the M6, but I still feel that the real route, my route, is along the paths and lanes that I walked then. The roads I drive are a kind of shortcut between different points on the long route that is my line through Britain.

Since walking to Iona I have extended the line a bit at a time, walking to link up other places that are significant for me: where I moved to in Somerset a couple of years later, places that I had stayed in Devon and Cornwall, Birmingham where I first went to university and Lichfield where I was ordained, and the area in Surrey I knew well as a child. I now have a sense that there are paths winding along lanes and tracks that are my network, joining up what might have been disparate locations but making them, in one sense, all one place.

And now if I think of how far it is between these places I will also have a sense of how far it is on foot. Of course, measured on a map it is the same regardless of how one travels, but that is not how it feels. From Bristol to Edinburgh is six hours by car, and an hour by plane. It is six weeks on foot. And on foot you see, touch and feel the places in between.

My path beside the motorway joined a small road that sloped up to a roundabout and a bridge. I crossed over, and fell for the lure of a Little Chef. For the previous two nights I had camped. The main reason for this was that I was on a very limited budget. I had worked out that I could manage the journey if I stayed each night at hostels. However, I knew there weren't going to be hostels in many of the places I needed them, so I decided that I would have to camp when I could, and use bed and breakfasts from time to time. So far I had camped two nights and used one B and B, so I was in credit. And I really fancied a coffee.

Occasionally until now when I had wanted a drink I had got out my stove and had a brew beside the path. It was possible now but I would have felt more than a little self-conscious sitting beside the A556 brewing coffee, and the Little Chef was there, with its simple menu and, also attractive, its toilets. So in I went, dropping my rucksack at the door and squeezing my boots under a table. I imagine that my own earlier sense of the bizarre when I came to the motorway was now reciprocated. All the customers were smart. Suits and well cut skirts. Morning coffee often combined with business. Salesmen making rendezvous and catching up about possible clients. And here was a sweaty and grubby hiker with muddy boots. But I enjoyed the coffee and it set me up for the challenge of the suburbs.

I had an offer of accommodation in Sale. Some friends were away but very happy for me to stay in their house. I should be there by late afternoon, having walked through Altrincham. But first I had to pass Tatton Park, a house and walled park owned by the National Trust and promoted as a good day visit. Which may well be true. But I did not want to visit. I just wanted to pass by. The trouble was there was no footpath between the wall and the road, nor on the other side. The verge was very rough and it would be hard to balance there, so the safest thing would be to walk along the road. But it was not wide and it was quite busy.

This was the first of a number of occasions when I realised that Britain is now geared for motorists, and not for walkers. I made it without injury, but it was not relaxing and I was very aware that if there had been what the emergency services call 'a collision between a vehicle and a pedestrian' it would have been a bit one-sided. A particular irony was that the National Trust encourages people to visit Tatton Park, but as far as I could make out there was no safe way to do it apart from driving.

Walking alone you are very aware not only of the sights, sounds and smells of the place you are passing through, but also of the changes in gradient, particularly of steep hills, up and down. With a rucksack even slight gradients are noticeable. And on footpaths you also notice changes in the soil. There are sandy soils which even after rain are quite easy going, but then there are clay soils which, when wet, can build up in layers on your boots so that you begin to feel like a you're in a diving suit.

Some days later I was walking beside the River Wharfe on a morning of broken cloud. At one point everything seemed to get lighter and without particularly thinking about it my half-awake mind registered that the sun had come out. Then I noticed that it was still cloudy. I stopped to try to work out what had happened, and realised that the rock of the riverbank had changed. I had walked from an area of grey millstone grit into much lighter limestone. The riverbanks and the stones of the nearby walls were reflecting more light. The same thing happened much later on the Isle of Mull where the rock of the mountains changed from basalt to granite.

There are also changes among the people. When, on an earlier journey, I had set off walking across Wales, people in Shropshire simply looked at me as I walked by and did not even return a greeting. But the further west I went the more people were inclined to speak. In Newtown I had a shopkeeper ask me enthusiastically about my route to Aberystwyth, and later I had a woman who ran a cafe in a town deliberately involve me in a conversation she was having with two friends. Years later I walked across the north of England and found myself being ignored by people I passed while I was in Cumbria but once I had crossed the Pennines into County Durham I had to break away from a conversation with a drystone waller which could clearly have gone on all afternoon. And further down Teesdale workmen waved to me from a bridge as I passed below.

When people do say hello, they do it differently in different areas. There are always some who will say, 'Good morning,' but among others there are such terms as 'A'right', 'OK?', and in the South-West, still, ''ow be?'

Also noticeable in a long walk are the regional variations of accent and dialect. The hum of voices in a shop will be quite different in Manchester from that in Leeds, or in Edinburgh compared to Glasgow. I think of it as the music of speech. It is about intonation, and the colour of the sounds that are used as people from a particular place or subculture talk to each other.

In the South-West of England there is a question about whether Gloucestershire and Wiltshire are really the West Country. Walking beside the River Severn on my way from Shropshire to Somerset I noticed a clear boundary at Tewkesbury. To the north, in Worcester, the speech music in shops and pubs was of the Midlands. To the south in Gloucester there were the rolling r's of the South-West.

Walking though Shropshire and Cheshire people sometimes asked where I was going. To this I rarely said, 'Iona.' Partly it was because I did not want to start a lengthy conversation about the purpose of my journey, but also I wasn't actually convinced I would make it beyond the first few days. The journey to Iona by car or train might be quite demanding but when I thought about it as something to do on foot it felt like a serious challenge. It seemed like a very long way. So I simply said I was going 'up Manchester way'. That was all I was confident of. And it was true. I was going Manchester way. I just wanted to go a lot further on, but I was not at all sure that I would.

As I had been there before by car and by train, and had looked at maps and worked out possible routes, I had some idea of how far it was. I could imagine medieval pilgrims setting off to Rome or the Holy Land with no idea of the distances involved. They were travelling into the unknown. They certainly would have had no confidence of arriving. Apart from the distances and the possibility of not being strong enough to keep going, there were dangers from the weather, from robbers and tricksters, from disease and injury, the possibility of getting lost, and some very hard country to cross. Many never made it to their destination. Only a fool would have said confidently that they were going to Jerusalem or wherever. Most would have approached the journey with a certain amount of humility.

I did not face the dangers of a medieval pilgrimage. Robbery was possible, but not likely. I could shelter in bad weather. If I got ill I could probably get to a hospital. The most likely dangers were becoming ill or having an accident when there was no one else around, or being hit by a car or truck. The most likely reason for not reaching my destination would have been that I did not actually have the physical strength or the determination to continue. Unlike medieval pilgrims I could get a taxi to the nearest station. That was a temptation they did not have. Theirs was a very different experience.

Nevertheless, looking back I think that my attitude in not saying, or really believing, that I was going to Iona could be described as humility. And during the first few days that sense of uncertainty grew. My legs began to hurt, quite badly. The rucksack seemed to get heavier all the time. And when I thought of how many maps I was going to use I was reminded of how far it was to go. Having been there before I could imagine myself arriving on foot in Edinburgh or Iona, but I was not at all sure it was going to happen.

The word 'humility' has become associated with a sense of undervaluing oneself. Of refusing to realise one's potential. Or accepting injustice without dissent. But in origin the word means an earthiness. It is linked to the word 'humus', the fundamental ingredient of soil, and to the word 'humour'. Humility is basically about having one's feet on the ground. Being realistic about one's strengths and weaknesses, and about how one is dependent on other people and on the world as a whole.

It seems to me that there is a lot in our society that disconnects us from the soil and gives us an unrealistic idea of ourselves. We lack humility as individuals and as a society. As individuals we rush around the country in our cars, which other people have made. We buy food in shops and restaurants which we cannot grow ourselves. We communicate with each other by phone and computer, and most of us do not even understand how they work, let alone have the resources to make one. As a society our minds are largely focused on the future, which does not exist, and on money, which is a mental construct. And yet we are a part of the life of the earth and we cannot escape that.

We are made of what we eat and everything that we eat comes from the soil. The water essential to our lives comes to the ground as rain. We need clothes to protect us from the cold and heat and these are made from wool, plants, skins or processed oil from the ground. We need shelter, and so we build, and for that we need stone or wood. These are the fundamentals required for life. At the most basic level we belong to the earth. If we forget that, or are never aware of it, we ignore a fundamental aspect of what it means to be human. We need to remind ourselves of this, not simply as an idea, but as something of which we are deeply aware. And there are many ways of doing that.

For me walking is a powerful way of reconnecting with the earth. Walking, I am aware of the wind and the rain, the sun and the light and shadow, all that is growing and living, and the sound and motion of life. When it rains I get wet. When the sun comes out I get hot. These are not just things I observe; I am caught up in them. And walking, as I was discovering, can also link up places, making them one and in so doing connect the memories associated with them. But walking is not for everyone. Some people can't walk, or can only do so with great difficulty. Even for those who are able to walk, it may still not be the best way to reconnect with the earth.

When I am walking I see people working in gardens. For many gardening is much better than walking. They have their hands in the soil. They nurture the plants. They feel the rain and the sun, and are sensitive to how these affect what grows in their patch of ground. And if they grow vegetables or fruit they have the satisfaction of eating what has grown in the soil they have worked.

I had a colleague once who went off to run a centre where people could go sailing, and he saw it not just as a leisure-time activity but also as a way of connecting with the world we are part of. Anyone sailing needs to be sensitive to the movements of the air and water, and respond to them, and will feel, smell and possibly taste the water. Other people I know turn wood, or make furniture. Handling the wood they become very sensitive to the grain, texture and colour, and they are often also aware of the kind of tree their wood has come from. They will sometimes have known the actual plant.

Other people will get a similar sense of connectedness from handling and sculpting stone. Martin Thornton, a clergyman and writer on spirituality, after writing a book would go and build drystone dykes as a way of clearing his mind and connecting with the basics of life. There are people for whom making bread is a fundamental activity. Many senses are involved in handling the flour, yeast and water, kneading it by hand, smelling the bread during baking and then feeling the texture and appreciating the taste when it is eaten.

I have known other people for whom keeping animals is what roots them in the reality of life. Animals, be they pets or farm animals, literally have a life of their own and a character. Handling and engaging with animals, particularly if there are not too many of them, give a sense of our connection with other living things.

There are many ways of reconnecting with the earth. In a society where most people's homes are heated by electricity or gas, where they travel in a car to work which involves mostly sitting in front of a computer or making decisions about things they never handle, where their food and drink come ready-prepared from a shop or a restaurant, and where their spare time is spent watching television or playing computer games, there are few opportunities for this to happen without deliberate effort. But if we live separated from the soil we may mistake our dreams and ideas for reality. We may have too great a sense of our own worth, or too little, leading us to make decisions which take too little account of the real world.

I am not suggesting that we all, somehow, go 'back to the land', working our own plot in a subsistence economy. The highly technological society of which we are a part has great benefits. And there is not enough land. What I am suggesting is that we should not become cut off from our roots. Somehow we need to build into our lives ways that help us remain aware of how we are a part of the living earth, not apart from it.

I was now coming into the city of Manchester. Living in cities we mostly travel around by bus, car, train or underground. It is a matter of time. Walking through a city can be slow going and the transport is available. But this can lead to our having no sense of how one part of the city connects up with another. A walk or a cycle ride between the two gives this feeling of connection. There are many people who choose to walk or ride a bike in the city because it makes them aware of being a part of what is going on around them. Inside the bus, car or underground they feel cut off.

Walking across Cheshire towards Manchester I had used many footpaths, some of which were well marked with signposts. It is significant that the drive to improve access to the countryside by the public came from city people. Country people had for generations walked along paths to work and to market but accepted that the great estates on the moors or behind park walls were out of bounds to them unless they were employees. It was city workers who pushed for the registration of public rights of way and for access to open land, even if it was privately owned. The Ramblers Association was born in the early twentieth century not as a result of country people exploring their neighbourhoods but by city people determined to get out of the smoke into the fresh air and not being deterred by gamekeepers and fences.

Traditionally people in British cities have found other ways as well of connecting with the living world they are part of. Sometimes keeping chickens or pigs in a back yard has been a means of improving the food supply for those on poor wages, but it has not always been just that. People have also kept pigeons and dogs. They have had allotments where they have grown their own vegetables and which have also been places to unwind, get a bit of peace and quiet, and some fresher air than there was in the factory or office or at home.

There is now a resurgence of interest in growing food in cities as well as in the country. There are urban farms in many places. Almost every allotment society in Britain has a long waiting list. People grow food in window boxes and in pots on balconies, or together in groups rent a piece of land for gardens. No doubt some do this because they feel it is better for them and for the earth if they grow food locally and reduce the amount of oil and other chemicals used in the process, but mostly it is for the satisfaction that comes from handling soil, watching seeds grow, and harvesting and eating the produce.

It is not a choice between one or the other. Developing our sense of connectedness with the earth not only leads us to treat the earth better; it also benefits us. It increases our sense of well-being and gives us a greater appreciation for and enjoyment of life.

Being in touch with the earth gives us a sense of perspective. If we are very concerned about the state of the world it is possible to feel weighed down by a need to save the planet. Life on the planet is certainly in a bad way, but we are not going to save it. We are part of it.

Taking time to connect with the earth by walking more, handling the soil, riding a bike, keeping animals, cooking food, working with wood, swimming, sailing, or simply pausing to feel the wind, sun and rain, can help us become aware that we are a very small part of the whole. We can all make a contribution to the well-being of the whole, but true humility helps us develop realistic schemes, campaigns and plans. It also helps us appreciate the life we have and the greater life we are part of.

References

1. Ivan Illich, *Celebration of Awareness* (Harmondsworth: Penguin, 1971)
2. Kosuke Koyama, *Waterbuffalo Theology* (London: SCM, 1974) and *Three Mile an Hour God* (London: SCM, 1979)
3. John Hillaby, *Journey Through Britain* (London: Constable, 1968)
4. Bruce Chatwin, *On the Black Hill* (London: Cape, 1982)
5. Bruce Chatwin, *The Songlines* (London: Picador, 1988)

Resources 2: Engagement

Benedict

Over two thousand years ago the author of Ecclesiastes said, 'Of the making of many books there is no end, and much study is a weariness of the flesh.'[1] But the ideas industry has continued to flourish, and long may it do so.

However, it is possible for us, as we think, worry, pray or plan, to lose touch with the physical world. The monastic movement began with people going out into the desert to pray. A number of people attempted to organise these solitaries, and to try to creatively channel the energy of the movement. One of the most influential of these in Western Europe was Benedict of Nursia.

Benedict founded a monastery at Monte Cassino in Italy in about 530 and here drew up his Rule, which was soon adopted by many other monasteries. This was designed as a guide for their life together and a protection for the monks from the possible vagaries and enthusiasms of their leader. The Rule set out a pattern for daily life, and a key component of this was work.

Work, at that time, normally meant manual work. It involved getting dirty, hot, wet and tired. And it involved being in touch with the soil, with wood, with plants, flesh and water. 'To work is to pray,' was the motto, and 'to pray is to work.'

That contact with the earth is easily lost in our society. In the foreword to a Church of England discussion paper Archbishop Rowan Williams wrote, 'To … sophisticated responses to the ecological crisis I should like to add a call for simple, accessible ways of learning again what it is to be part of the created order. Receive the world that God has given. Go for a walk. Get wet. Dig the earth.'[2]

References

1. Ecclesiastes 12:12
2. *Sharing God's Planet* (London: Church House, 2005) pviii

For reflection or group discussion

1. Think of things that you do that help you feel in touch with the world. Do you find these enjoyable, difficult, tiresome or fun? If you are in a group, tell each other what these things are? And notice the differences.

2. Are there engaging activities that you do not have enough time for? If so, what could you do about that? Would it help to commit yourself to doing it with a group? Either by joining a group that already exists or simply getting together with others for hill-walking, gardening, breadmaking, swimming, cooking, working wood, sculpting or whatever.

3. Have you had experiences which have brought you down to earth very quickly? Was it unpleasant or enjoyable? Painful or exhilarating? Was it significant for your life or of no great consequence?

Some Bible passages relevant to the theme

Genesis 2:4-7
In this story of creation humanity is made from the earth.

Exodus 3:1; 1 Samuel 16:1-13; Amos 7:10-17; Mark 6:1-3; Acts 18:1-3
Moses, David, Amos, Jesus and Paul: all these key figures in the Bible were people who worked with their hands.

John 12:1-8
Jesus greatly appreciated having his feet anointed with scent.

John 13:1-17
Jesus was willing to do a task which was both manual and thought to be demeaning, but which would have been pleasant as well as meaningful for his disciples.

Action

1. If you have a journey that you often make by car, bus or underground, walk it sometime. Take your time. If it is too far for one walk do part of it and then another time pick up the trail where you left off. Then do other walks linking more places with which you have an association, so that you develop a sense of their being part of one place.

2. Take up an activity in which you can engage your mind and your senses with the material world: making bread and kneading the dough by hand; growing vegetables, using tubs or window boxes if you do not have a garden; walking through woodland or open spaces when it is windy or raining, or walking barefoot sometimes; carpentry or woodcarving; modelling with clay; building walls or landscaping using your hands and hand tools; etc. Choose one that suits you and do the amount that suits you. You can grow vegetables without trying to become self-sufficient. You don't have to make all your bread. Walks in the rain don't have to be hikes.

3. Watch a piece of land through the seasons. Take a look at it regularly and see how the plants change through the seasons and the colours change with the weather.

Further reading

T.J. Gorringe, *The Education of Desire: Towards a theology of the senses* (London: SCM, 2001)
Drawing on a wealth of sources the author takes the reader on a journey, exploring how our senses engage us with the world, each other, and God.

Carolyn Scott Kortge, *The Spirited Walker: Fitness walking for clarity, balance and spiritual connection* (New York: Harper Collins, 1998)

Walking can be simply a way of getting from A to B but it can be so much more.

Anne Richards, *Sense Making Faith: Body, spirit, journey* (London: CTBI, 2007)
A beautiful workbook on tuning into the senses as a way of engaging with the world and God.

Any book on breadmaking, cooking, growing vegetables, wood-carving, carpentry, or whatever it is that you choose to do that helps you engage your mind and senses with the material world.

Three

Travelling Light

Walking along the lanes of Tatton and Ashley and then into suburban Hale and Altrincham I probably made quite an unusual sight. The most notable and noticeable thing would have been my rucksack. People wander around with rucksacks all the time. There is nothing unusual in that. They are a convenient way of carrying things, and at times they become fashionable. But these are usually small rucksacks. 'Haversacks', they were once called. Some of them are tiny, with room enough for a phone and a pack of tissues. Others are suitable for a packed lunch and a waterproof. Mine was in a different league, and was very conspicuous.

From the moment I had conceived of this journey I had mulled over what I would need to take with me. I was going to walk, so I needed to be able to carry it all, or pull it in a cart. Although I read Gerard Hughes' account of walking to Jerusalem with a small handcart called Mungo, I decided against it quite early on.[1] I wanted to follow footpaths as much as possible: footpaths with stiles, mud, ruts and in places overgrown. A handcart was not an option. It would all have to go on my back.

Because of the tight budget I was working on I would need to take a tent. And something to cook on, or at least to be able to make tea with. Reading John Hillaby's *Journey through Britain* I noted that he regretted not taking a small stove.[2] As long as I had the money I could stop in cafes for hot drinks, but there would be many stretches, beyond Manchester, when there would be no cafes, pubs or restaurants for a long way. It would perhaps be a little luxury, but I decided to take a gas stove and a small pan and mug. And a sleeping bag, washing kit, clothes, first aid kit, maps, notebook and paper, water bottle, waterproofs. It soon added up.

As well as John Hillaby I read a few others who had done long walks. John Merrill never, ever carried water. 'A dead weight,' he called it.[3] But I don't like being thirsty. I would carry water. I had heard of people who cut the handle off their toothbrush in order to reduce weight. Walking from Compostela to Istanbul Nick Crane had a cunning scheme whereby he carried three socks: two to wear and one to be washed, and he wore them in rotation. He also had one shirt which he wore till it was falling off his back.[4] I would not go that far. I was perhaps a little concerned not to be too smelly or ragged, particularly when I was walking through a city or town or staying with friends. It was not just a matter of appearance. It was also about feeling emotionally comfortable.

I had also, in my youth, been a Scout. Probably, without that experience and training I could not, and would not, have conceived of doing a walk like this. I had a great deal to thank the Scout movement for. I had learnt and gained confidence in things which as an adult I simply took for granted. Occasionally when people heard what I was planning to do they would say, 'How are you going to find the way?' Well, with a map, of course. 'And what if it's foggy?' I would use a compass. Yes, I would take a compass as well.

The drawback with the Scout training was the motto: 'Be Prepared.' For what? Anything? I found myself running through things that might happen and thinking of equipment I would need in order to deal with that eventuality. So I had aspirins, and something to repair the tent with, and a bar of Kendal Mint Cake in case I got stuck without food in the Scottish Highlands, and shorts as well as trousers, and a whistle and a strong orange plastic bag in case I had an accident out on the moors and had to wait in my sleeping bag in the rain until I was rescued. And a few other things to help me be prepared for whatever might conceivably arise. But it all had to be carried. All the way.

Reading articles and books by other walkers I discovered some interesting things. One was that it is far less tiring walking with light shoes than with heavy boots. No great surprise really, but I found out that a hundred grams of weight on the feet was the equivalent of three hundred grams on the back. In other words, it would be best not to wear boots unless I actually needed them.

I also discovered that the technology had developed since the '60s when I did my Scout hikes. Tents were now a fraction of the weight of the old cotton one I had carried across Dartmoor as a teenager. Rucksacks were a completely different design and put much of the load onto your hips, thus sparing your back and shoulders a lot of strain. Waterproofs were more likely to keep the rain out. Boots were now like leather trainers, and not even trainers had been invented back then. We had carried plimsolls to give our feet a break from the boots, but they were not good for long walks. Walking was now high tech and I was not going to ignore the improvements.

The rucksack I already had was going to be too small for all the stuff I would need, and too uncomfortable on my back. So I would invest in a new one. There seemed to be two possibilities within my budget, both of which had adjustable backs and so could be made to fit well. There was a green one which looked strangely like the kind of ex-army bag I had carried several decades earlier, but which I was assured in the catalogue was a totally modern design. And there was one which was described as being dark blue with orchid-coloured side panels. Orchids, of course, come in all sorts of colours, so orchid is not a particularly precise way of describing a colour. This one was pink. A deep and lurid pink.

The point of this, I assumed, was that it would be very visible on mountainsides and open moors, so that if I had an accident I could easily be found by a search and rescue team, or, more likely, by another walker. That was a very good point. I was walking alone and so could not send off for help in the event of an accident. The problem was that I did not much want to be a form of visual pollution on legs, spoiling anyone else's view of the landscapes I was walking through.

But in the end, after much deliberation, I went for the pink. Not because I wanted to be visible in the mountains. I reckoned that if I had an accident there, short of being unconscious I could pull out my bright red waterproof, if I was not already wearing it, or my emergency bag. But the orchid pink would be very visible to the drivers of vehicles, which were likely to be a much greater danger.

In three hundred miles of road-walking I was not hit by a passing vehicle. I have no idea whether I would have been if my rucksack had been camouflage green, but it is possible – and no doubt more likely. But I never really liked the rucksack. Fortunately I did not have to look at it much. It was on my back. And maybe the colour was not a problem for other people. Perhaps, like the designer, they liked it.

So here I was now walking through Hale and then Altrincham with my big blue and pink rucksack, and its appearance was not my greatest concern. What occupied my thoughts much more was the fact that it was heavy. Probably fifteen kilograms or so. This was something I thought about in Altrincham and Rochdale, up on the Pennines, walking up Wharfedale, in Hawes, Kirkby Stephen and Carlisle. In fact the weight of my rucksack was something I thought about a lot of the time, at least in the first half of the walk. Was there anything in there I could do without?

Well, yes there was. If I had been fleeing for my life from an invading army I would not have carried all this stuff. If I had been willing to sleep out under trees in the rain, or only have a hot drink when someone else would give or sell me one, or I had not been bothered about how dirty I was or if my hair itched, or was willing to find my way by signposts and not concerned to take footpaths and back roads, I could have reduced the weight. Much of it was a matter of choice.

As I did not want to travel that way, nor worry about how I might manage if the weather turned really cold, or I sprained an ankle in the mountains, or if I ran out of clean water, I would have to carry that amount of stuff. And as it happened, there were very few things that I did not use at some point or other. Only the Kendal Mint Cake remained unused till the end.

I suppose I had a lot of stuff but when I did other long walks later on I carried much the same amount of equipment. There were one or two other things I took on later walks occasionally, depending on where I was going. Sometimes I took a very small pair of binoculars, French or German dictionaries, an ultrasound device for scaring off French dogs, which rush out of farmyards snarling and yapping, and then, later, a mobile phone.

It was a big full rucksack, and it often felt heavy. But this bag, with a capacity of eighty litres, could carry everything I needed for six weeks of walking and camping out. Compared to the amount of stuff I have at home it was tiny. And that was the other thing that ran through my mind from time to time. If I can manage with this amount for six weeks, why do I have so much more stuff at home?

The journey proved to me that I do not actually need all the other things I have. I simply like to have them, for a variety of reasons. Some are useful for my work, although medieval priests and many missionaries managed with much less. Some are beautiful, at least to me, and I like to have them around. Others help me remember people, places and things that have happened. Some help me to keep in touch with people, or be creative, or enjoy myself. I would not want to go for very long without a guitar to play, or music to listen to, or novels to read. You can cook a lot more interesting things if you have more than one pan. And while I could sleep in a tent wrapped in a sleeping bag I do prefer a bed, and to sit on chairs rather than the ground.

But even so, I have to admit that I could still lead a pleasant and comfortable life with a lot less than I have. And that is probably true of many of us. So why do we have it all?

That is not simply an academic or personal question. The situation is that many of us have not only more stuff than we need but more than we know what to do with. We own things we have forgotten we have, and only discover them when we clear out attics or cupboards and wonder why we kept them in the first place – but probably we then put them back again. Some people hire lockups because they can't keep all their stuff in their home. Some of us have more than is good for our health. We don't have room to move around because our living space is so cluttered, and we have things which we worry about losing.

While some of us have more than we need or really want, many other people lack things that would improve their lives considerably. I walked into Manchester past some big houses with big gardens and big cars outside, and, I assumed, a lot of things in the houses. A few miles further on there were small flats, and houses divided up with several families living in them, second-hand shops selling furniture and other items to people with very small incomes, and agencies working to help people with nothing to have at least the essentials for a small home. That contrast is within one city, in one country. Across the world the contrasts are enormous.

And the earth as a whole suffers for the amount of stuff that we in Western society want to have in our homes and offices. There is no shortage of iron and aluminium in the earth, but many of the rarer metals are already running short, particularly some of those used in the manufacture of electronic equipment. And while there may be no shortage of iron, processing it from iron ore to steel uses vast amounts of energy, much of which comes from coal or oil. Plastics too are largely made from oil, and most of them take decades or centuries to break down. Our desire to have more and more things adds to the pollution of the earth, depletes it of resources which other people now or in the future will need, and contributes to climate change.

It has been estimated that in order for everyone on earth to have the same material standard of living as people in Britain we would need to have three planets. To have an American lifestyle we would need five. We have only one. And yet, as a society, we go on wanting more and more. It is like an addiction – a social disease – and one that has frequently been analysed. The consequences for ourselves and for the earth have been described in many books and films, and there is no shortage of proposed economic programmes for sustainable living. But the disease continues. How do we overcome it?

In the '70s I lived for three years in Nigeria, teaching in a school in a small town. Once every few months I would drive or go on the bus a hundred and fifty miles to our nearest city, Kaduna. It was a place that most of my students had never been. They came from villages in the bush where their fathers were subsistence farmers and the biggest town they saw was the one where they went to school or one like it.

A friend of mine had earlier worked in a school in Kenya and on one occasion he had had to travel up to Nairobi and decided to take one of his students with him. He reckoned afterwards that it had been a big mistake. The teenage boy found the whole thing such a shock that it disturbed him for quite some time. The sheer size of the city, the numbers of people, the traffic and the noise were overwhelming.

Walking now into Manchester I did not have that experience. I did not know Manchester but I had lived, studied and worked in other cities. I just happened now to be living and working in the country, and for the last few days to have been walking slowly through rural Cheshire. But even so, the difference was palpable. It was perhaps because I had adjusted to moving slowly, and paying attention to my surroundings. In the country you look at the people you pass, and perhaps greet them.

Moving around in the city we are not normally attentive to what we are passing. We are focused. Moving on to the next thing. Getting to the next place. There are too many people to pay attention to them all. There is too much going on to try to puzzle it all out. And on buses and in cars we move too fast to be aware of how one place runs into another. But now I was going slowly and had been doing so for several days, and I noticed a lot that I would not normally have seen.

Coming into Manchester from the south-west, the transition from country to city is gradual. At first there are the expensive suburbs with big gardens, paddocks and fields, and slowly they become smaller and more compact. Not all city approaches are like that. Some have estates of flats and small housing on the city boundaries. Others just begin. One minute you are in farmland and a few minutes later you are walking down city streets.

Walking into Beauvais in Northern France was like that, and I was struck by the complexity of city life. In the ancient world cities were considered a marvel, and I could see why. Here were thousands of people all living together, their lives interconnected. People passing, walking, driving, talking, making things, selling, arguing, watching, eating and drinking, all this was a great complex web of urban life. For some reason, perhaps because I had spent a week or more walking only through the open spaces of northern France and a few small towns, I had a strong sense of a great web of activity. It was quite awesome.

Unlike rural Africa in the '70s, while the rural parts of Europe have more open space and a thinner population than the cities they are not something separate. People watch the same television programmes, read the same papers and listen to the same music. Phones, e-mails and social websites connect people wherever they are. You can phone someone now and not know if they are in Regent Street or on Snowdon. It has been said that rural Britain is mostly an expanse of suburbia.

But even so, there is more space and less noise in the countryside. During the day you can often see the sky changing with the weather, and at night there are stars. There are fewer people, fewer vehicles, fewer shops and less advertising. Buying things is something that one does more deliberately. You don't just find yourself buying something in the way that you might when you are walking past shop windows each day with money or a credit card. In the city the inducements and the opportunities are always there. And the pressure is strong.

Manchester developed as an industrial city, as did most of the cities of Europe. There is still a lot of manufacturing in Manchester, although it is not on the scale it once was. Like agriculture, manufacturing industry employs only a fraction of the number of people in Britain that it did fifty years ago. But these cities are part of the great global network of manufacturing and selling. The shops in Hale, Altrincham, Sale and Manchester are stocked with goods shipped in from China, Thailand, Korea, India, Brazil and Japan. And the hoardings, television and internet advertisements are carefully designed with skill and ingenuity to get people to buy the goods. Shop windows are often deliberately set out to encourage the random passerby to call in and buy.

But they did not encourage me. There was no way I was going to buy anything from these shops for the simple reason that I could not carry it. My bag was heavy enough already, and I did not want to be weighed down with unnecessary baggage. I was taking my time, walking slowly down these streets, but my aim was clear. I wanted to walk to Iona, and I did not want extra weight to stop me.

I had some shopping to do, but it was all for necessary stuff. I needed a new gas bottle for my stove, and had to shop around to find one. In Altrincham there was a medium-priced outdoor shop and a rock-climbing boutique, but neither of them had what I needed. Finally I found an army surplus store beside the market and there among the camouflage jackets and khaki socks was just what I needed. I left content.

I then followed it up with food. Next door was a cafe that served pie, peas and chips, with a cup of tea, for little more than the price of a coffee at a Little Chef. I then needed to work out my route into Sale where I had an offer of accommodation with friends. A bath and a bed were a welcome thought. All I had to do was find the place.

These were the days before satnavs, GPS and Google Earth, so I had to do it the old way. I had an Ordnance Survey map but they are of less use in the city than the country. I needed either advice or a street plan, and the obvious place to get that was a Tourist Information Office. And Altrincham had one. I had not expected that. It had not occurred to me that Altrincham might have tourists. But there was the office, and inside were helpful people. I was given a street plan, and leaflets about interesting things between there and Manchester city centre. They also helped with another request, beyond my imagining.

I had worked out that if I stopped that night in Sale I would need accommodation on the north side of the city centre for the next night. Cities are not made for fast walking. You have to keep stopping to cross roads and wait for red men to turn green. I could not expect too much for the next day, although the towpath of the Bridgewater Canal looked promising as a route into the centre. So I asked about possible accommodation in Failsworth or Moston.

'I'll see,' said the smart lady in her mid-'50s. 'I'll phone the tourist office in Oldham.'

I had never been to Oldham. All I knew of it was that it was a former industrial town on the northern side of Manchester. And they used to make car batteries there. When I worked in a garage in the '60s there was an old enamel advert for car batteries. 'I told 'em Oldham' was the slogan. The enamel panel was probably worth more now than a car battery cost then. But that was the extent of my knowledge, until I now discovered that Oldham has a Tourist Information Office. It was clearly holding its head up and saying, 'Don't just go to Bath, Stratford and Canterbury, come to Oldham!'

The assistant was not able to come up with any addresses of bed and breakfasts, but I was encouraged anyway by the sheer existence of a tourist office in Oldham and I left for Sale, ready to try my luck when I got to the north side of Manchester.

The cycle of manufacturing and consumption clearly needs to change. A great deal of energy and material is used up in making things that people do not need or really want and in persuading them that they do. The life of the earth is being irreparably damaged as a result and people are not substantially any better off. The air and water are polluted by metals and plastics as a result of many industrial processes, and the atmosphere is being changed by the carbon dioxide output. Many people have more things but they have to live at a frenetic pace. In Manchester now the waterways and air are far better than they were a century earlier, but that is not the global situation. Manufacturing has moved to China, India, Brazil and South-East Asia. Conditions are better in Britain because many of the industrial processes now take place elsewhere. But in Britain people are aware that their lives are far more pressured than they were thirty years ago. They work at a faster pace with more stress.

There needs to be a way for people's energy and resourcefulness to be directed towards making life better for each other: providing decent food, shelter and clothing for all; making things which have individuality and beauty; and celebrating life with art, music, and an appreciation of the world we are part of. But such an alternative is not just going to happen. What we have and are part of is a system that has to be changed. And that is going to involve people standing up to the pressures to consume and developing ways to do things differently.

I was able to resist any lures to buy other than what I needed from the shops in Manchester by the simple fact that I had a clear aim I wanted to keep to. I wanted to walk to Iona and did not want to be encumbered by anything that would weigh me down. It was that simple. I didn't even think about buying anything else.

That is one way of resisting the pressure to consume. Have an aim. Preferably have a worthwhile aim. And creating an alternative society in which people value each other and the planet seems a pretty good one.

A second thing that helped me was, I suppose, the idea I had of myself. I was a pilgrim, not a shopper. Maybe that is a second way to resist the pressure to consume more and more. Stop being a consumer. Move out of the flow of humanity that defines itself by its ability to have more and more things and think of yourself as someone who does things. Who makes a difference to the world. Who appreciates life as it arises. Who creates beauty, or laughter, or friendship. There are plenty of possibilities, all of which are better than defining yourself as someone who buys stuff.

As Gandhi put it, 'A person is defined not by what they have but by what they are.'

Moving out of the flow is not easy. It takes courage. It has been said that standing up to your enemies is easy; it is standing up to your friends that is hard. Being different from the people around us, the ones we work with or live with, is not easy. The constant enticement through advertising to acquire and consume is hard to resist anyway, let alone when it is reinforced by our peers. One thing that can help here is knowing what makes us think and feel in particular ways. Knowing ourselves, in other words.

Making a long solitary journey on foot is helpful. Walking every day, you get to know your body quite well, particularly when you work it too hard and then pay for it with several days of pain, as I did on my first days of this walk. I was so pleased with my progress on the first day that I foolishly pushed my pace on the second. By the third day I was feeling it badly, and walking through Altrincham on the fourth I had a noticeable limp. The pain never went away completely. At times it was worse than others. For the first week or so I thought that maybe I would wake up one morning and my feet and legs would be OK. It never happened, so eventually I decided I would either have to put up with it or give up. I decided to put up with it, and became familiar with the soreness and stabbing pains, like the rattles in an old car.

Being quiet and alone you also have space to be aware of your emotions: frustration, pleasure, tiredness, hunger, loneliness. There is also plenty of time to think and to be aware of the tracks that your mind habitually runs along. And these are not unique to the journey. The ways I worry, and become anxious, or mull things over, or find ways of leaving these aside and attending to the present moment are aspects of the person I am. I have just become more aware of them by doing long walks on my own, and walking is only one way of doing this.

Various ways of understanding yourself and other people have been developed. Some are quite technical. Among the means of describing different types of personality I have found the Myers Briggs Typology Indicator quite helpful. And the Enneagram. I find Transactional Analysis a useful method of recognising both how I respond to other people and how they deal with each other.

There are other ways that do not involve such technical analysis. There are plenty of people around who have a clear understanding of how they think or feel, and of how other people behave, simply by giving themselves time to reflect on what is happening, and paying attention to their own responses.

But there is a difference, perhaps, between understanding yourself and knowing yourself. This is true of places. I could know a lot about Manchester but it was only by being there and walking through it that I could claim in any sense to know the place. Similarly I was hoping on my way north from the city to stop with a man I had met a few weeks earlier. Before that I had known something about him. Now, having met him, I could claim to know him, though not well. Stopping overnight with him and his wife would help me get to know him better.

We can be the same with ourselves. We can fill our lives with activity and ideas so that our minds are continually moving from a memory of the past to a concern for the future, to fantasies, plans, schemes and theories. Much of this is good and it achieves great things. But many of us seldom stop. Some of us do not know how to stop.

Mindfulness is a way of stopping. Of sidestepping the thinking, worrying, ruminating and planning with which our minds are continually occupied, and, as it were, standing outside those processes. It involves being aware of ourselves, what we feel physically and emotionally, and of what our minds are doing.

There are various ways of doing this. Mindful walking involves paying attention to the feeling of the feet on the ground, and the movement of the toes, ankles and legs, and slowly attending to them. Other forms of mindfulness can be done sitting, or lying down, or moving slowly. Many of them involve attending to one's breath. Sometimes one can attend to what one is hearing or seeing, in such a way as to simply register the sensation rather than describe it or analyse it. Much of this derives from Eastern practices of yoga or Buddhist meditation. The outcome is a sense of being in the present moment, as a timeless moment, and of being oneself.

This has several outcomes. One, which many people who are prone to being chronically unhappy find, is that it enables them to step out from under their cloud of anxiety and depression, and slowly move into a brighter sense of living. Another is that it enables a person to stop identifying with their ideas or their achievements and gain a sense of being. As the Christian contemplative Thomas Merton put it, 'One moves across the ocean on a ship, not on the wake of the ship.'[5] A third outcome is that it can enable a person to accept and value himself or herself as valuable, just as they are.

An underlying principle of these approaches to personal understanding and to the practice of mindfulness is that you are yourself and do not need to become another person. Change by all means. Grow. Develop. But this comes from within. It is not a matter of trying to push yourself into a mould. You yourself have value. You don't have to try to be someone else.

On this journey I was aware of the achievements of other long-distance walkers. I had read some of their books. But I did not need to try to match them. This was my walk. Similarly, you are living your life. And you do not need to do a walk at all.

The word 'simplicity' has been used in the past to describe this sense of self. It indicates a way of living that is not encumbered by unnecessary trappings, striving or guilt, and points to a centredness that enables such a life to be lived.

Two twentieth-century writers on simplicity come at this in different ways. For Richard Foster the key is having a direction in life.[6] He refers to Jesus' teaching about anxiety in which he says, 'Seek first the Kingdom of God and his righteousness (or justice), and all the rest will follow.'[7] It is like my having a clear sense that I was on a pilgrimage and not a shopping expedition.

Richard Rohr describes simplicity as the freedom of letting go.[8] Let go of the need to acquire, to compete, even to be acceptable to others, and what remains is a simple self, unique and valuable. He finds that both the self-understanding that comes through the Enneagram and spending time in contemplation are aids to letting go. Rohr's idea of contemplation is akin to mindfulness. It is more than attending to the world we are part of, which I have described in Chapter One. It encompasses that but also includes paying attention to oneself. He draws on the work of Christian mystics down the centuries and there finds a kind of prayer which is, in fact, very similar to the Buddhist practice of mindfulness.

I find both Foster and Rohr helpful. And on this journey, walking slowly through towns and cities and beside busy roads, I was aware that the rush and haste around me was typical of my normal existence. Somehow, when the pilgrimage was over, I would need to take back into my daily life something of what I had seen and learnt on the journey. It would not be easy. It could easily fade away like a holiday after two weeks at work.

In fact, I am still working on it. There is no quick fix. Simplicity is not acquired like a new television but developed like physical fitness. And, like fitness, it is easily lost.

References

1. Gerard W. Hughes, *Walk to Jerusalem* (London: DLT, 1991)
2. John Hillaby, *Journey through Britain* (London: Constable, 1968)
3. John N. Merrill, *Walking my Way* (London: Chatto & Windus, 1984)
4. Nicholas Crane, *Clear Waters Rising: A mountain walk across Europe* (London: Penguin, 1997)
5. Merton, *No Man is an Island* (London: Search Press, 1977) p103
6. Richard Foster, *Celebration of Discipline: The path to spiritual growth* (London: Hodder, 1980)
7. Matthew 6.33
8. Richard Rohr, *Simplicity: The freedom of letting go* (New York: Crossroad, Revised edition 2003)

Resources 3: Simplicity

Cuthbert

Off the east coast of Northumberland are the small, rocky Farne Islands. They are now a bird sanctuary, but for Cuthbert they were a place of retreat.

Cuthbert was in turn a monk, a wandering preacher and pastor, the prior of a monastery, and then a bishop. He lived in the 600s and travelled widely around Northumbria, between the Forth and the Humber, and had a reputation for going into valleys and wild areas where other ministers would be loath to travel. He mixed with all sorts of people, from kings to the poorest farmers – and was willing to argue his case and speak out when he felt it necessary.

It was a demanding life, and he needed times of solitude and quiet. The Farne Islands were one place where he found it.

Many other very active people down the centuries have found they needed places to get away. To recharge. To reflect. To be themselves as they are in themselves, rather than in response to others. This is a key to simplicity.

Some people are able to take time out, perhaps even for days at a time. For others long periods of retreat are not possible, but moments of quiet are. And there are ways of using those moments of quiet to let go of the clutter in our minds.

The Shakers used to sing,

> *''Tis the gift to be simple, 'tis the gift to be free;*
> *'tis the gift to come down where we ought to be.'*[1]

Simplicity is a gift. It is not something you strive for, earn or achieve. It is something you are given.

The problem is that often our hands are too full of other things to be able to receive the gift. So we need to let some of them go.

Reference

1. *Come and Praise 2* (London: BBC, 1988) No 97

For reflection or discussion

1. Have you ever had a good 'clear-out'? Turned out a cupboard, or a shed or garage, and got rid of things you don't need or really want. How did it feel? Why do you think it felt this way?

2. Do you ever buy things you don't really need or want? Why do you do it? How do you feel afterwards?

3. William Morris said, 'Have nothing in your house which is neither beautiful nor useful.' Do you think that is good advice?

Some Bible passages relevant to the theme

1 Samuel 17:1-51
In this tale of the young David he is willing to fight the giant warrior Goliath but must do it with his usual sling and stick. He cannot do it with the armour and weapons of the king.

Psalm 46
In this poem God exhorts readers to pause, and be still, and know that God is God.

Matthew 4:1-2; Luke 4:1-2
According to both these gospel writers Jesus followed the ancient practice of fasting when he had to pray and think about how he was to carry out his work, following his baptism by John the Baptist.

Matthew 6:24-34
Jesus tells his disciples they are not to be anxious, even about the basic things they need for life, but to instead focus on God's reign and justice.

Matthew 13:44-45
In these two stories Jesus says that sometimes it is necessary to give things up in order to have what is really valuable.

Action

1. Imagine that you are going to leave your home and be away for a long time. You can decide where you are going to in this exercise. Perhaps it is a long holiday. Perhaps you are emigrating. Maybe you have to leave in a hurry because of some great danger.

Then make two lists. What would you need to take with you? What else would you like to take with you? And why?

How much stuff are you leaving behind? How do you feel about that?

2. Draw a time chart of your life. On a big sheet of paper draw a line and mark on it with words or pictures significant things that have happened in your life up to the present moment. Take your time. You may have strong feelings about some of what happened. Identify what those feelings are: sadness, happiness, disappointment, grief, anger, regret. At the end of the line draw yourself now, or write your name. Then draw an arrow to continue the line. Look at the whole thing. The line is past. The arrow is into the unknown future. You are now.

3. Find a place to sit where you will not be disturbed for ten minutes or so. Sit upright and comfortably. This probably means having your feet squarely on the ground, your hands in your lap, and your head balanced at the top of your spine so that your neck muscles are not pulling in any direction to keep it upright.

Close your eyes and be aware of the sounds around you. If you can identify what they are, acknowledge that, but do not think about the cause. Just let there be a sea of sounds with you quietly in the centre of it.

Then pay attention to your breathing. Do not deliberately breathe in any particular way. Just let it happen as it was before but pay attention to either the feel of the air coming in and out of your nose or mouth or to the movement of your abdomen as it rises and falls. Be aware of the air coming into you and going out again. Pay attention to this for several minutes.

While you are doing this, your mind will wander. Perhaps to plans for what you must do later, or to remembering things that have happened. Or to things that might happen. Be aware of those thoughts, and the emotions that go with them, and gently bring your attention back to your breath.

It might help to set a timer, perhaps to ten minutes for the whole exercise. But not longer. Less would be fine. Then when the time is up open your eyes and pay attention for a few minutes to what you can see: looking for the colours, shapes and textures of the things before you.

Repeat this exercise on a number of occasions. You may find after a while that you find it easier to be still in other places, and to move into stillness for a few minutes on a bus or train, or at your desk or computer, developing a greater sense of being yourself: a person who has ideas, plans, worries, possessions and relationships, but is other than all those.

Further reading

Richard Rohr, *Simplicity: The freedom of letting go* (New York: Crossroad, Revised edition 2003)
A collection of talks on contemplation, community and how less is more.

Richard Foster, *Celebration of Discipline: The path to spiritual growth* (London: Hodder, 1980)
For the author the key to the discipline of simplicity is to focus on the bigger picture, the Kingdom of God. Everything else follows, as Jesus said.

Eric Fromm, *To Have or To Be* (London: Jonathan Cape, 1978)
Contrasting two modes of existence the author analyses the pathology of the consumer society and drawing on the wisdom of many religious and philosophical traditions advocates a cure.

Mark Williams and Danny Penman, *Mindfulness: A practical*

guide to finding peace in a frantic world (London: Piatkus, 2011)
Based on recent scientific developments and ancient practices.

Anthony de Mello, *Sadhana: a Way to God: Christian exercises in Eastern form* (St Louis: Institute of Jesuit Sources, 1980)
A practical guidebook from an Indian Catholic teacher and leader of retreats.

Four

Noticing Strangers

After crossing the motorway I had come first into the suburbs and then into the Manchester conurbation. Shropshire and Cheshire are hardly a wilderness but even so in a day's walking I had met few people and I was walking alone. I had no phone and Madron and I had agreed that I would only phone home in an emergency. We would keep in touch with occasional cards and letters. Now there were people all around, all going about their lives, with me – with my pink rucksack – weaving among them.

A couple of days earlier I had been walking alone beside a canal in Cheshire. There were few boats on the canal, and no other people to be seen, only the houses of a small town beyond the hawthorn hedge. Then I came to the edge of a chemical plant: pipes, cylinders, valves, gangways, factory buildings, and still no people. I had no idea what they were making, or how it worked. And while it might have warmed the heart of an engineer or the factory owner, it seemed to me something of an eyesore. I would have preferred to see more trees and fields.

But, as I adjusted the rucksack on my back, I was aware that the material of this bag, and the adhesive of my boots, and the fabric of my tent, and the gas for my stove, and the fleece of my jacket, in fact a large part of what I had with me, was made in a factory much like this. I could walk in the pretty countryside if I chose, but my ability to do so depended on places such as this. I might be spending a lot of my time walking across fields and beside trees and hedges, but I was part of a network of activity and production that included mines, mills, factories and chemical plants. I might be walking alone but I was dependent on other people who made the things I was using. I could not have made them myself. And I might be walking quietly beside an old canal but the equipment I had and the food and drink that I would need had all been moved around in trucks, trains, and possibly ships. I had not stepped out of industrial society, I was simply weaving my way through it, travelling slowly and on my own two feet, but still a part of the whole.

That network of human industry stretched back into the past. Two hundred years ago the canal had been the most efficient way to move goods around the country. The processes in the chemical plant had been developed over hundreds of years. As had the skills of weaving fabric, making boots, growing and processing food, and constructing the transport systems that were now used to move goods.

The Cheshire countryside, with its fields, trees, hedges and lanes, is not a natural environment. There are in Britain a number of areas designated as Areas of Outstanding Natural Beauty which have special by-laws applying to control development and to maintain the scenery. Many of us appreciate these areas and are glad they exist. But they are not natural. Most of them, if left untended, would become bog and woodland in a matter of a few decades. The British landscape that many people love is actually a human artefact.

Sometimes when I am walking I am reminded of the people who were involved in forming what I am now walking through. A ruined shed, an overgrown wall, an ancient track, a standing stone all point back to the activity of those who lived long ago. Once, these things were new. Life has moved on, but what they did has become a part of what followed, and is, occasionally, still visible now.

At other times there are few material reminders but the place itself has a significance which makes the past almost palpable. Some years after my walk to Iona I walked to Italy. The route I chose was not the simplest but, again, I wanted to link some places that had significance for me. Thus I used the Simplon Pass to cross the great ridge of the Alps south of the Valais in Switzerland. It was not the first Alpine pass I had crossed, so I knew I just had to accept that what I was doing that day was walking uphill. It was steep and I needed to take my time. It was hard work.

I was away from the modern road, climbing what was the old path, fortunately now well maintained as a walker's path. On that day it was deserted except for me climbing up through the trees and across the streams. But I had a sense of others long ago, struggling up that same path. Porters with badly fitting footwear and baskets, without the benefit of modern boots and a well fitting rucksack. Pilgrims, possibly praying their way with each step. Delegates and merchants with business in Italy cursing the struggle to get there. And refugees, carrying all their goods and hoping desperately for peace, shelter and food on the other side.

Before this I had walked through northern France, from Calais to Paris, and my route took me through the Somme. Periodically there were small graveyards with their rows of uniform stones. The land around was quiet, and the sky big and open. Occasionally I could see a car passing on another route across the plain, or a tractor working in a field, but I was walking alone. Apart from the ghosts. Hundreds of thousands of men had tramped along these roads, many of them to their deaths. I had seen the pictures. I had read the poems. I had even sung some of the songs. Now these were all in my mind as I steadily walked on and on through the day across this still and quiet land.

In the fields of Cheshire and the streets of Manchester there has not been slaughter on the same scale, but there has been struggle. Over generations labourers have tended the land, working in all weathers, clearing, ploughing, hoeing, harvesting, and often for little more than a meal a day and a roof over their heads, and sometimes not even that. And in the city people have worked long hours away from the sun and slept in overcrowded houses with poor sanitation and insufficient heating in winter. The names of most of the twentieth-century war dead are recorded somewhere, on stones or in records. The names of many of those who struggled year by year over the centuries to get by in the countryside or the industrial cities are now lost. But what we have, we have inherited from them. Europe as it now is. The landscape, the technology, the stories, the ideas, the songs, and the language.

My walk to Italy was an attempt to connect up my trails in Britain with a place called Bobbio in Italy. I knew that Irish monks had not only sailed to Iona and established a monastery there in the sixth century but had also travelled through Europe, and one in particular, a character called Columbanus, had established a monastery at Bobbio. On the way, I wanted to walk via a small town in Switzerland which I had visited in my teens when it had left a big impression on me.

From Canterbury I had walked to Dover, and then, some time later, I had taken a ferry from Dover and set off from Calais, walking through the Somme area, to Beauvais and to Paris. A couple of years after that I had another opportunity to go walking for several months and set off from Paris to walk to Bobbio.

Three weeks later I was in Dijon and hit a mental block. It would not normally have taken that long to get to Dijon but I had been ill and had to take some time out to recover. By the time I got to Dijon I was fine, physically. But as I sat there in my room in the youth hostel, I could not face picking up my rucksack and setting off again. So I took a day out to wander around Dijon and spent time sitting in cafes and visiting the art gallery. For two more days I did the same thing, because still each morning I could not face continuing my journey.

This had never happened before. Normally, however tired I had been the previous night, by the morning I was ready to go again and would set off through the city or country or across the hills. But not this time. I really did not want to do it, however much I told myself that it would be OK once I got going, that there would be interesting things to see, and I would have the great satisfaction of completing the walk I had set out on. I could not face picking up the rucksack and setting off across the town into the countryside.

After three days of this I caught a train southwards, and then a bus to Taizé. I had thought of visiting Taizé on the walk but had decided on another route. Now I would go there, and see what happened.

Taizé is a small village in Burgundy and the home to a Christian community established during the Second World War to pray for peace and reconciliation. By the '90s it had become well known and was receiving thousands of visitors every year. I knew quite a number of people who had been there, and was familiar with some of the songs that the Taizé Community used in their worship. Now I would go and see the place for myself, and meet some people there.

That was the big attraction. Meeting people. And there were plenty of them. Many of those who go to Taizé are young. Under thirty. Hundreds go there from Germany, the Netherlands and Scandinavia, others from Italy, Poland or other parts of France. They camp or stay in huts and through several days together they worship in the distinctive Taizé style, with lots of songs and candles, and take part in discussions about their lives and the world.

It is a place that has a reputation for honest discussion and exploration of issues and sharing of concerns and ideas. Many of the young people come in groups with youth leaders, and in order for them not to be inhibited by their leaders, the older people stay in another part of the site. I was not there as a youth leader but I was certainly one of the older people so I was allocated a place among the over-thirties, and was given a bunk in a wooden hut and invited to attend the talks and join a discussion group.

The talks were by one of the members of the Community, and they were quite good, although I can't remember what they were about. The discussion group I joined had a dozen people in it from various places, and no common language. We could only discuss by translating for each other. Three Italian women only spoke Italian, but a Catalan man could speak some Italian, and French and Spanish. There was a Swedish woman who spoke English, and I could get by in French. There was an American who spoke only English, but altogether we got by, with some understanding and a lot of laughs.

At the end of a week in Taizé, as the others in my group left, I too set off. I took a bus, and then a train to a place called Lons le Saunier. I had intended to walk there, and it would have been about four days' walk from Dijon. From there I set off again on foot, with the thought that now I had broken the journey. Even if

I got to Bobbio, I would not have walked the whole way. I would walk a bit and then maybe catch a bus.

I never did catch a bus. I did take a boat along Lake Geneva, hitch two miles after climbing a thousand metres of Alpine pass, take a cable car down a pass when I could not find a path, and once accept the offer of a five-mile lift when it was getting dark. But apart from that I walked all the way into Italy, although not as far as Bobbio.

A couple of years later I walked the stretch in France that I had missed out, just for the sake of completion. But when I was at Taizé, and afterwards when I started walking again, I was puzzling over two things in my mind. I felt disappointment, and to some extent that I had failed by not walking the whole way. But who had I let down? No one else was relying on my completing that walk. Perhaps if they had been I would have carried on. I don't know. It was not something I needed to do. I had decided to do it. That was all. In that it was a pilgrimage I could say I was doing it for God, but I could not for one second believe that God was somehow going to hold it against me that I had not done every inch on foot. For all I knew God could well have thought it was a pretty crazy idea anyway.

I remembered walking the Pilgrim's Way to Canterbury and stopping overnight at Aylesford Priory. At the evening meal a fellow guest asked me what I was doing there and I told him that I was on a pilgrimage and had set off from Winchester on foot.

He turned round and said to an Irish priest sitting next to him, 'This man's walked all the way from Winchester!'

'Oh,' said the priest. 'Did he miss the bus?'

Normally on a long walk I would keep quiet about what I was doing, unless someone asked. I did not want to appear to be on an ego trip. Though perhaps I was really. On any walk the question of why I was doing it would often arise. I was rarely sure. But if I had any ideas at all they were a fair mixture of motives.

But the other thing that puzzled me as I walked on after Taizé was why I had hit that mental block on this walk and never before. I had spent six weeks walking to Iona alone and was no less fit now. In fact I had far less pain in my legs and feet than I had at times on that earlier walk. My rucksack was no heavier. The scenery was no less interesting. My destination was attractive, and I was anticipating some exciting walking before I got there. I eventually came to the conclusion that I had a greater sense of isolation.

On the walk to Iona I had become aware that one effect of spending day after day walking on my own was that any contact that I did have with people took on a greater significance than it would normally. Small acts of friendliness or hospitality were precious. And I was much more sensitive to rejection.

There was a time in Argyll when I stopped to have my lunch on a beach by a campsite. It was an idyllic spot, and the weather was good. People on holiday were messing about in boats. A few were swimming. I had originally thought I might camp there for the night but I had arrived earlier than planned and decided I did not want to spend the afternoon sitting around watching people enjoying themselves. I would carry on. But first I would use the toilets at the campsite.

As I came out I met a man staring at me with a 'What do you think you're doing?' look on his face.

'I hope you don't mind me using your toilets,' I said, guessing that only a man with a sense of ownership could look like that when confronting an unauthorised urinator. 'I had thought I might camp for the night, but maybe next time.'

'There won't be a next time,' he said.

At first I thought he was suggesting that the campsite would be closing down, but then I realised that as I had used his loos without asking his permission I was to be banished from his campsite. For ever. It was laughable.

The problem was that this act of pettiness did not make me laugh, but niggled me. As I walked on it kept running through my mind. I intended to stop at another campsite about eight miles further on. Perhaps I would find that he owned that one too. I became quite anxious.

It was several miles further on that the phrase 'forty days' came into my mind. I had not actually been on the road for forty days, but it was getting on for that, and forty days is a symbolic time. It occurs in the Bible as a significant period. Jesus, the gospels say, was in the wilderness for forty days and then he was tempted.

I had been on the road for a significant period of time, and it was taking its toll. If I had had someone with me we would no doubt have laughed it off together. We might even have told him there and then not to be so stupid. But I was on my own. The solitude was becoming loneliness. It was getting to me.

When on the way to Italy I arrived in Dijon I had not been going that long, but I had a greater sense of isolation. Partly, I decided, this was because walking to Iona, even though I was walking alone, I had had various points where I would meet up with people I knew, but this was not the case in France. On the trail to Iona I stopped in Rochdale with a Member of the Iona Community I had met a few weeks earlier, and with a friend in Westmorland. In Edinburgh I stayed with my sister, and then on Iona there would probably be one or two people I had met before. It was certainly a place I knew well. But on the way to Italy there were to be no such meeting points, and the destination was unknown to me. I just knew of it from other people.

Even more significant, I reckoned, was the language. I can get by in French. At Taizé I had managed to do some translating for our group discussions. But my French was not good enough to be able to pick up phrases with no context. And so much talk on a solitary walk is of this kind.

In an evening I might get talking with someone, and as long as the other person was patient and their local dialect not too strong, I could have a conversation. But if a French person I met on a path or in a shop would say something to me, after the inevitable 'Bonjour', I often could not catch what they were saying. So I might ask them to repeat it and that would be embarrassing for all. It was usually not something significant. It would be the French equivalent of 'Could rain later' or 'It won't last'. The content of the statement or question was not important. They were simply indicating that they were taking notice of me. But whereas in Britain I could normally reply and extend the greeting, or turn it into a three sentence exchange – 'Nice yesterday though' or 'Is that what they say?' – in France I could not do that. It was like dropping the ball. If I asked for it to be repeated the flow would be lost. So I would mutter something and beat a retreat.

Sometimes I could not do that. Once I was walking beside a road in the afternoon and a man pulled up beside me in a car. He leant out of the window and spoke. I was not sure what he had said so I guessed. 'No thanks,' I said. 'I'm enjoying the walk.'

But he was not asking me if I wanted a lift. So he said it again. At the third attempt I realised he was asking me how far I walked in a day. 'Oh, twenty-five kilometres,' I said. He nodded and drove off. He wasn't going to keep up the conversation.

And so in France each day the sense of isolation grew. At Taizé there was conversation. Music. Laughs. And most of the people in my part of the camp were on their own, or at least wanting to meet others outside their own group. As often happens in such circumstances people quickly got talking, explaining why they were there, where they had come from, even telling their life history. When the time came to move on I was recharged.

There are people who can survive for long periods of time out in the wild on their own, who have learned the skills of extreme bushcraft from their tribe or their commando trainers. But most of us are dependent on others for the things we need. This dependence links us into great networks of production and exchange. Our food comes from many places, the clothes we wear are manufactured in one place from fabrics made somewhere else, our homes are constructed with materials which have been transported over long distances. In a simple act like making ourselves a cup of tea we are connected with numerous other people. Growers, processors, packers, transporters, merchandisers, store managers, shelf stackers, checkout operators are all involved before we have even taken the tea out of the shop. We then have to get the tea home, fill a kettle with water and boil it. Add it all up and a lot of people are involved in our cup of tea. Sitting and drinking it we might be on our own, but we are still linked up with others.

Some of us like to have a cup of tea quietly on our own. Many others like to sit and have a chat with someone else at the same time. But even the solitaries among us occasionally need other people, and we certainly do at the beginning of our lives. In our childhood we acquire from others a language and the basic skills of thinking and making sense of what happens to us. And when we want to buy the tea we probably need to be able to speak or at least communicate in some way or other.

We do not just need occasional meaningful exchanges. Without the small comments we make to each other – in shops, in passing – without at least eye contact, we wilt emotionally. Chat is not just about information. It is a way of doing with words what people also do with touch. We affirm each other's existence. We energise each other through contact, because we cannot function effectively in isolation for too long.

We are mostly aware of ourselves as individuals, at least in Western society, but we are not just individuals. We are connected with others. We are part of networks. We engage with others in a multitude of ways. And we cannot avoid that. It is simply an aspect of our lives.

It is sometimes said that one of the things we need is community. People move into villages looking for a community to belong to. They join clubs and associations in cities in order to try to find community. Some people join intentional religious communities, like the Iona and Taizé Communities. But 'community' is a vague word. News reports will talk about 'the Muslim community' or the 'Gay community', even though many of these Muslim or gay people have nothing much to do with each other. Sometimes they might be antagonistic. We can say that we need 'community' but we must then think about what kind of community we are actually looking for.

We are inevitably in some kind of relationship with many people. Some of these relationships are long-standing. Some are very much of the moment. It is a question of what these relationships are like. So far in this book we have thought about how contemplation can lead us to have a greater respect for the world we are part of. We have thought about the value of engaging with the world, of feeling the earth and of linking different aspects of our lives. And we have thought about the value of simplicity. All these are things we do as individuals. But our individuality is only one aspect of our lives and we will think now about our relationships with other people.

Resources 4: Community

Brigid

At Brigid's monastery in Kildare in Ireland there was a fire that never went out. It was tended day and night at the heart of a place of welcome for all who needed shelter and help. For centuries it burned, continuing the flame that was first lit by Saint Brigid herself.

Or so it is said. A lot is said about Brigid but very little is known. As a historical figure she fades into legend and myth. She is associated with places across Ireland and the west of Britain but historians are reluctant to commit themselves as to whether there even really was a woman called Brigid who gave rise to the stories. Perhaps, they say, her name and much of her character is derived from the myths of an Irish goddess.

But what is certain is that in Ireland, Scotland, and across the world, this spirit of welcome and hospitality has been lived by countless women and men down the ages. That flame has never gone out.

In the seventeenth century, long before globalisation and the development of ecology, John Donne wrote, 'No man is an island, entire of itself. Each is a piece of the continent, a part of the main.'[1]

None of us exists in isolation. From before our birth we have needed other people simply in order to survive. We learn our language and other basic skills from others. As fit and healthy adults we can be reduced to emotional weakness by solitary isolation. As we get older we return to needing the support of other people.

We can pretend that this is not so, or we can accept it, and welcome it. We can open the doors of our minds, our imaginations and our emotions to other people, and welcome them.

Reference

1. John Donne, *Meditation 17*, 1624

For reflection or discussion

1. Make a cup of tea or coffee or pour yourself a cold drink and while you are drinking it make a list of how many people might have been involved in producing it.

2. Do you have experience of a group which has or had clear boundaries? Where people definitely belonged or did not? Do you have experience of a group in which it was not really clear who was or was not a member? How did you feel about each one? Why do you think that was?

3. Can you remember ever being welcomed by a person or a group of people? How did it affect you at the time? And in the long term?

Some Bible passages relevant to the theme

Genesis 18:1-15
The nomadic herdsman Abraham shows hospitality to three strangers, who then promise him that despite their age he and his wife Sarah will have a son.

Leviticus 19:9-18
The commandments given to Abraham's descendants, the Israelites, are to guide and enforce good community relations and support for strangers. These are a small sample.

1 Kings 19:1-21
The prophet Elijah wanders into the desert to the mountain of God, convinced that he is the only person left who is faithful to the God of Abraham. In the stillness after a great storm, an earthquake and a bushfire, God assures him that he is not alone, and that he still has a task to do.

Mark 1:14-20
As Jesus begins his preaching he gathers a small group of disciples.

Mark 6:7-13
When Jesus sends out his disciples to preach, teach and heal on his behalf, he sends them in pairs. They never go alone.

Action

1. Draw a diagram to identify the various communities that you belong to.

2. Consider your list of friends and contacts. Are there any that you wish you communicated with more frequently? Choose one and write, phone or text them to renew the contact.

3. On a short journey pay attention to the people you pass or meet. What do you think they are feeling? How does their life seem to be for them? Speculate on where some of them might be coming from, and going to. You will probably be wrong but it helps to remind you that they have lives beyond the short time that they are near you.

Further reading

Jean Vanier, *Community and Growth* (London: DLT, 2nd edition 1989)
The founder of the L'Arche Community explores how a community can be a place of belonging and openness, of challenge and growth.

Brother Roger of Taizé, *His Love is a Fire: Central writings with extracts from journals* (London: Geoffrey Chapman, 1990)
Formed during the Second World War the Taizé Community, founded by Brother Roger, has had a profound impact on the world church and on society.

Norman Shanks, *Iona – God's Energy: The vision and spirituality of the Iona Community* (Glasgow: Wild Goose, 2nd edition 2009)

A Leader of the Iona Community describes how it aims to combine work and worship, prayer and politics, action for justice and church renewal.

Frank G. Kirkpatrick, *The Ethics of Community* (Oxford: Blackwell, 2001)
A study of the history, philosophy and theology of community, and its significance for individual, religious and political life.

Ian Bradley, *Colonies of Heaven: Celtic models for today's church* (London, DLT, 2000)
The sharing of a common life was central to the ancient Celtic strand of Christianity. The author believes we have a lot to learn from their way of doing things.

Five

Mind and Heart

I spent the night near Sale and then, next morning, walked into the centre of Manchester beside the Bridgewater Canal. It was a clear morning. A Saturday. There were a few people with dogs also walking the canal bank. And one or two early anglers. The dog walkers and I looked at each other and nodded. The anglers looked at their floats.

The canal is wide. Big enough for large barges, and much wider than canals I had followed in Cheshire. And I had things to look out for. At the tourist information office in Altrincham I had picked up a leaflet about the canal, when it was built, what it was for, and things to see. Places specially built so that horses that fell in could be brought out. I had never thought of that, but when barges were pulled by horses a few horses as well as people must have ended up in the canal on a busy and wet day, when the tow-path was muddy. And there was a place where the night soil was unloaded. No main sewers in this industrial city back in 1800. Falling in the canal would not have been a joke.

But now it was clear, and the water clean enough for fish. I passed through Old Trafford, where the de Trafford family had made a lot of money selling off their estate for industrial development. And there was Manchester United's ground. A holy place for some. And a food factory, warehouses, and roads weaving over and under. Approaching the city centre the canal had been restored as a feature and leisure facility. The area around the new concert hall was a far cry from the industrial complex it would have been in the days of horses.

In the centre I found a small cafe, and with a coffee and a bun I thought about the city. I had lived in Birmingham and Edinburgh, and knew the west side of London quite well, but Manchester I had only visited a couple of times. It was not a place I knew. But it was one I could come back to. I would not spend time now exploring the centre but press on northwards.

I had no idea where I would spend the night. One possibility was Rochdale, but it was some way ahead. A few weeks before leaving I had met Stanley Hope, a Member of the Iona Community who lived there. I had told him about my walk and he had said if I wanted a bed for the night I could stop over with him and his wife. That was a possibility, but it was still quite a long way. I decided I would give it a try and if I couldn't make it I would have to find a bed somewhere else. The route to Rochdale was easy. There was the Rochdale canal from the city centre winding its way up to this former cotton town to the north. All I had to do was find the canal and keep walking.

I found the canal after a bit of wandering around back streets with my map, but I was not going to try walking beside it. Unlike the Bridgewater Canal it had not been done up at that time. The tow-path was overgrown and was strewn with bricks, concrete and plastic. After decades without use the canal itself was cluttered with supermarket trolleys, old tyres and bits of bike. It might lead to Rochdale but, if it were possible at all, it would be harder to follow it than to walk beside the road. I looked at the map again.

The simplest route would be to follow the main road which would mean that I would see a bit more of Manchester than I would following the canal. On the canal towpath I would only have seen the backs of houses. On the road I would see a slice of the city from the centre to the outskirts. But there would be one big drawback.

If you are walking with a large rucksack it is easier if you can keep to a steady pace. Stopping and starting is particularly tiring. So walking across moorland on a firm path is much easier than crossing fields where there is long grass, gates to open and stiles to climb. Canal towpaths are ideal, as long as they are still in use. They usually have a firm surface which is not as hard as tarmac, and they are mostly level. There are short climbs around bridges and locks but nothing much. And old canals twist and turn and are often overgrown by trees so they make for pleasant walking. Country lanes are also easy going, as long as there is not much traffic. But on city roads you have to keep stopping to cross other roads that join them from the side or negotiate roundabouts and wait at traffic lights. They do not usually have steep hills, although occasionally they do, but they are tiring. Still, the A664 to Middleton and Rochdale looked like a better option than trying to negotiate the Rochdale Canal towpath, so I set off that way.

In his book *Still Waters Rising* Nicholas Crane talks of having a sense of aloneness walking into a Swiss village on a winter evening when the lights are coming on. There is a tinge of loneliness, he notes, but it is nothing to the loneliness he has felt living in a big city. Many people can identify with that.

One of the things, I believe, that makes a difference is eye contact. I now live in a village in Somerset and if you are walking round the village, even if other people don't speak, and they often do, they at least look at you. Sometimes visitors don't do that and it is quite noticeable. If you speak to them they look at you in surprise, and it takes a moment for them to realise what has happened. Then they will usually happily reply. But they will not initiate the contact.

It is understandable. They come from cities where people don't make eye contact with each other. Perhaps it is because there are too many of them. You can walk through a village and pass half a dozen people, if it is busy. But on a city street there are hundreds. They are simply part of the scenery. They are obstacles to be avoided, not people to engage with, even in the most superficial way.

And many people in the city will have a network of friends or acquaintances whom they will acknowledge. Out of the thousands they live among they have a circle of tens, maybe hundreds, they actually know and see occasionally. That is enough for them to cope with. But it makes it hard for someone who does not belong to such a network. Or who is feeling particularly vulnerable or excluded. Then, being unnoticed by other people can be painful. Loneliness in the city can be harder than loneliness in the mountains.

What struck me in Manchester as I walked out along this main road was that so often people did notice each other. I called into a shop for some chocolate and the assistant spoke to me as if she saw me every day. At one point I was called by a young woman on the other side of the road. She wanted to operate the pedestrian lights and the switch on her side was broken. Could I press the button on my side? And then at one point a car stopped in the main road to let me cross a side road.

I was going to have to stop and wait for the car to turn into it but the driver clearly saw what I was doing. Maybe he went walking in the hills. I don't know. But he clearly registered that it would be helpful to me if I could just keep going so he stopped and waited. And the traffic backed up behind him as I walked across the road.

Ten seconds later he had probably forgotten about it. It was not a big issue. But it made a difference to me. A small difference was that I used up slightly fewer calories of energy. What made a bigger difference was that I had been noticed. Not just that someone had seen me, a walker, striding along the pavement, but that he had in that moment registered what it was like for me, and had responded in a helpful way. That stuck in my mind.

On this journey there were a number of occasions when similar things happened: where in different ways people picked up how things were for me and reacted in a manner that would help me. It happens all the time, of course. Not just to people on walks. But perhaps because I was spending so much time alone, with plenty of time to reflect on what was happening, I noticed many of these.

About ten days later I was in Kirkby Stephen in the Pennines. I had stopped a couple of nights in Wharfedale, and then been two days back on the road and was feeling tired. It was a grey afternoon. I arrived in the town about four and went into the church to look around, but more to the point, to sit and to think. I was very aware of pain in my legs, and my back was beginning to ache even when I didn't have the rucksack on. Although I had only left home a fortnight before it felt like a long time. And Iona was still a long way away. If it had been easy I might have got on a bus home. But it wasn't, and at five o'clock I crossed the road to the youth hostel.

Outside the hostel was a minibus. 'The Redfoot Goose is on the Move' said a banner on the window, with a cartoon that looked like a duck in red wellies. I checked into reception and made my way to the allotted dormitory. When I opened the door I was hit by a wave of smell. Sweat and liniment, like a rugby changing room. Apparently, the Redfoot Goose was the emblem of an Air Force squadron and some of the airmen were doing a charity walk. As I changed out of my boots I found out more from the man sitting on the bunk opposite mine.

One of their colleagues had been greatly helped by Stoke Mandeville Hospital following an accident and now, in appreciation, they were doing a sponsored walk to raise money for it. They were walking the Coast to Coast path from St Bees Head to Whitby. The minibus was their support vehicle. But what was I doing?

'Just walking to Scotland,' I said. Although I might have said I had been walking to Scotland but was now thinking of giving up.

'Where from?'

'Telford,' I said, referring to the nearest town to the village where I had started.

'Hey, this guy's walked from Telford!'

How? Which way had I come? With no support? I was carrying all my stuff? Going to where?

They were genuinely interested. And as we talked I realised that I had by then walked quite a long way. And though I was not trekking across the fells, it was still a serious walk, and I was doing quite well.

Over a meal some of us talked into the evening, about walking, and pilgrimages. They told me about the hospital, and their friend's injuries that the hospital had treated. And the next morning I left to continue to Scotland, and they set off across the Pennines.

A few days later, at Samye Ling, it was simpler. I had heard about the place some months before leaving. Some Tibetan Buddhist refugees had set up a Buddhist centre at Eskdalemuir in the Southern Uplands of Scotland and it seemed like an interesting place to stay that would be on my route. There was no way I could book ahead as I had no idea when I would arrive. I was not willing to walk to a schedule but would find accommodation as I needed it. That was OK, I was told when I rang them before leaving home, there is usually room.

As I approached Eskdalemuir from Gretna on a small road that wound between Crawthat Hill and the Grange of Tundergrath I crossed the Water of Milk and the Black Esk to follow the White Esk into several miles of conifers and on to Castle O'er. I had camped the night before and there had been a light rain when I started that day. It grew heavier as the day went on, and the word 'usually' kept going through my mind. Usually is not the same as always. Usually means that sometimes there is no room. But, I told myself, there would be other places around, or somewhere to camp. That was certainly true. There would be places to camp in the forestry plantations, amongst the sodden bracken and broken branches. I plodded on along small roads winding through the wooded hills and met no one. Occasionally a Land Rover would splash past. Otherwise the views were of trees, and occasionally grey hills through falling rain.

Eskdalemuir, I discovered, was not really a village. Or not one that I could see. There were a few cottages scattered around, but no sign of a Buddhist centre. I found a house which had a sign saying, 'Shop. Please ring.' I rang the bell. A woman answered it and I stepped, dripping, into her hall. Along one wall were two shelves with matches, sweets and a few cans. I bought two bars of chocolate and asked for the Buddhist Centre.

'That way,' she said, with little enthusiasm and pointing vaguely out the door. 'On the Ettrick road.' It was the way I wanted to go anyway so at least I was not going to have to make a detour of several miles. So I set off and the rain continued.

After a couple of miles the rain eased off and I came round a bend to a place that looked like the home of a Himalayan Government Officer, surrounded by prayer flags. A sign said 'Retreat House: No Entry'. And another pointed, 'Samye Ling'. Half a mile further on I came to a sign that showed I had found the right place, and a neat drive lined with prayer flags and trees. Four young men were laying stones to tidy the edge of the drive and a flower bed. Everything dripped.

'I'm looking for somewhere to stay,' I said.

'You'll need to go to the office,' said one of them. 'They're quite friendly in there today.' He left me to make my way. I turned slowly.

'Are you tired?' he said.

Yes, I was. I was very tired. Why hadn't I thought of that? I was knackered, but for some reason I had not realised. It was simple. He had guessed how I felt and by asking the question had helped me to recognise how I was feeling.

He then went with me into the big house at the end of the drive and showed me the tea-making area where the urn was always on. Then he pointed out the office. There someone took my name and someone else showed me a room with two sets of bunks and a mattress on the floor. One of them ought to be free I was told. I made a bed, went downstairs and made tea, took it through to what I was told was the library and collapsed in a chair. People came and went, as did the rain outside. Later, in the dining room, there was soup and wads of brown bread with peanut butter and jam and salads. That night I slept well, and the next day I stayed, watching the rain from the library, and, when it stopped, walking around the place and visiting the temple, a magnificent building completely in the Tibetan style. I rested. I talked. I thought and I prayed. People were friendly. I was welcome. No one made a fuss.

Common to many religions is the idea of compassion. Compassion is the ability to experience or endure something with another person. These, I believe, were all examples of compassion. The driver of the car in Manchester was able to see the situation from my point of view, to realise what would be best for me, and then he did it. The airmen in Kirkby Stephen, probably without thinking about it, picked up on my sense of isolation and lack of enthusiasm for the journey I had set out on, and they asked, listened, affirmed what I was doing, and brought me into their conversation. The young man at Samye Ling realised how I felt and asked a question that helped me realise it too. They were all simple actions which arose from an insight into how things were for me.

The word 'compassion' has dropped out of use now in English. If it is used it perhaps now suggests an overwhelming feeling. But compassion is not a gushing or overwhelming emotion and it is not the same as pity. It is to be able to put ourselves into someone else's shoes, to feel something of how they feel, and to respond in a way that is helpful to them. It is what therapists mean when they talk about 'empathy'.

This is not the same as sympathy. With sympathy one is sucked into the pain of the other person. With empathy one retains a foothold outside it and so is able to think and act in helpful and constructive ways that might not be possible if one were caught up in the emotion. In all these cases the other people could sense how things were for me but they were not drawn into my frustration or discomfort. And I did not want them to be. It was most helpful to me that the driver simply, immediately stopped as he did, that the other walkers did not allow themselves to become dispirited with me, and the young man at Samye Ling simply showed me in and made me feel at home. I got the practical help I needed, without fuss, and without pity.

Jesus in the gospels is described as being angry or upset by the distress of other people. He then acts or speaks in ways that are helpful to them and to others. The situation gets to him emotionally, but it does not overwhelm him. He feels for the people he comes across who are suffering, but is also able to act in ways that liberate them from their often debilitating situation. In doing this he is in tune with the God of the Hebrews who in the Book of Exodus responds to the cries of the slaves in Egypt and acts to set them free.

At Samye Ling I was told that the difference between Mahayana Buddhists, such as the Tibetans, and Theravada Buddhists, such as the Burmese, is that the Mahayana Buddhists believe that when the Buddha was enlightened he did not enter Nirvana immediately. Out of compassion he chose not to enter Nirvana until he could take every living thing with him. He is thus seen as continually at work bringing all life towards enlightenment.

In our time, as so many people in our world suffer from a lack of the basics they need for survival, let alone a comfortable life, and in a society where many people feel they are insignificant, and as the whole network of life moves into a state of crisis, surely compassion is needed. If we look at what is around us, and see it as it is, surely it will evoke compassion. But often it does not, and it is worth wondering why.

Empathy, or compassion, requires imagination and intuition. We need to be able to join the dots or read between the lines. We see a face, but we cannot actually see what the person is feeling. We work that out on the basis of a multitude of signals and our own experience of how other people have looked. We hear what a person is saying and from the sound, the tone, we guess how they are feeling. Even when someone tells us what is happening to them and perhaps how it feels, we still need sometimes to notice the gaps, to hear what is not being said and to imagine what might be within the silence. And if no one is actually telling us, and all we know is a few facts about a situation, we imagine what that might mean for the creatures involved.

All this takes time, and practice. Often we are driving our lives and only seeing from the windows the things that concern us. We have our routes, our destinations and our tasks to be done, and there is little space for much else. We do not have the time to read what we cannot see, and if we gave it to ourselves we might be distracted by what it stirs up in us. We might find ourselves stopping and using up even more of our precious time.

Sometimes the haste is a way of avoiding compassion. We do

not want to feel how life is for other people. There is simply too much pain around. We construct patterns for our lives, routines, appointments and targets which keep us on the move and stop the rest of the world with its pains, griefs or disappointments breaking into our lives.

If we take a moment to glance at what is around us there is too much for us to deal with. All that hunger and poverty, homelessness, pain, frustration. We feel powerless in the face of it. We do not know how we can begin to respond to it all in any meaningful way. Anything we do will be lost like a drop in an ocean of need. Best not to look.

And that sense of powerlessness is just one of various emotions that can arise from attending compassionately to what is happening in our world. Among them may be anger and great sadness. These are characteristic of grief. If we look at what is happening it is likely we will grieve the loss of the future we thought we would have. Like the occurrence of a terminal illness when we are expecting another twenty years of health, the news of what is happening in the world points to something very different from what we had assumed.

Economic decline or collapse, shortages of oil and other finite resources, climate change and extreme weather all point towards something other than that future of increasing wealth and comfort that many of us had expected, or dreamed, for ourselves or our children. And that hurts. It is a very deep grief. It is more comfortable to ignore the facts, and avoid the pain, like an ill person in denial.

When I arrived at Samye Ling the young man's question helped me become aware of how I felt. Once I acknowledged that, I could deal with it. I spent the rest of the afternoon, and the next day, sitting around and taking it easy. I was tired and so I rested. It was not of great significance. And I was fortunate in being able to take the time to relax. But the point is that unless I had realised how I was I could not have responded to my own need. It seems at first like a contradiction, but we need also to be compassionate towards ourselves. We need to be aware of how we feel, and to acknowledge that. Sometimes we can then give ourselves space or time to recover, or make changes in our lives so that things are different. Sometimes we are not able do that. We simply have to accept that this is how we are. We are tired. Or sad. Or angry. Or frustrated. Or feeling powerless. Or lonely. Or whatever.

Being compassionate towards ourselves is not actually a contradiction. We are complex beings, and we all know that we often drive ourselves hard, beat ourselves up for things we feel we have done wrong, or keep criticising ourselves for our weakness, our looks or our limited abilities. Some of us have a stronger inner critic than others. Some will think the critic is the voice of God, and others reckon it is their nagging mother always on their back. However we see it, we are aware, sometimes, of being set against ourselves. To be compassionate towards ourselves is simply to allow ourselves to recognise and realise how we are, not set against ourselves but alongside ourselves and not demanding we be something different.

It allows us to own our feelings of hurt or loss, or of anger at how we have been abused or misled or at what people are doing to each other or to the world. Perhaps sometimes we are afraid that if we allow ourselves to feel pain for another person, or for ourselves, we will be stuck for a long time in a state of frustration, anger or deep sadness. But actually it is refusing to feel that drains us of energy and hems in our lives. Giving ourselves a break allows us to regain the energy we need to move on a bit further.

Though we might sometimes treat ourselves like machines, pushing ourselves hard to get things done or to reach targets, we are in fact organisms. We grow. We change. We have within us the potential to heal ourselves. And this is true not only of our bodies but of our whole being. Our minds and emotions can also move through changes into new patterns, and do so without our pushing them.

Many of us find that when we are struggling with a problem

or a dilemma we need to leave it. In time a solution often presents itself. As the old folk wisdom had it, we need to sleep on it – not continually turning it over but actually leaving it on one side, for our mind to sort it out in its own time.

Similarly many people find that a good way of getting through depression is by mindfulness. By developing an awareness of what their mind is doing, they are able to stand back from the issues or worries that they are continually turning over. In the process, their emotions stabilise and their energy returns.

So too, grief is not something to be worked at, or to be numbed, but to be acknowledged and allowed. In doing so, energy returns in the course of time and the person is able to adjust to the new normality of their life.

In all this, of course, like a plant or a baby animal needing protection, a human being needs an environment where these processes can be allowed to happen. And often what compassion calls for from us is not direct action to solve a problem but a giving of support so that the person can regain the energy or the stability or the insight they need.

The walkers at Kirkby Stephen and the people at Samye Ling did not do anything for me except allow processes of recovery to take place. These were very small examples of what is so often needed, and often in much bigger and more significant ways. Examples of what we can do for each other.

Compassion often leads to hospitality. This is what I was given by the people at Kirkby Stephen who welcomed me into their company for an evening. It is what the people at Samye Ling provided, as did many others on my journey.

Further north, in Argyll, I visited a place called Dunadd which in the sixth century had been the principal fortress of the kingdom of Dalriada. This was the time when Columba came from Ireland to Iona and established his monastery there. The Scots of Dalriada were immigrants, or the descendants of immigrants, from Ireland. So they were his people.

I was interested in the history, and the links between the church and this Celtic kingdom, so I went and I had a look round. The ancient hill fort was on a small hill almost surrounded by level ground which had clearly at one time been marsh. I climbed to the top and stood in the strong west wind imagining how the place might have been back then. Near the entrance was a carving of a boar on the rock, a bowl hollowed out of the stone, and a carved footprint. It is assumed these were all to do with a king-making ceremony but no one now knows. It was an intriguing place.

When I was walking back from this small hill fort, an elderly lady at a cottage gate asked me what I thought of it. I told her and we got talking.

'Would you like a cup of tea?' she said.

'Well, yes please,' I said, not expecting to be invited in by a total stranger. But we sat in her sitting room and continued the conversation about Dunadd, the local woodlands, the Celtic kingdom and Iona.

'I went there once,' she said. 'Shortly after my husband died. It was group of very intense arty people. I didn't really fit in.'

We were not sitting surrounded by paints and canvases but the house and the garden outside were something of a work of art. There were books, paintings, comfortable furniture, and a garden that spoke of harmony between the climate, the plants and the person.

'I found it all very difficult,' she said. 'I shouldn't have gone really. I thought I was over my husband's death but I wasn't. And it was very hard. Then on the third day someone said, "Are you all right?" and I just burst into tears and couldn't stop.' She paused. 'They were wonderful. I don't know what happened but I've been back with the same group every year since then. It's a great refreshment. Then I am glad to be back at my house and garden. Would you like another cup of tea?'

I took one, and a piece of cake, and we talked about gardens. Then she said, 'I get told off by my family for inviting strangers in. "You don't know. One day you could have someone who causes trouble." I suppose that's right. But I enjoy it. I meet such interesting people!'

Then she said, 'I was talking about it once with a friend of mine and she sent me this.' She showed me a small card and on it was a quote from the Letter to the Hebrews in the New Testament.

'Do not fail to practise hospitality,' it said. 'For some in so doing have entertained angels unawares.'[1]

'So there you are,' she said.

I was reminded of the way that among the ancient Celtic Christians, as among so many others, hospitality was a fundamental virtue.

We saw a stranger yesterday,
We put food in the eating place,
Drink in the drinking place,
Music in the listening place,
And with the sacred name of the Triune God,
He blessed us and our house,
Our cattle and our dear ones.
As the lark says in her song:
'Often, often, often goes Christ in the stranger's guise.'[2]

As I left I felt like neither Christ nor an angel, but I had new energy. It was not just the cake and the tea that had done it but the meeting. More than simply a greeting, but a meeting, and conversation about things that mattered to us.

References

1. Hebrews 13:2
2. *The Iona Community Worship Book* (Glasgow, Wild Goose Publications, 1988) p11

Resources 5: Compassion

Francis

If we get involved with other people we can get hurt. Not only might they hurt us, but we might also begin to share their pain. That is what is meant by 'compassion'. Suffering with another person. And we often want to avoid it.

We want to avoid it because we are afraid it will weigh us down and stop us doing what we want to do. It will sap our energy or take up our time.

Or we suspect that it will stir up in us some of our own pain that we have carefully buried. We do not want to feel again what we have felt in the past. Compassion for someone else might open up old wounds.

There are also the fears we might have for the future, which we do not want to feel. The world is a frightening place. These are frightening times. Or they are if we think too much about what is happening.

Francis had a great fear. It was leprosy. Francis was good-looking and fit. His life was ahead of him. But time and again he would see solitary lepers, or even small groups, shuffling around. They would be wrapped in rags so no one could see their disfigured faces or hands, and they would call a warning so that people could keep out their way, though hopefully also leave something for them to eat.

Then, one day, Francis was walking along a lane, and round a bend, coming towards him, was a leper. He could turn and run, or step aside and hide. But as the leper approached him he saw, amidst the rags, a man, suffering. He stood where he was, and as the leper came to him Francis spoke to him and embraced him. The leper returned Francis's greeting, and then continued on his way. After a moment Francis looked round at the leper, but there was no one there.

From then on, in his wandering Christian life, amidst his

preaching and teaching, caring for lepers was important for him.

For reflection or discussion

1. Has there ever been an occasion when someone has realised how you felt? How did they respond? Was it helpful or unhelpful to you?

2. Has there been an occasion when someone assumed you felt a particular way but was quite wrong? Why do you think they got it wrong? How could they have done better? Do you find you are able to know how someone is feeling?

3. Are you comfortable or uncomfortable expressing how you feel? What difference does it make, if any, whom you are talking to? If there is a difference, why is that? How true do you think that is of people generally?

Some Bible passages relevant to the theme

Exodus 3:1-10
The Hebrew descendants of Abraham have become slaves in Egypt, and God has compassion for them.

Psalm 103
The poet praises God for his compassion, justice and forgiveness.

Hosea 11:1-9
Though God is hurt by the Israelites' disloyalty, he continues to be compassionate towards them.

Mark 1:40-43; Mark 6:30-34
Jesus is described as 'having compassion' in many translations. The Greek word that Mark used means literally that his guts turned over.

Hebrews 13:1-3; 1 Peter 4:8-10
In these letters leaders of the early church encourage the members to show genuine hospitality.

Action

1. Take time to still yourself (perhaps as in Resources 3, action 3) and identify how you feel. It may be a mixture of emotions. Acknowledge them.

2. On a future occasion, when someone begins to tell you about something that has happened or is happening to them, give time to listen and try to understand how the situation is for them. It may not be the same as it would be for you. Then decide what might be the best response you can make for them. You may well not be able to solve their problem. They may not want you to. Nor might they want advice. And you might not be able to give them what they want. But what can you do? It may be no more than providing the opportunity to talk to someone, which you have already given them. The likelihood is that this in itself has been helpful.

3. Take a newspaper report and think how things might be for the people involved. Give yourself time to reflect on that before moving on to the next item.

Further reading

Karen Armstrong, *Twelve Steps to a Compassionate Life* (London: The Bodley Head, 2011)
For the author compassion is more than empathy but is the way of life taught by all the major world religions, and essential not only for human flourishing but for survival. In this book she sets out a programme for how we can develop it.

Daniel Goleman, *Emotional Intelligence: Why it can matter more than IQ* (London: Bloomsbury, 1996)
A bestseller on developing awareness of our emotions and deploying that awareness for a more full life for oneself and others.

Brian Thorne, *Infinitely Beloved: The challenge of divine intimacy* (London: DLT, 2003)
A profound and readable exploration by a person-centred therapist of the significance of divine and human compassion.

Novels: long ones, short ones, it doesn't matter, but choose ones that give you an insight into how the characters feel rather than just what they do. And think how realistic or unrealistic the novels are about this.

Six

Lighting Candles

Leaving Manchester I was heading for a place called Scargill House, near Kettlewell in Wharfedale. It was a place where Madron and I had received very welcome hospitality some years earlier.

After three years living in Nigeria where I had been a secondary school teacher we returned to the UK with a two-month-old son, not knowing what we would be doing or where we would live. I was in the process of exploring whether I could train for ordination in the Church of England and had a three-day residential selection conference lined up for a few weeks after we got back to the UK. If I was selected we would go to Durham where I had a provisional place on a course. If I wasn't selected I would have to find a job somewhere. As it was, they wanted me.

We bought a house in Durham, which I thought I would do up while I undertook my studies. I embarked on the course and also threw myself into student politics. Madron spent most of her time in the cold and gloomy house, coming into the college for lunchtime. And she got pregnant again. The baby was due at Christmas of our second year there, a time when I would be looking for a job as a curate.

Miriam was born shortly before Christmas and was quickly diagnosed as having an acute form of brittle bone disease. She already had a number of broken bones from the womb and from her birth and she needed to be sedated. She survived until early January.

My memories of that time are disordered. I remember the Warden of the college arriving on my doorstep with his family in the car outside, off for Christmas elsewhere, and him telling me he knew how I felt because his mother had died some months ago. He didn't know how I felt. No one did. But then there was another member of the college staff who called while we were out and left a small card saying simply, 'Sorry. With love.' That was better.

I remember the minister of the church we attended prattling on at Miriam's cremation service about how a death like this was a challenge to someone like him who believed in healing, as if this death was some kind of theoretical problem. I also remember sitting in the Galilee Chapel in Durham Cathedral, while Miriam lay sedated and in a coma in her incubator, and reading the words of the Venerable Bede on the wall above his tomb: 'Christ is the morning star who when the night of this world is past brings to his saints the promise of the light of life and opens everlasting day.'

And there was Christmas Day. I went into the hospital and Santa Claus had obviously visited the children's ward. Hanging on the end of Miriam's incubator was a small rattle. She was not left out.

By the end of January Miriam had died and her ashes were interred in the lawn of St Margaret's Church. I had a job fixed up in Staffordshire and we would move there in the summer. Our toddler son still did not sleep through the night and the house that I had intended to do up was nowhere near done. We were both exhausted, and hanging over us was the fact that the disease that Miriam had was congenital. Although our son was fine, any further children we had might have it too. There were various thoughts and fears turning around in our minds amidst the pain.

A friend of ours at the college had worked at Scargill House before coming to Durham and she suggested we get in touch and see if they could have us to stay for a few days. They could. They had a policy of always keeping their best room free from regular bookings just in case someone needed it in a hurry. It was offered to us at a cheap rate, and in the early spring we went for a few days.

We were welcomed without fuss. There were no questions or counselling, although I am sure that if we had wanted to talk with someone it would have been possible. We were simply given good food and an excellent room, and the time and space to rest and sort ourselves out a bit. We recovered the energy to return to Durham and begin preparing for our move in the summer.

We went back to Scargill several times after that. It was a good place to be. Set on the edge of Wharfedale with magnificent views across the valley, open space for walking, and a pleasant library and lounges for wet days. It was a place where children were able to act their age in the lounges and at mealtimes, so parents like us could relax. Now I was going back on foot, linking my present home in Shropshire with this place where I had never lived, but which had been very significant for me. I also felt that when I got there I would have completed the first leg of my journey to Iona.

But I was not there yet. I was on my way out of Manchester on the Rochdale road. When I had contacted the people at Scargill to tell them about my walk to Iona and my wish to stay at Scargill they were happy for me to arrive any time. This was helpful, as was the similar offer I had received from Stanley Hope whom I had met in Birmingham a few months earlier and who lived in Rochdale, on my route to Scargill. I did not know how far I would be walking in a day and so could not say when I would arrive. In both cases my intention was to phone and at least give them a bit of warning of when I would get there.

It dawned on me when I was a mile or two from the centre of Manchester that I could possibly arrive in Rochdale that day. I might not need to stop for the night in Middleton. So I had better phone Stanley. I tried, but there was no reply.

I pressed on, enjoying the movement, the life and the humour around me. A launderette which could have been called 'Washerama' or the 'Harpwhey Laundry' was 'Ocean World'. Local buses were run by The Bee Line Buzz Company. Graffiti on a closed public toilet told me that for alternative facilities I should 'Call International Rescue'.

I stopped for pie and chips in the Three Cooks Cafe in Middleton and phoned again. Still no answer. This was in the days before ubiquitous mobiles and voicemails and for each phone attempt I had to find a public call box. I found another later that afternoon. This time Stanley was in. I reminded him of our conversation in Birmingham.

'So, when are you coming then?' he asked.

'This afternoon,' I said, 'if that's OK.'

There was a pause and he asked me to wait a minute. It occurred to me that he had possibly not informed his wife Kathleen of his offer of hospitality and was now off to discuss it. He returned after a short while and said, 'That'll be fine,' and explained how to find the house.

The route was not difficult. I found the canal again and followed it for a couple of miles. It now had a clear towpath although it was not usable by canal boats, not least because it flowed under the M62 through a pipe. At a major road junction I called into a supermarket for some flowers for Kathleen and by five o'clock I was at the door of their small terraced house in Rochdale. I was warmly welcomed. Over tea and sandwiches I was able to talk a bit about my walk so far and explain the difficulty of trying to make arrangements in advance. All this was accepted and understood. I was given a bed, offered a bath, and told to make myself at home for the evening.

I had walked the final stretch into Rochdale along the main road and noticed on the signboard that the town was twinned with Bielefeld in Germany and Tourcoing in France. Such twinning arrangements were not uncommon, intended to help the people of the two towns to get to know and to understand and respect each other. What was unusual was that Rochdale was also twinned with Sahiwal in Pakistan. I asked Stanley about this.

He was reluctant at first to explain how this link had come to be developed. I realised that this was not from embarrassment about the link but because he had had a significant hand in it and was not comfortable talking about himself. However, he did tell me the story.

Stanley had grown up in Rochdale and then, during the Second World War, he had been in the army in India and had learnt Urdu. He returned to Rochdale after the war and in the '50s and '60s a number of people from Pakistan moved into Rochdale. They were encouraged to come. The British economy needed more workers so there were campaigns to encourage immigrants from the Commonwealth. But once they got here they encountered enormous problems.

Some of these arose from the attitudes of local people, but others were a result of officialdom and bias in the legal system. Racism was not only widespread in the populace but also systemic. There was no race relations legislation in those days and the law concerning house tenancies meant that property owners could exploit their tenants. The people coming into Rochdale had a raft of problems to try to deal with.

Stanley knew about this because he talked with them. As he spoke Urdu he was able to chat not only with those who were fluent in English but with others as well. He offered practical help but realised that this required more than simply one person lending a helping hand.

He was a member of Rochdale Methodist Church and for a while he had the support of his church, but when one minister left and another came that support declined. However, Stanley pressed on. He decided that he had energy either to try to change the attitude of his local church or to try to help the immigrants, and he chose the latter. For him this was not just a matter of hospitality but of justice, and working for justice was an essential aspect of being Christian.

Justice is often considered a matter of making sure that people get what they deserve: weighing up one thing against another and interpreting or making laws and rules so that things are fair. But in the Bible justice is a matter of doing what is necessary to help those who are disadvantaged. And it is a theme that runs right through the Bible.

Early in the whole Bible story the Israelites are oppressed slaves in Egypt. God 'hears their cries' and, through Moses, leads them out of slavery to freedom in their own land. This is the archetypal story of justice, retold every year at the Passover festival. But the theme is brought up time and again, not least by prophets like Micah and Amos who remind the people that God's desire is justice rather than piety. 'Take away from me the noise of your songs, says the Lord. I will not listen to the melody of your harps. But let justice roll down like the waters and integrity like an ever-flowing stream.'[1]

Then in the New Testament Jesus works continually to restore marginalised people into a position where they can make a creative contribution to the community, by healing them, affirming their forgiveness and their freedom to make a new start, or by reconciling people who are at odds with each other. And St Paul sees God's activity in Jesus as one of justice in restoring people into a right relationship with himself, each other and themselves.[2]

Unfortunately, the word used by St Paul and others, while it is often translated as 'justice' in English Bibles is also sometimes translated as 'righteousness', which, if it means anything at all to people, tends to suggest an aloof moral goodness. Justice is far from being aloof. It involves getting involved in making a difference. It is what the writers of the Bible see God as doing, and as God requiring people to do. This is what Stanley saw his church in Rochdale as needing to do, and he would get on with it whether or not he had his church's support.

He worked in the Town Hall and changed department to become a Community Relations Officer. What continually annoyed him was not the immigration laws but the way that they were frequently, almost consistently, interpreted in a racist way. He told me of a number of such situations. One simple example sticks in my mind.

An American friend of his who was working in the UK had to return quickly to the States for family reasons and did not have time to renew his visa. Stanley rang a contact at the immigration service to ask whether he would have difficulty getting back into this country.

'Is he black or white?' said the man in immigration.

'White,' said Stanley.

'Oh, he'll have no problem then,' was the reply.

Time and again Stanley met this kind of situation. He supported families in Rochdale that were divided: one partner living in the UK and the other in Pakistan and unable to get here. And he knew full well that if the families had been white the problems would have been overcome.

Slowly, over a period of time, attitudes and relationships in Rochdale improved, and as a result of campaigning by people like Stanley, British law changed. The death of Stephen Lawrence in London and the failures of the Metropolitan Police in investigating the murder led eventually to a greater understanding of institutional racism. And while there are still problems, injustices and prejudice the situation is better now in most places than it was in Rochdale in the '60s.

The twinning of Rochdale with Sahiwal was symptomatic of that change. However a twinning arrangement works out in practice, the principle behind it is that there are two communities that each have things to learn from the other. It is not about one helping the other out but about mutual recognition and respect. This is what lay behind Stanley's work.

The people he met up with who came from Pakistan were disadvantaged and Stanley was concerned to give them help as they needed it, but this was not a paternalistic kind of help. It arose from a respect for the people who had come to Rochdale, who had a contribution to make to the community as a whole. And here is another important component of the biblical idea of justice. The prophet Amos, for instance, does not castigate the rich of his society, lolling around in luxury, because they are failing to give handouts to the poor. He condemns them because they take advantage of the poor in their weakness, and the poor people are entitled to justice.

Walking across Manchester in the early '90s I was aware of considerable differences of wealth and living standards within the one city. The suburbs around Tatton Park, with large houses set in gardens where gardeners were at work, were in sharp contrast to the low-rise estates bordering the Rochdale Road. But I was also aware of how much better life was for even the poorer people in the city than it had been a hundred, let alone a hundred and fifty, years earlier. At that time the city was booming, and expanding. The canals were working hard. Railways were beginning to be built. People were migrating from the country because there was the possibility of employment in the city, whereas the work opportunities in the country were declining. Mechanisation was gradually reducing the amount of manual labour needed on the land. Without work people went hungry.

But in the cities the streets were not paved with gold. Friedrich Engels catalogued the living conditions of the working classes in nearby Salford, and they were not unique to that town. Living conditions were squalid and much of the available work was tedious, dangerous and poorly paid. People toiled for very long hours for little return in places where there was recurrent danger and often a long-term risk to health. And they were not just adults. Children worked in factories because their families needed money, there was no schooling, and they were sought after for some jobs. In mines and chimneys small children could get into places that adults could not. In the cotton mills around Manchester their nimble fingers were able to reach into moving machinery to clear snags and other problems in places adults could not reach. There were inevitable frequent injuries and sometimes deaths.

For all the poverty of Manchester in the 1990s life was a whole lot better for most people than it had been back in the mid-nineteenth century. The improvement had not, of course, happened overnight, nor was it the result of one person's efforts. Numerous individuals had been involved in different ways in bringing about this change. There were developments in technology, and in public health engineering; changes of attitude, and legislation; universal education and the organisation of labour.

Rochdale had seen the birth of the co-operative movement, as people clubbed together to give themselves purchasing power for basic foodstuffs, thereby improving their families' living standards. It was a movement that grew worldwide. The organisation of labour and the right to strike was a long time coming, but many of the people involved in the trade union movement in the early days were members of Methodist churches and had developed the skills and self-confidence to speak in public as local preachers. They had also acquired a sense that the improvement of life for their colleagues and families was not a matter of waiting for charity but of working for justice.

The Methodist Church was not alone in this. In other spheres Anglicans were active, even though they met with opposition from some powerful members of their own church. Some members of the Church of England used their position as Members of Parliament to bring in legislation that took children out of dangerous workplaces and gave them access to education, and other Acts that protected adult workers, controlled their working hours, and gave them better, safer conditions and, eventually, the right to vote.

In the rural areas too life improved. Most of the villages I had walked through had not only a church but also a school. Often now the old Victorian building was closed and the children had better facilities elsewhere. But these old school buildings are a monument to another aspect of this slow change that might be called a movement of justice. These schools were established for the children of the working classes and the poor of the villages. The wealthy already had schools: the Grammar Schools in nearby towns and the Public Schools scattered across the country. The idea of educating the poor was controversial and behind the establishment of these schools for the wider populace often lay a battle between a cohort of wealthy locals – perhaps the local squire, traders and industrialists who had moved out of the smoke – and a local vicar and his allies who were determined that education should be for all, and was for the good of all.

Other churches, and people of no religion, played a part in this gradual change. They argued with each other. Their priorities were different and many 'freethinkers' believed that religion was an obstacle to justice, not a creator of it, but slowly changes were made. And still need to be made. When Stanley Hope returned to Rochdale from the war, the Welfare State was being developed. There was a massive house reconstruction programme and full employment, and successive Factory Acts meant that working conditions were relatively safe and healthy compared to those of a hundred years earlier. But now new issues had emerged, and in the pursuit of justice Stanley involved himself in the one that he could do something to address.

Walking out of Rochdale alongside the canal the next day I passed the backs of derelict cotton mills. The industry had moved. There were issues now of finding other ways to use the skills of the people of the town. There was a workforce here, needing their time and skills to be used creatively and for the good of society. This might be seen as an investment opportunity. It could also be seen as a matter of justice. The two are not mutually exclusive.

The people of Rochdale are not without clothing. The shops and markets of Britain are flooded with clothing, much of it cheap. There are issues of justice here too. Often no one knows what the working conditions are of the people who made them. They are often cheap because the workers are very badly paid, and might even be children labouring in conditions not dissimilar to those of early nineteenth-century Lancashire. There were people who looked at the situation in Lancashire then and said nothing could be done. But it could, and it was. The same applies now.

But much of the work to be done is not dramatic or exciting. It is slow and tedious. It involves investigation, campaigning, lobbying and argument. And in a market economy those who buy have influence as well as those who produce. We can choose not to buy goods which we suspect might be made or traded unjustly. We can buy from suppliers whom we know will ensure that the producers and the traders get a fair return for their labour, and are able to live in healthy conditions. That may mean looking for the Fairtrade brand, but not necessarily. There are plenty of manufacturers of clothing and of other goods who ensure that their workers are treated fairly. And there are websites and publications in which the results of investigations are published so that these can be checked out.

There is also talk now of 'environmental justice'. This can mean one of two things. It can refer to the way that those who are poor often end up living in a less healthy environment. This is particularly true in cities, and has been for a long time. In Britain it is often true that the greener suburbs are on the west side of the city, like the part of Manchester that I walked through into the centre. The east side is often the most industrialised and densely populated. This is because the prevailing wind in Britain comes from the west. The east side was the one that got the smoke and fumes. The west had the fresh air. In other places, and where hills and rivers come into play, there are different patterns, but in a market economy where people are concerned about their local environment the housing in the greener areas fetches the highest prices. Justice, in this situation, will mean ensuring that the local environment of those who cannot buy their way out is still a good one. That means good housing, parks, play facilities, traffic control, law enforcement, noise control, tree planting, urban farms, some of which may need local government action and others grassroots initiative.

But environmental justice is also a way of looking at wider environmental issues in terms of justice. If justice is to be seen as balancing rights and wrongs it is hard to see how this can work, but if justice is seen as working for the good of those who are disadvantaged, then it can become a useful way of contemplating many of the environmental issues we face. Acting in ways that are good for birds, animals or plants can be seen as a matter of justice. They cannot speak for themselves. They are often powerless in the face of our technology and its side-effects, the waste and pollution. They need us to consider them with respect, and work for their good.

Decisions are not going to be easy. Sometimes it will come down to weighing up conflicting interests, and the well-being of plants, animals or ecosystems against human need. But environmental justice means bringing them into the equation and giving them a place there as of right, considering them as of value in themselves and not just as a resource or hobby interest. And like the movement for human justice it will be enacted in a million decisions, in planning and policy meetings, in legislative changes and in simple choices about what to eat and where to buy it.

Some words are hard to translate from one language to another and one such word is the Hebrew 'shalom'. It is often rendered as 'peace' in English but it means much more than a cessation of hostilities. At times it would be better translated as 'healing'.

When an individual is healed, that is 'shalom'. When there is reconciliation within a divided community, that is 'shalom'. When two communities cease to be in conflict but instead work to support each other, that is 'shalom'. When people treat the land and the life within it with respect and work out ways of living that are good for all life, that is 'shalom'.

The prophet Micah's vision of 'shalom' was, 'They shall beat their swords into ploughshares and their spears into pruning hooks; nation shall not lift up sword against nation, neither shall they learn war any more; but they shall all sit under their vines and under their fig trees, and no one shall make them afraid.'[3]

Justice is when people work towards developing 'shalom'. So when the Scargill Community offered hospitality and space to people like us so that we could rest and get our lives a bit more together, that was justice. When campaigners and politicians in Manchester worked to improve the well-being of the people in the city, that was justice. And when Stanley Hope met with the Pakistani immigrants in Rochdale and acted as an advocate for them in the Town Hall and to Government, that was justice.

And now, when people in Britain burn less oil and coal in order to reduce the impact of climate change for people in South Asia and Africa and for future generations, that is justice. When negotiators hammer out a deal which means that more energy can be generated from the tidal flow in an estuary and migrating birds can still have a feeding ground, that is justice. And when a clothing retailer insists that its suppliers' employees work in safe conditions and receive fair wages for the work they do, that is justice.

Compassion leads to action for justice. That is how it was with Stanley. Meeting with the immigrants from Pakistan and hearing their stories, he could imagine how things were for them and he used his local knowledge to work to overcome prejudices and to improve their opportunities. He helped them to become a part of one community in Rochdale and to contribute to the local commercial and industrial life. His compassion gave him the energy to do what he did.

Part of that work involved getting policies changed, as well as attitudes. He campaigned for changes in national policies regarding immigration and race relations as well as in his local government procedures. This was important. Without policy changes, and in some cases new laws, compassion simply becomes sad feelings or anger. And policies and laws can enable justice to be practised regardless of the strength or lack of compassion.

A very simple example of this was the Scargill Community's policy of keeping a room or two spare for people who needed them in a hurry. They had realised at some time that this could happen and made it a part of their normal procedure. It meant that when I contacted them following Miriam's death and said that Madron and I needed a place for a few days' break I did not have to go into details and tell the whole story. The person I was speaking to on the phone did not have to imagine how things might be for us. They simply had to make a decision about whether this was the kind of situation that the rooms were kept for. And when we arrived from Durham there was nothing that made us feel they were putting themselves out for us, but rather that this was the way things were meant to be. We needed a break, a bit of space, food and shelter, and they would provide it as well as they could.

I have little doubt that in the case of Scargill if they had not had this policy and I had told my story to one of the leaders they would have done what they could to find us space and to help us. But it would not have felt the same for us, either in asking for the room nor when we arrived. Charity is good, but it is better when it is translated into policies, procedures and laws which promote justice.

When he retired from Rochdale Town Hall Stanley continued to work and campaign for racial justice. He had not been an active member of his church for many years, although Kathleen his wife was. But he saw his work as a Christian commitment. Back in the '50s he had heard George MacLeod on the radio and been attracted by the Iona Community that George had founded. One aspect of the Community's life was working for peace and justice. He joined, and, as Stanley put it to me, the Iona Community helped him 'keep the faith'.

He died a few years after I met him. Almost until he died he was writing and urging others to join in working for justice. One of his favourite sayings was the proverb, 'Light a candle. Don't just curse the dark.'

Stanley Hope lit a lot of candles. Some are still burning.

References

1. Amos 5:23-24
2. 2 Corinthians 5:14-6:2
3. Micah 4:3-4

Resources 6: Justice

Two reformers

People knew that the Church needed to change. It was corrupt in many ways, and it was powerful. And even those in power who wanted to change it seemed unable to do so. Sermons were preached, books were written, and learned people exchanged letters about what needed doing. But not much changed.

Martin Luther was a teacher at the University of Wittenberg. From his lecture notes on the Bible it is clear that between 1513 and 1517 he developed what James Atkinson called Luther's 'reformation consciousness'. It was another way of understanding key words like 'grace', and thinking about what it meant to have faith.

But this remained part of an academic discussion until 1517. Then Johan Tetzel, a Dominican teacher, appeared in Luther's part of Saxony selling indulgences. Basically, he was saying that if people paid money into the Church's coffers for rebuilding St Peter's Church in Rome, then their relatives could be freed from years of torment in purgatory.

To Luther, now, the whole business of selling indulgences was wrong. But it also exploited the compassion of poor people. Luther made a statement for public debate about indulgences in the usual way, by nailing a list of theses to the church door. And it was like throwing a lighted match into a load of straw. People who had had little time or inclination to discuss the theological niceties of church reform were now mobilised, because this was not merely about ideas but about justice.

At the same time, in Zurich, Huldrych Zwingli had developed a similar way of seeing things to that of Luther. He too was involved in an academic debate which cut little ice with most people.

But then he argued publicly against the way that people were having to pay high rents and tithes to support a wealthy church when they themselves were impoverished. For many of the men their only way of getting money was to serve as foreign mercenaries, and from his experience as an army chaplain Zwingli knew what suffering that meant.

And so there began the revolution in the church that came to be known as the Reformation. Behind it lay a new way of seeing things. But the energy for change came from a concern for justice.

For reflection or discussion

1. What is the difference between 'justice' and 'mercy'?

2. Have you been involved in a campaign or other kind of work for justice? If so, what was your aim and who were you involved with? What was the result of what you did, as far as you know? Were there any outcomes which you had not intended? Were they good or bad?

3. In the television or internet news that you've seen today, or in newspaper reports, what can you see as campaigns or struggles for justice? What is stopping justice coming about?

Some Bible passages relevant to the theme

Exodus 3:1-10
God not only has compassion for the Israelites but will act to rescue them from their slavery.

Exodus 20:1-17
On their way to the land God has promised them he gives the Israelites instructions as to how they are to live. These concern not only their worship of God, but their relationships with one another, and serve to protect the weak from the strong.

Micah 6:6-8
Micah declares that what God wants to see is not flamboyant worship but justice.

Luke 4:14-21
In Luke's gospel Jesus begins his work by going to his home town and declaring that he is doing what the prophet Isaiah wrote about, bringing justice and a time of healing and liberation.

2 Corinthians 5:14-6:2
In this letter Paul speaks of how God carried out a great act of justice, engaging with the world in Jesus so that people could be reconciled to him and join in his work of bringing justice. Unfortunately the Greek word *dikaiosyne* is sometimes translated as 'righteousness' rather than justice.

Action

1. What issues of justice are there in your local community, church or place of work? Make a list of them. Then think what you could possibly do to help bring justice into that situation. It might involve talking with people, or joining a campaign, or raising money, or writing letters. You cannot do everything. Choose one of them to work on.

2. Of the things you buy how many of them do you know are traded justly? Do the producers get a fair deal? Is the way the things are produced and transported good for the environment? Do the suppliers pay their staff a fair wage and provide decent working conditions and good terms of employment?

Of the ones you don't know about, try to find out. The websites of the Trade Justice Movement and the Ethical Trading Initiative can help here.

If they do not operate justly, change to a supplier that does.

Think also about the bank that you use. Does that operate in a just way? Compare it with others and move to a bank that operates with greater justice.

3. Are there national or international issues that you can see are matters of justice? Choose one that concerns you. Find out what

organisations are working to bring greater justice into that situation and join or support one. This may involve giving money, or fundraising, or writing letters or cards or campaigning in some other way. Join in doing what you can.

Further reading

Kathy Galloway, *Sharing the Blessing*, (London: SPCK, 2008)
The author works out the significant social and political implications of the fact that all that we have is a gift.

Jim Wallis, *Faith Works: Lessons on spirituality and social action* (London: SPCK, 2002)
The founder of the Sojourners community writes not only on the basis of theory but from years of working with socially deprived people in Washington DC and elsewhere.

Hans Kung, ed., *Yes to a Global Ethic* (London: SCM, 1996)
International leaders and thinkers write on the need for justice within and between nations, and the paths we can take towards it.

Walter Brueggemann, *The Prophetic Imagination* (Minneapolis: Augsburg Fortress, 2nd Edition 2001)
How compassion leads into justice in the life of Moses, the preaching of the prophets, and the work of Jesus.

John L. Bell, *States of Bliss and Yearning: The marks and means of authentic Christian spirituality* (Glasgow: Wild Goose Publications, 1998)
Speeches and sermons with humour and a cutting edge which relate faith to life as it really is.

Seven

Choices and Changes

At Mankinholes Youth Hostel there was an enormous cartoon of Obelix on the wall of the stairwell. Obelix was, or perhaps still is, the companion of Asterix the Gaul. Getafix the Druid has a way of making a magic potion which gives Asterix and his companions superhuman strength, enabling them to fend off the Romans and to rush around Europe having all sorts of satirical adventures. But Obelix is denied the potion because when he was a baby he fell in it. The result was that he developed great size and strength, and was employed carrying enormous stones for menhirs and henges. And here he was, carrying a great rock on his back, striding along with a grin on his face.

I was interested in Celtic culture and particularly in the Celtic strand of Christianity. I also enjoyed Asterix cartoon books and had taken my children to the Asterix theme park in France. I had not connected the two, and I doubt if Goscinny and Uderzo, the creators of *Asterix the Gaul*, connected their characters with history or faith either. But on my walk to one of the centres of early Celtic Christianity in Britain it was good to be greeted by this smiling cartoon Celt.

However, the reference at Mankinholes was not to anything Celtic but to the Pennine Way, for which the youth hostel is a staging post. It begins sixty miles to the south, in Derbyshire, and winds its way, mostly following the ridge of the Pennines, to Kirk Yetholm, just across the Scottish border. From spring to autumn walkers can be seen striding or trudging along the path, carrying their rucksacks like Obelix's rock. I arrived a few minutes before the hostel opened and several arrived as I waited for opening time, one of them caked in mud. He had, he said, slipped over.

The Pennine Way was the first national long-distance footpath to be officially recognised in Britain, so it is historically significant. It weaves its way mostly on the high ground, so if the weather is good the views are excellent. If the weather is bad there are no views. But among British walkers the Pennine Way has almost mystical significance. Was I going to walk it?

Not the whole of it, clearly, but I could have walked part of it.

John Hillaby on his '60s walk from Land's End to John O'Groats had joined the Pennine Way at the beginning and walked the length of it. It was his route northwards. I had thought quite seriously of doing the same. Scargill is not far off the path and I could have made a small diversion and rejoined the Way after a break there.

I knew early on in planning my walk that I wanted to link up Wrockwardine, where I lived, with Scargill, Edinburgh and Iona. But I was a long time deciding which routes to use. Interested in history, and particularly the Celtic church, I thought for a while of perhaps following the routes that Celtic missionary monks would have used to travel on foot around northern Britain, which were basically the Roman roads. But most of those had been tarmacked over during the twentieth century and turned into motor roads. Not good for walking.

Modern long-distance paths, like the Pennine Way, were another option I considered. I could have started at the south end of the Pennine Way, and then when I reached the northern end transferred to part of the Southern Upland Way towards Edinburgh. Then, in the west of Scotland, I could follow part of the West Highland Way. The lines were all there on the map.

Finally I decided that I was not trying to tick off a set of walkers' challenges but to link up places on foot. To that end I would simply go by ways that were good for walking. I would walk along country lanes, bridlepaths and canal towpaths, and use waymarked routes if they suited me. But I did not set off with a detailed itinerary already planned out. I knew the rough direction I wanted to go and a few key places I wanted to visit. Apart from that I was working it out as I went along. I had walked to Mankinholes from Rochdale, mostly following the canal as it climbed slowly into the Pennines. And now, here, I had come to a waymarked path stretching away northwards across the moors. Was I going to take it, or find another route?

I spent the evening mulling it over while a few other walkers arrived, and some conservation volunteers who told stories about the damage being done by the large number of walkers. My decision was of little significance to anyone else. My additional pair of feet would cause further erosion, but not a great deal. And if the path became too damaged it could be rerouted. This happens from time to time. Unlike many places that suffer environmental damage, there are alternatives for the Pennine Way. Part of it can be closed off while the ground recovers. In many situations this isn't possible.

For me, the main issue in using this path was one of stamina. The Pennine Way would be harder work than walking the back-roads and bridle paths on either side of the Pennine ridge. And I did not know how much I could manage. I was not an experienced long-distance walker, nor an indestructible twenty-year-old. I was walking alone and was a bit concerned that if I set off up the Pennine Way and then got driven off the fells by incessant rain, or camped and got flooded out, I might not have the energy and determination to keep going. But, on the other hand, it was an attractive challenge.

I slept on it, and when I woke up decided I would go northwest across to Wharfedale and then follow that dale northwards. With the decision made I had some breakfast and set off, stopping for a moment to look at the Pennine Way winding northwards, dropping down into the Calder Valley and then on across Heptonstall Moor. But I did not follow it. Instead I walked down into Hebden Bridge and then up onto the moors and across to Haworth which I had in mind as my next stop for the night.

Before even starting this walk I had been aware that one of the crucial things for completing it would be the matter of pace. In many ways walking alone is easier than walking with a group. Alone, you can go at the speed that suits you. A group goes at the pace of the slowest, and someone who naturally walks quickly, as I do, finds that more tiring. Walking alone you can also stop when you choose and move on when you feel like it. I had all that in my favour.

But I still had a problem with pacing myself. Even though I realised that I had walked too far and too fast in the first few days, resulting in a lot of pain, I still found it hard to cover the right distance each day. Right for me, that is. There was no other criterion. I was responsible for this walk. No one else had told me to do it, let alone set out where I should go and when I needed to be in each place. But finding my pace was hard. Each day there was always a bit more that I might be able to do.

There was also, for me, a problem with stopping early in the day. What would I do then? My usual way of amusing myself in a place was to go for a walk. In which case I might as well keep walking along my path. Or I could read a book – but I was not carrying a book to read. In actual fact, there is always plenty to do anywhere because there are things to look at and to watch. But while I often tuned into the scenery around me when I was walking and noticed the details of the hedges or trees, I found it hard to do the same when I was camped somewhere or booked into a hostel.

As a result I no doubt missed a lot. Rushing on to the next place I not only hurt my legs and feet but missed some of the flowers and birds, the scenery, the faces of the people, and the stonework and brickwork of the walls and buildings – so much that would have been good to see. I would have been better off slowing down. But that would have meant giving something up. I wanted to complete the walk, and the more quickly I got some of it behind me the more confident I would be of that outcome. If I had given up the goal, I might have seen more on the way, and would probably still have completed the whole thing.

There were times when the distance I walked was beyond my control. I arrived in Haworth in the early afternoon with the thought that I would stop in the youth hostel there for the night. It was a big one and it was May. Not, I would have thought, a peak time. So I amused myself looking around Haworth, the town where the Brontë sisters had lived, their father Patrick being the local vicar. At five o'clock I walked into the youth hostel. I was the first one in.

'Sorry, we're full,' said the warden.

'Full?' I said. 'It's only five o'clock!'

'Aye,' he said. 'I've got a school coming.' And as he said it the doors opened and a flood of children burst in. I stood there like a rock in a torrent as they swirled around me and a few teachers tried to channel the flow.

Sorry, no, I could not camp in the grounds. That was not permitted. But he could give me the phone number of a bed and breakfast.

I could have simply set off to see what happened. Perhaps I would pass a B&B sign. Many days I did that: just walked till I found a place to stay, trusting to God or serendipity. But this day I was not in the mood. I phoned round and booked a bed in Keighley, four miles further on.

Then on the way to Keighley it began to rain. By the time I got into the town it was cold and it was pouring. I stopped and bought fish and chips in a cafe, just as it was closing, and then set off into the downpour to find my bed for the night. I had worked out where it was on the map. Unfortunately the map did not match reality. Changes had been made to the roads. I walked on. I looked around. At one point I had to turn back and try a different route.

Why was I doing this walk? This was not the first time I asked this question, nor the last. There were no prizes. I was not being sponsored. No one was making me do it. I could give up at any time. But I wanted to know what it would be like to link on foot several places that were significant for me. I wanted to know what it would be like to arrive on Iona and think back over my long, slow journey there. I thought it would be good. But more than that I did not know, and I wanted to find out. In order to find out, I was putting up with this. With pain in my feet, the weight of a rucksack on my back, solitude that sometimes turned to loneliness, and cold rain in Keighley. Eventually I found the right place and stepped into dry warmth, for a bath and bed.

Walking to Iona was an unusual thing to undertake, but much of what I was doing was what we do all the time when we want to achieve something. Whether it is a small thing, like preparing for Christmas, or something big, like working for environmental justice, the same processes apply.

Firstly, we need an idea of what we are trying to achieve. That might be a specific achievable goal, like replacing our light bulbs or reducing our carbon footprint by ten per cent. But it might be something vague, like creating a better local environment, which only in the course of time breaks down into specific objectives. But however big or small our vision, the way forward involves many decisions.

Then, in making these we need sometimes to leave aside the immediately pleasurable for a longer-term goal. That might mean struggle or pain, but it might involve simply forgoing something pleasant that would be unhelpful. We need, as they say, to be able to delay our gratification. This sometimes means letting our mind direct our actions rather than instinctively responding to our emotions. This is the way, and we follow it. And if it seems muddy, or steep, or we would feel more comfortable sitting in a pub, too bad.

But while we are looking forward to the greater good, we also need to be able to attend to immediate challenges and demands. While I had a vision of arriving on Iona after many weeks of walking, day by day I had to plan my route, and moment by moment I had to attend to the details: to this particular signpost, to the road I needed to cross at that moment, to where there might be a food shop or a public toilet, and to how I could keep the rain off my map.

If I had spent too much time thinking about my final destination I would have become discouraged. After two hours of walking in Yorkshire, Iona was not much closer than it had been when I started. With a vision for the future we need to be able to attend to the present, partly so that we can make appropriate decisions, and partly so that we can enjoy being where we are and receiving the energy that comes from that enjoyment.

When I took a wrong turning in Keighley in the rain it was, if anyone's, my mistake. Perhaps if I had looked more carefully, or taken my time, I could have gone straight to the house I was looking for. There was no point in blaming someone else. It was my walk, and they were my decisions. Similarly, I had chosen to spend the afternoon in Haworth. The hostel was full and I had to walk on, but there was no point blaming the school trip organisers, or the warden. They had their plans and their ways of doing things, and those were good. It was my judgement that there would be room in the hostel and I got it wrong. In other decisions too we need to take responsibility for our choices.

We also have to travel at our own pace: to work at the things we can do and not burden ourselves with the things we cannot. There is always a lot to be done. There is always a long way to go. We are only ourselves. With others we might do great things. But individually we can only contribute our part. And for many of us finding our pace means giving up schemes and projects that are too grand, and accepting our limitations. Other people might have clocked up the Pennine Way on their walk northwards, but I could not.

And sometimes we need to change our direction. Or even to go back a bit and start again. In Keighley it would have been stupid for me to continue walking when it was clear I was going the wrong way. A number of times on this walk north I had to alter my intended route because what I found on the ground did not fit with what the map suggested. This was particularly true of footpaths across fields, which did not always go where I was expecting, or, sometimes, did not actually go anywhere. I needed to change my plans to fit with reality. As we all often do.

There is a word sometimes used in Christian prayers and in the Bible which refers to this kind of change. It is 'repentance'. Like many traditional Christian words it often carries a lot of unnecessary baggage. The word repentance simply means to change. It does not mean to feel bad about something – although one might

– but to do things differently, or to live in a different way.

When I was trying to find my bed and breakfast in the rain in Keighley and changed direction because I realised I was going the wrong way I was, quite literally, repenting. As I was when I changed my route across fields in Cumbria, or at various other times on this journey when I decided to take a different route from the way I had set out. But we rarely use the word in that literal sense now. More often we use it to refer to a change in the direction of our life or to a change in the way we do something.

It is in this metaphorical sense that Jesus and prophets and preachers in the Bible use this word. In Hebrew how one lived was often described as the way that one was going. To change direction, to repent, was to change how one lived. And the challenge was often made not only to individuals but to society as a whole.

From Mankinholes to Keighley I had spent much of the day walking along small roads in big open spaces, with wide views across the moors, the sound of skylarks and lapwings ducking and diving like acrobats, and only occasionally a passing car or tractor. But in the Calder Valley at Hebden Bridge I was in a transport corridor. It is one of the ancient passes over the Pennines and beside the road was a railway and a canal: successive generations of transport systems. And in the cafe were a number of truckers tucking into their fry-ups with mugs of tea.

Out on the moors I could pretend that I was not part of this world. But I was. Even though I was travelling the way that people have travelled for tens of thousands of years, I was only able to do so because I am a part of the industrial society that gives me the equipment, the health, the money and the leisure to take this time out. The factories and offices of Leeds and Manchester, the trucks on the road, the cars and the trains, the power lines and the tractors are features of a society in which I belong, and from which I cannot escape.

But within it I still have some choices. As do we all. Together we have choices, and we can shape how our society functions. And as the increasing carbon in the atmosphere causes changes to the climate, and the oil supplies diminish, and the seas become more polluted, clearly it needs to change.

When Jesus began his preaching he called for repentance, by individuals and by his society. As did the prophets when they described the injustices of their society. This change is what many Christian preachers have called for when they have realised the way their society is going.

I believe it is something we need now, as a society and probably as individuals. We need to change our way of living, for the sake of future generations, and for all other life on the planet. Clearly we are limited, as individuals, in what we are able to change, but that does not mean there is nothing we can do. Our lives, like a long journey, are made up of many choices and decisions: what we buy, how we travel, where we take holidays, what we work at, and how we spend our leisure time.

We have some choices, and many limitations. So do other people. But we cannot make their choices for them, and are not usually party to the reasons why they make the decisions they do. It is probably unhelpful to make them feel guilty if we think they are living the wrong way. Better to present or model a better way of living.

Nor is there anything to be gained by blaming those who lived in the past. The people alive when the industrial revolution began had no idea about climate change. It would be unfair to blame Watt, Newcomen and Diesel for their inventions. Or even to blame ourselves for our own earlier choices. We are where we are. The past has happened. We need to acknowledge it: both the good and the bad. The good that we and others have done, and the bad, and the things that have just happened but have shaped our lives or shaped the world. Recognise them. Accept them. Embrace them. And then move on. The significant question is: where do we go from here?

After a night in Keighley I set off on a small road across Rombald's Moor to Ilkley on the River Wharfe. Here there was a path beside the river, sometimes on the river bank, sometimes crossing fields or running beside roads, but always following Wharfedale northwards, gradually climbing into the hills.

I spent the next night in a bunkhouse barn at Bolton Abbey and then continued beside the river. This was a day of flowing clouds, with breaks of sunshine. It was perhaps only ten days since I had left Wrockwardine but it seemed longer. Spring had moved on. The hazels beside the river were opening into full leaf. There was a chorus of birdsong.

In a few places the river ran through small woods. These were possibly remnants of a forest that once covered the whole area. It is good that people in Britain campaign to stop the destruction of the world's rainforests, but we need to acknowledge that our own landscape is only as it is because our forebears cleared the forests and successive generations of farmers have stopped them regenerating. Likewise, while many people in Britain are rightly concerned about the rapid increase of carbon emissions in China and India, these countries are only trying to achieve the level of material wealth that we and mainland Europe enjoy. And some of those emissions come from the manufacture of goods which people in Britain want to buy. One reason that Lancashire and Yorkshire are cleaner now than they were a century ago is that the things that were made here are now imported from elsewhere.

At times a road ran near the river and I walked to a rush of traffic noise. On two occasions low-flying fighter jets roared overhead. I wondered about the traffic. Was it all really necessary? And about the planes, burning more fuel in a minute than the cars in an hour. Did we really need them? Maybe we did. But I was sure that there was much in our country's armoury that was not necessary, or even desirable. This was before we were taken into a war to remove from Iraq weapons of mass destruction which did not exist. Our own certainly existed, and still do. It is not only from our consumer lifestyle that we need to repent.

At Grassington I bought fish and chips and ate them on a bench in the town. Chaffinches bobbed for the crumbs. From a call box I rang Scargill and left a message to say that I expected to arrive that afternoon. I then found a footpath which ran along the side of the dale at a high level. I could have taken one nearer the river but I remembered this path. Once, staying at Scargill, I had walked it into Grassington and now I would follow the path the other way.

It skirted the edge of the open moor, where the stone-bounded fields of the dale give way to miles of open land of rough grass, heather and bog. Sheep graze. Crows watch. Clouds pass. And the sound of the wind in the grass is sometimes backed by traffic in the valley below or drowned for a moment by the roar of a passing jet. Finally I came to a gate I recognised.

From Scargill House a path runs up the side of the dale, through the garden and then a little conifer wood to a small gate, giving way to the open moor. Each time we had been there I had walked up that path, and though the gate onto the moor. I remembered it from my first visit and would walk up that way on my own every visit after that. Now I came to that gate from the other side, and walked through it and down the path.

I was not prepared for what happened. It was as if I met someone coming the other way who was myself years earlier. This was the place we had come to following the birth and death of our daughter with brittle bone disease, and here I was, walking up the path, angry and grieving. This was the place where I had taken short breaks away from my first job as a parish minister, and now here I was from that time, tired and frustrated at everything I felt expected to do. This was where we had brought our two children for holidays during that period, and here I was, guiltily aware that I neglected them for my work and was now leaving them again with Madron to take some time alone up on the moor.

Now, twelve years on from that first visit, I walked down towards that place and my past. For a short while I stopped and filled with tears. Then my present and past embraced. That was how it had been, but now was a new time. I laughed, I smiled, and moved on down the hill to the house that I would make my home for a couple of days.

There would be mail waiting for me. Some maps I had posted on ahead. Better still, perhaps, a letter from Madron with a bit of news of the family in Wrockwardine. And there would be people to chat to, a comfortable bed, good food, and no need to walk anywhere the next day or so while I prepared to move on towards Edinburgh.

Resources 7: Repentance

John Newton

It is unfortunate that the old word 'repentance' has come to be associated with feeling bad or guilty. The original word 'repent' simply means to change direction or turn around. Repentance is about moving on in a new direction and we often do it. We realise we've made a mistake so we do things differently. We realise we've got into a mess so we get out.

But whether we are thinking about change on the big scale or the small, we cannot undo the past. Often if damage has been done, it cannot be undone. And sometimes that can be hard to live with.

John Newton had a varied career. He lived in the late 1700s and was, at one time, a sailor and was caught in a violent Atlantic storm. He wasn't a religious man but he prayed that he would survive, and he did. From then on he took his relationship with God very seriously. And as time went on he came to realise that the slave trade he was involved in was wrong. He got out, and joined the campaign against it. It was not a popular movement. It had been started by Quakers and some Christians of other denominations joined in, but for decades they were a derided and unpopular minority.

Newton was aware that there was nothing he could do about the harm he had inflicted by shipping people from Africa to the West Indies, or to their deaths at sea. He could not carry the exiles back or resurrect the dead. All he could do was ask forgiveness from God. And he was confident that he had it. This confidence meant that he did not have to try to justify what he had done in the past, or be weighed down by it. It gave him the freedom and energy to work for a better future.

Many of his hymns capture that theme, but probably the best known does it most clearly. What had saved him, he said, was 'amazing grace'.

For reflection or discussion

1. Think of a time when you have made a significant change in your life. How did you feel before you made the change? And afterwards? And now? To what extent was the decision based on how you felt and to what extent on your thoughts about the situation? In future would you want to place more weight on either your feelings or your thoughts when making such a decision?

2. What changes, if any, do you think you need to make in the way you live?
   - For your own sake
   - For the sake of your friends, family and other communities you belong to
   - For the sake of the environment

3. Are there changes you would like to make but feel unable to? What might help you? What can you do to get that help? If you cannot make a change, how do you come to terms with that?

Some Bible passages relevant to the theme

Joel 2:12-13
The prophet Joel foresaw an environmental disaster and said people needed to change. This was not just a matter of being upset. The 'heart' in Hebrew thinking was not the centre of emotion but of the will. People needed to change how they were living.

Amos 5:4-24
The prophet Amos's message is that God condemns the powerful and wealthy who oppress the weak and the poor, and calls them to be less concerned with worship but instead to act with justice.

Matthew 3:1-12
John the Baptist preached that the reign of God was breaking in and people needed to change how they were living. Matthew then

says, in 4:12-17, that after John was arrested by the authorities Jesus began to preach the same message.

Luke 19:1-10
In Jesus' society tax collectors worked for the occupying Romans and had plenty of scope to get wealthy at other people's expense. Here one tax collector responds generously to Jesus' interest in him and Jesus declares that salvation, or healing, has come to his household.

Romans 12:1-21
As in many of his letters, Paul goes on from writing about what God has done through Jesus to how this needs to affect what his readers in the first Christian churches do in their own lives.

Action

1. Assess how you use your time. To what extent are you free to choose how you use it? Think about whether the way you use that time is good for you, your friends and family, and for other communities you belong to. If it could be used better, work out how to make changes.

2. Assess how you spend your money. How much choice do you have about how you spend it? If you have some choice, think how you might use your money better for other people, the environment and yourself. For example, would it be good to give more away? If so, to whom? Should you buy things from a different source, such as a local market instead of a supermarket? Or buy things that are made or traded in a different way, such as fair-trade products or items that are made to last, even though they probably cost more initially? Decide what you are going to do differently, and how. And do it.

3. Think how you might reduce your carbon footprint. For example, instead of using a car, can you use public transport, walk

or ride a bike? Can you insulate your house better, or reduce the temperature? Can you buy food that is produced nearby or produced and transported efficiently? Check out websites or resource books for advice. List the changes you could make, and put them in the order you can achieve them. Start with the first and when that is done move on to the second. One step at a time.

Further reading

Rowan Williams and Joan Chittister OSB, *For All That Has Been, Thanks* (London: Canterbury Press, 2010)
For those struggling and striving to make their life different, this is another way of looking at how it already is.

Yvonne Burgess, *The Myth of Progress* (Glasgow: Wild Goose Publications, 1996)
Our society assumes things will get better and people get very anxious when it appears that they are not. The writer tells where this idea has come from, and questions its value.

John L Bell, *Hard Words for Interesting Times* (Glasgow: Wild Goose Publications, 2003)
Not a book for those who want to carry on with their lives in the same old way.

Andrew Simms and Joe Smith, editors, *Do Good Lives Have to Cost the Earth?* (London: Constable, 2008)
The answer, obviously, is no. This collection of pieces by a number of well known writers and journalists suggests why.

Horace Dammers, *Lifestyle: A parable of sharing* (London: Hodder, 1986)
A classic book that calls for another way of living and started the movement with the slogan 'Living simply that others may simply live'.

Eight

Windows onto God

Scargill House was built in the nineteenth century as a country lodge for a wealthy industrialist. In 1959 it was bought by a trust to be the home of an intentional Christian community. Their aim was to run it with permanent paid staff and volunteers as a place where people could go to get some space in their lives to recharge their personal energy levels, to reflect and pray and to study and learn. They were inspired by a community at Lee Abbey in Devon which had been set up shortly after the war for this purpose. The idea was to have somewhere similar in the north of England. By the time I first went to Scargill it had been running for twenty years.

The original house provided the core of the building with lounges and a few bedrooms. But added to it were further lounges and a large meeting room, a lot of residential accommodation and a chapel. The chapel was built in a contrasting design to the original house but fitted in well with it and with the valley as a whole. It was made of local stone and wood, with a high apex and roof lines that matched those of the conifer trees that at this point clung to the side of the dale. The interior was simple. There was little ornamentation, and at each end was a large clear window.

Through one window you could see the side of the dale rising up behind the house: a steep craggy slope with fir trees clinging among the pale rock. Through the other window was a view of the far side of the dale. During the few days I stayed there on my journey north I spent some time watching the changing light as clouds moved across the sky. There were sheep on the hillside, and occasionally crows passing, and trees moved in the wind. At times the far side of the valley faded away behind heavy rain, but then it slowly reappeared. It was a chapel but the view beyond it was not obscured by pictures of saints, or Jesus, or angels. Here was just a small part of the world with all its own colours and movement.

One evening I joined in a communion service. The table was plain wood, with candles. There was bread and wine. Words were spoken. Songs were sung. The bread was broken to commemorate Jesus. He was well known for his meals with all sorts of people:

meals in houses, on hillsides, beside a lake. It seems he had a particular way of taking bread, blessing it, and sharing it out. But now, as always in a communion service, there was mention of the pain of Jesus. The bread and wine were commemorating the meal Jesus had on the night before he died, or on the night that he was betrayed.

Now, in this service, the focus of my attention was not the sky and the trees outside, the world of the present moment, but Jesus back then, and the other people in this chapel now. We were a mixed bunch from different places but together we sang, shared the bread and wine, and committed ourselves to continue living as disciples of Jesus.

On a couple of other occasions I sat alone in the Scargill chapel not looking outside but thinking, praying, and being still. There was something about the plainness of the place that, for me, was conducive to stillness. It was not busy or fussy and so I found it helped my mind settle into the present moment, to see future possibilities more clearly and present concerns with an altered perspective.

Different people find different kinds of settings helpful in this way. Some years later, after walking through Burgundy and the Jura mountains I arrived in Geneva. On my way I had called into a lot of French churches and several cathedrals, all of them furnished with statues of saints, pictures, and often stained-glass windows. There were candles and ornaments and memorial plaques. In Geneva I called first into a modern Catholic church which was starkly different. There was a large coloured-glass window that depicted space: the cosmos, galaxies, stars and planets. For a time I sat and looked at it and as I did so the sounds of the city outside, the movement of cars, buses and pedestrians, the turmoil of life in this international hub with its urgency and self-importance faded into a different perspective. So much less important. So ephemeral compared to the grand scheme of the universe.

I then called into the Protestant cathedral: a medieval building which had once had its statues and pictures like Beauvais, Notre

Dame and Sens, but at the Reformation had been cleared out and since then had had a plain interior with rows of pews for the faithful to sit while they prayed, sang and listened to the preaching of the word. For me it was as refreshing as walking onto open moorland – astringent and spacious.

Then, a few days later, in the mountains I came to a village church that was open for anyone to call in and I spent a few minutes just sitting and appreciating the simple beauty. Less is often more. The walls were painted white. The seats were pine. At the centre of the front was a stone font and to the side a reading desk. And high up round the walls was painted a short text from the New Testament about the love of God. Later, when I was taken into a number of highly ornate Italian churches, and then arrived at St Peter's in Rome, I recalled that place as a point of stillness and simplicity.

But that is my preference. There must be people who love the decorations, statues and crucifixes of the French churches, and certainly some travel miles to wonder at the decorations of the churches of northern Italy. We have our varied languages, both those we speak and those we use when we create images of what is beyond words. Our lives are different stories and our past experience influences our response to where we are and what we are seeing and hearing. What for one person evokes a sense of mystery for another might simply create confusion. So trying to speak of what is mysterious is difficult. And creating spaces in which people can pray, meditate or worship is not going to be easy either. For me, the chapel at Scargill was a helpful space. The simple cross and the bread and wine were useful pointers to essentials of the Christian story, the story of Christ. It was a good place to be for a few days.

I left on a bright morning, the first of May, and for the next eleven days wound my way northwards to Edinburgh. At Hawes Youth Hostel in Wensleydale I met up again with the walker who had arrived muddy at Mankinholes a week before. He had stuck to his route of following the Pennine Way and while I was sitting dry and warm in Scargill House he had been out on the open moor and had then camped at a farm. I admired his determination. I enjoy open moorland but did not regret my decision to follow Wharfedale rather than the Pennine Way across the moors.

A high path took me over into the Eden Valley where at Kirkby Stephen the group of RAF walkers following the Coast to Coast Path encouraged me to carry on. Between Appleby and Carlisle I followed hedged lanes through rich farmland and there came across a strange symbol beside the road. It had clearly been created deliberately, but I did not know whether what it said to me was what the creator intended. There was a fence hung with dead rooks and one was nailed onto a wooden post with a crossbar.

It was once a common practice for farmers and gamekeepers to hang up dead vermin. Moles. Rooks. Buzzards. Anything that was thought to be a pest. Perhaps it was supposed to be a warning to others to keep away. Perhaps it gave the killer a sense of satisfaction to display his trophies. Here the practice was clearly being continued. A number of rooks, which can eat their way through a lot of freshly planted seeds, had been shot and were now displayed. It was the one that hung separate from the others which impressed me most as it looked as if it had been crucified.

I do not know if that was the intention of the man, and I assume it was a man, who had killed the birds, but it was how it seemed to me. And, like a crucifix, it spoke of much more than one rook on two pieces of wood. A depiction of Jesus on a cross can evoke not just the torture and death of one innocent man but the unjust suffering of millions of people down history: people who have been and continue to be 'crucified' to protect the interests of those with more power. Here it was not humanity that was crucified, but the rest of life. The dead bird represented nature: the living world apart from humanity, suffering and being destroyed to satisfy and protect human interests.

Walking for some distance through a country you become aware of the shape of the land, and how it changes from one area to another. Upper Wharfedale was rocky and rugged, but now the Eden Valley had rolling hills. I had walked from an area where the underlying rock was limestone into one of sandstone, which was very different. What had also changed was the dialect of the place names. Moving from Cheshire to North Yorkshire I had passed from a land where there were settlements called Worlesdon and Winsford set among hills and valleys to one with names like Yockenthwaite and Oughtershaw set among fells and dales. I had walked from an area which centuries ago had been settled predominantly by speakers of Old English to one where the settlers had been Scandinavians.

The physical landscape was influenced by the texture and strength of the underlying rock, and how prone it was to being eroded or dissolved by water, as well as by the courses of water and ice that had flowed over it. The human geography was influenced by the waves of settlement and the place names by the languages of the settlers. In a similar way our attitudes are shaped by the stories and images which we hold to be significant.

In ancient Germanic and Scandinavian mythology the origins of earth lay in a titanic struggle between the powers of rock and ice and those of the gods. Then, following their birth, humans struggled one with another and with the forces of the world that threatened them. The purpose of human life was to fight and to win: to win food from the land or the sea or to win in battle. And for warriors who died in battle there was Valhalla, a place of continual drinking and fighting. The deep nature of reality was seen as continual conflict.

The earth born out of struggle is a common theme of myths across the world and it is hardly surprising. Anyone who watches the living world – whether in a park or garden, or in a television programme – sees a struggle. For one to live others have to die. Sharks, lions and thrushes show no mercy to their victims. They kill and they eat in order to breed, and live to kill again, till they die in their turn. And those whose livelihood depends directly on producing food easily see any being which challenges that production as an enemy, whether slugs, rabbits or rooks. This view is not confined to the former inhabitants of Cumbria or anywhere else. It is widespread. And here beside this lane it was being represented by a dead rook hanging on a cross.

As many times before, I found Carlisle a friendly place: a place where people speak to you and tell you what they think. Aware that I had several days walking through the Borders ahead of me, and that I was likely to be travelling long distances between shops, I decided to stock up on lightweight food. I found a shop that sold outdoor equipment and searched the shelves for dehydrated meals. The proprietor was checking his stock lists.

'Do you have any dehydrated meals?' I asked.

'Up on the left,' he said, without looking up. 'But I wouldn't have them if I was you. Bloody awful things. You're better off with a bit of cheese and a bun.'

OK. Nicely blunt, and more help to me than to himself. I bought just two, in case I could not get any cheese or buns.

Two days later I arrived in the rain at Samye Ling Tibetan Buddhist Centre in Eskdalemuir. There I had a bunk, food, shelter from the rain, people to chat to and access to the temple for meditation should I wish to use it. I stayed two nights

The temple at Samye Ling rose in the midst of the wet grounds like a lotus out of the mud of a pond. I visited it on my own, as I had the chapel at Scargill, and sat for a while. Later I joined in a time of communal meditation. It was led by a monk and there was no explanation. There were bells and chanting, but no sermon, bread or wine. And no songs. The words, as far as I could tell, were repetitive. But I understood that they were not to convey ideas but to aid meditation, which was a stilling of the mind and the development of awareness.

At the front of the temple was a great golden image of the Buddha, the Enlightened One, seated in meditation. Around the statue were dozens of others. I was told later that this was a pointer to the fact that the Buddha is encountered in many different ways.

There is no one path to enlightenment, though those who have travelled towards enlightenment can help others on their way. And the statue of the Buddha portrayed a person at peace. His face had no trace of striving, let alone of pain. He sat amidst the struggles of the world but he was somehow beyond them.

I was comfortable with the thought that there is no one road to insight into the truth of life. In the Christian tradition the variety of styles of architecture and worship reflect this, except to those who are convinced that all others are wrong. I was also comfortable with the thought that different religions can lead people towards God. I had long ago realised that the statement of Jesus in John's gospel, 'No one comes to the Father but by me,' so often quoted by those who are convinced that only Christians have a right relationship with God, could be heard in two ways. It could be taken as meaning that only by knowing Christ can someone come to God, but also that all those who come to God are taken there by Christ whether they recognise him or not. Given that the gospel in which the phrase occurs begins with the statement that Christ is the light that enlightens every person it seems to me that this saying should be taken in the second way.[1]

But the image of an Enlightened One as untouched by pain or by joy was a challenge and a puzzle. To me the life of the world was a woven tapestry of pain, pleasure and joy. Being a part of the world would involve knowing and experiencing this, not escaping from it. In my weeks of walking I had been immersed each day in a great symphony of colour, sound and movement. Time and again it appeared like a great work of art in which I had a part. And somehow the pain that I saw around me in the faces of some people, and could imagine in the situations in which they lived, and the pain that I felt frequently in my legs, feet and back, and the times of sadness and loneliness and of exhilaration and pleasure, were all a part of the whole.

The ancient Hebrew picture of the relationship of humanity and the world was different from that of the Germanic and Scandinavian myths which portrayed the world as an arena of conflicting forces. In Hebrew thinking, the world as a whole was God's creation. And in the creation poem at the beginning of the Bible the earth is called into being by God. First it is simply land surrounded by sea and covered by a dome of sky, but then the land is populated by plants, insects, birds and animals, and the sea by fish and monsters. Then humanity, male and female, is called into being to represent God the creator. Humans are created to be an image of God who has called everything else into being and has seen that it is good. This is a very different picture from one in which humanity is fundamentally in conflict with the rest of the world.

The world as presented in the Hebrew scriptures is not without its struggles, and these are not just the struggles between person and person, tribe and tribe, nation and nation. The collection of stories at the beginning of the Bible moves swiftly from this opening narrative to one in which Man and Woman are sent out of a garden where food simply grows for them on trees to one in which the production of food involves toil and childbirth involves pain.[2] Adult life is no idyll in the ancient Hebrew picture. But the idea remains that the whole world is God's creation and humanity is a part of the whole. And this remains as the first statement in Christian creeds: God is the creator of heaven and earth.

In the first centuries of the Christian church there were movements which taught that the world was not the creation of the good God about whom Jesus spoke but of some other power. Others taught that human life was meant as a process of purification and escape from the struggles of the world and the power of the flesh. But this attitude was resisted and refuted by what became the mainstream Christian church, although such views have resurfaced time and again in Christian history and are still present now in one form or another. The mainstream view, Catholic, Orthodox and Protestant, is that the cosmos is God's creation and humanity has a part within it. The sense that I had, slowly making my way northwards through Britain, was that I was indeed a part of a whole complex web of life, and that it was like a great work of art.

That, of course, bristles with problems. If the world is made by God, how is it made? What is the process of creation? If God is the creator, God is necessarily not a part of everything that we can feel, touch or see, so how can we know about, or even speak meaningfully about, God? And if the world is God's creation, and it is good, why is there so much pain and suffering? Why is life so often a struggle for all living beings, including humans? If you are on a long walk and inclined to think about these things, you have plenty of time to do so. Which I had.

I had no simple answers to these big questions but I had a deep conviction that the statement that the world is God's creation points to something true about the deep nature of reality. And that being at home in the world was not just a matter of my relationship with what I could see, touch and feel, and with other people, but also with God within and beyond the world.

As my mind turned over these questions on the journey north from Samye Ling, several intriguing memories repeatedly surfaced. One was of a conversation in the lounge during a heavy rain shower. There was a woman there who had come to the centre for a short break from a stressful and distressing situation, and as we all talked one of the monks listened to her, and spoke with her, with great compassion. Another was that image of the Buddha, seemingly beyond the pain and struggles of life. And a third was of the temple itself, bright red and shining gold amidst the mud and damp woods around it, reminding me of the Buddhist image of a lotus, or water lily, which has its roots in the mud of a pond but its flower in the air and sunlight above the water.

Perhaps these were clues to the puzzle. Without its roots in the mud the lily flower would die. The plant is neither roots nor flower but both. The compassionate monk is not detached from the woman's pain but shares it while also living beyond it. The temple is a part of the whole landscape. The Buddha has not escaped from the world but remains, not to give answers to endless questions but to bring enlightenment.

Time and again on my journey I had come across intriguing signs pointing towards a waterfall, a lake, or a town with an interesting name, but I had chosen instead a path that would take me towards my chosen destination for the day. And often I thought maybe one day I would come back and take that other road. Samye Ling was like one of those signs. My short time there gave me glimpses of another way, another discipline, another room with different views from the windows. Perhaps another day I would find out more of what it had to offer, but for now I was on a pilgrimage to Iona, an ancient centre of Celtic Christianity.

From Samye Ling I continued north, following small quiet roads up through the hills of the Borders, over from the valley of the Esk to Ettrick Water, then skirting Black Knowe Head, I crossed the Yarrow Water and took the road across Blake Muir to Innerleithen. For those two days there were showers and periods of sunshine, winds blowing white and grey clouds across lively skies, and the browns and greens of the hills changing texture as the light and shade moved. There was very little traffic, and few people who were not in cars. But there were crows, thrushes, finches and tits, the occasional buzzard circling high, and small outbreaks of colour where spring flowers were opening in the shelter of conifers and walls.

I came into Innerleithen on a Sunday afternoon and took high tea in a small cafe well filled with day-trippers from Edinburgh. Scargill had been my first destination. Edinburgh was my second, and I began to feel I was getting near. From my map I could have worked out the distance, but the nearness was not about miles. It was the voices in the cafe and the registration plates of the cars on the roads. It was the place itself. I knew Edinburgh well and the architecture of Innerleithen had much of the same style. I was tired but this sense of the place gave me a new energy. There was a campsite near the town but I lashed out on a room in St Ronan's Hotel. I had no idea who St Ronan was but it sounded like the place for a pilgrim, and I slept well.

My idea was to spend the next night at a place I had identified called Windy Stack in the Moorfoot Hills. It looked on the map to be suitable for camping and from there it would be a day's walk to Colinton on the edge of Edinburgh, where I would stay with my sister. But I reached Windy Stack by lunchtime, and over bread and cheese decided to carry on. It was as its name suggested, and the ground was rough and wet. I could make it to Penicuik. I did that and once I was in this small town decided to go further, up and over the Pentland Hills. So it was that in the early evening I came over by Allermuir Hill and walked down to Bonaly with the city of Edinburgh spread out before me.

There, of course, was the castle on its rock, the spires of St Mary's Cathedral, and Arthur's Seat looking over it all. There were the grey roofs, and I knew that within the centre were the wide streets of the New Town and the wynds and closes of the Old. To the west was Corstorphine Hill and beyond it the towers of the Forth Bridges. This was my second home.

I had moved to Edinburgh when I was seventeen, having grown up in the south-east of England, and I spent a year working in the construction industry before going to university in Birmingham. It was a year of significant changes. I had left school and was earning my living. Not much, but it was something. I learnt to drive and made new friends. And there was all the buzzing life of the city, its colours and contrasts, its wealth and poverty, its entertainments and dangers. It was cold. It was black and grey. The air smelt of breweries. The buildings told of history. The voices, the money and the food were those of another country, which very quickly became my country. By the time I left on a train to study in the English Midlands, Edinburgh had become my home.

My way of seeing the world had changed too. I had grown up going to an Anglican church and arriving in a suburb on the west side of Edinburgh I found a church and went on a Sunday morning. It was Anglican too but it looked and felt very different. There were no candles on the altar. There was no altar. It was referred to as the

Communion Table. There were no coloured hangings, pictures or stained glass, and there was not even a cross. The words of the service were from *The Book of Common Prayer* that I was familiar with but the hymns were different, the sermons were long and the preaching energetic. And the people were friendly.

I was invited to join the church youth group, and I did. Then over the next few months I came to see things differently. Regardless of what I had heard before in sermons and had read in prayers and hymns, I had an idea that God was someone I somehow had to please. It was not that God was a kind of celestial exam board – I had too good a knowledge of stories of Jesus to have that idea – but that God was either a friendly teacher of long ago or a remote disciplinarian. However, for these people faith was a close personal relationship with God, and for many of them it was a very friendly relationship. In their services they would read prayers from a book but on their own and in informal meetings they would talk to God like they might phone a friend. They believed God guided them towards what they needed to be doing and had given them the Bible as a source of both guidance and eternal truths. In the course of the year I was there I too moved into this way of thinking and praying. And when I went off to university I had it in mind that I would become a civil engineer, as I had previously intended, but now I would do it not just so I could earn a living but so I could do something useful for God.

It lasted four years and then it fell apart. I had worked out what I believed about God, Jesus and the Bible, but then my ideas collapsed. I had prayed to God as a man talks to a friend, or a child to a kind father, but then I felt that it was phoney and God was not there. I had followed what I believed was God's guidance and it had led to a dead end. After several years of walking in the light I had ended up in the dark. It was an uncomfortable place to be. But several things happened.

One was that while most of the Bible had become pretty meaningless, the story of Jesus hanging on a cross and crying, 'My God, why have you forsaken me?' became remarkably real. There I was.

Here he was. And a million other people down the ages who have cried out to a God who has abandoned them. I was not alone in the dark.[3]

Some friends were concerned to try to pull me back to where I had been before but others saw this as a part of my journey. Someone suggested I read a book by Paul Tillich whom I had avoided before because my knowledgeable Christian teachers had said that he was too liberal and therefore dangerous, and he did not really know the Lord. But I read Tillich's sermons and they were what at that time I needed to hear. I had no idea now what I believed about God, or Jesus, or the Bible. I could not even use the word 'God' with any meaning, but I saw that did not matter. In my confusion I could simply trust that I was valued, even though I was not able to give a name to what or whom I trusted in.[4]

Then I went back to Edinburgh and to that same church. My friends there wondered what had happened to me and were puzzled or concerned that I was no longer enthusiastic about the evangelistic activities they got up to. Or the prayer meetings, and the Bible studies. But I sat in the church during a service in which the old words were being read, and they washed over me. And I thought, 'I haven't got a clue what all this is supposed to mean, but it doesn't matter. For now, I can just be here.'

Slowly over the following months and years I began to be able to make new sense of the Christian words, ideas and symbols. I learnt that prayer is so much more than talking to God. I began to read the Bible again but in a very different way and I found it exciting and valuable. Faith was like a journey, and more like a walk across moors and through river valleys than a stroll in a garden. A long journey where there is always more to discover, where sometimes you are not sure where you are, and where you sometimes have to turn round in order to find the way ahead.

It was twenty years later that I walked through Edinburgh on my way to Iona. I did not call in at that church. It would have been locked anyway. But I walked past it. I have been back since and it has changed a bit. Its spirituality or theology would no longer be my style, any more than would that of a French cathedral. But belonging to that church was a part of my life journey, and an important one. It was there that people helped me see that faith is not fundamentally a matter of what I believe but a relationship of trust in God.

Since then I have found that this was not just their view. It squares with that of Christian teachers down the ages and of many different traditions. It ties in with the way Jesus often called for faith but never once asked people what they believed about God. My experience, which I know I share with many other people, is that this relationship is not one that is always comfortable and friendly. God in whom we trust is beyond our understanding so our faith inevitably involves exploration, questions, uncertainty, and at times confusion.

Trying to get our ideas sorted out is a part of living with faith. Often faith is implied in what we do but we may be reluctant to put into words what lies behind our way of living. Sometimes for good reasons. For a start, our words can make the whole thing seem too simple. For example, the experience of awe is not uncommon and many people give attention to the world they are part of and come to value it greatly. They often see the world as having value in itself but they might be reluctant to say that it is valuable because it is created by God. This may be because the idea of creation has been tied up with unbelievable concepts of it all being made in six days, as if the opening chapter of the Bible were a scientific explanation rather than a poem. It may be because for them the word 'God' conjures up an image of a supreme being rather than the ground of all being, and they find such talk unhelpful. It may be because talk of God inevitably makes God into an object and they have a sense that whatever it is that they experience with wonder and awe it is not a thing, but beyond every thing.

Nevertheless, while aware that any talk of God can oversimplify what is often profound and mysterious, I still want to say that we experience wonder and awe at the world because it is God's creation. And that God is not only beyond the world, God is within it, and so true life is to be found not in abstraction but in engagement. Each person is valuable in their uniqueness because they are of value to God. God is compassionate and concerned for justice, and so in having compassion and working for justice we are in harmony with what God is about. God is forgiving and knows the social tangles we are caught up in, so that while we work for justice we can be honest with ourselves and others about the inevitable compromises we make.

In other words, the forms of spirituality that I have suggested can help us become the people we need to be in the crisis of our time are in accord with what Christians believe about God. Of course, many people use them and are helped by them who do not accept, or find it hard to accept, Christian doctrines. For me that is not a problem. Faith is a relationship of trust in God. It is not a set of ideas about God or a trust in particular teachings about God. God is beyond all ideas. The words, the images, the symbols and the rituals can at best be windows onto God.

And from any window what you can see is a limited view. But it is better than no view at all. All our words, images and symbols are limited, but they are still useful. Improving them, discarding ones that have ceased to be useful, and discovering or developing new ones is a part of life. We do it in art and science and we do it in religion.

We need to do this because our understanding of how things really are affects what we do. Our understanding of the deep nature of reality affects how we live. If you see the world one way you might end up hanging dead rooks on your fence. If you see it another way you might spend years seeking enlightenment through meditation. If you see it a different way again you might devote your energies to always having the latest electronic game or gadget or to having a comfortable house and long holidays in sunny places. How we respond to the ecological crisis will depend on how we see the world and our relationship with God the Creator.

It is clearly going to be helpful sometimes to stand back and take stock of this: asking ourselves what we really believe, and whether our way of living fits with that. If we believe that the world is God's creation and therefore we are a part of God's creation, we need to think about our side of that relationship. To think about the part that worship, prayer and meditation have in our lives, and whether our lives might be better if that were different. To consider whether the other aspects of our spirituality need to be developed or changed in some way. To face up to what are big questions for us, turn them over in our minds and think them through.

Such things as prayer, worship, meditation and theological thinking are not in themselves faith. Faith lies behind them. They arise from faith, which is an underlying trust in God. But they can enhance faith, and help our faith grow, and help us engage our faith with the other aspects of our lives. So they are important.

And while we live in many ways as individuals and make our own journey of faith, we are not alone. There are plenty of other people around us who are on similar journeys, and others who have been along the same paths before. They can help us, encourage us and challenge us, and sometimes they have things to teach us.

References

1. See John 14:6 and John 1:9
2. Genesis 3
3. Matthew 27:46 and Mark 15:34.
4. Paul Tillich, *The Shaking of the Foundations* (Harmondsworth: Penguin, 1962) especially p155f.

Resources 8: Faith

Dietrich Bonhoeffer

Religions come in various shapes and sizes. They often have creeds, hymns and liturgies, special places, venerated people, sacred books, and rules or guidelines for life. Religions help some people to live good lives and drive other people to do terrible things.

Faith is not religion. Faith is a relationship. Basically, it is a relationship of trust. Time and again in the gospels Jesus commended people for their faith. Never once did he do this because they believed certain things about him, or went to the synagogue or the Temple, or even because they were good. What he was talking about was the fact that they trusted him.

Dietrich Bonhoeffer was a Pastor in the German Protestant Church in the 1930s. When Hitler came to power many in the Church supported him. Bonhoeffer was among those who did not and who formed what was called the Confessing Church. For a while, until the Nazis closed it down, Bonhoeffer was the head of a training college for new pastors in the Confessing Church.

When it was clear that war was about to break out Bonhoeffer was in the United States. Although people tried to persuade him to stay he caught the last boat back to Germany. He believed he needed to be there, as part of the church working against the Nazis. He worked for a while as a double agent, ostensibly for the Nazis but in fact keeping in touch with the church outside the Reich. He was also involved in a plot to assassinate Hitler, which failed.

He was arrested and spent months in prison before being hanged shortly before the end of the war. While in prison he wrote letters, poems and papers. His actions had not been thoughtless. As a theologian he struggled with what it must mean to be a faithful disciple in such extreme circumstances. He speculated on the idea of a 'religionless Christianity', which was conceivable because faith was something deeper than religion.

But he was also clear about the importance of the Bible, and how the traditional practices of prayer and of singing hymns were essential for his own life of faith. They were like the bass that underpins a complex piece of music, giving it a foundation that might not be noticed, but is essential for the whole.

For reflection or discussion

1. What kind of places do you find helpful for thinking about God, praying, meditating or worshipping? What is it about them that you find helpful?

2. What people have influenced your thoughts and feelings about God? How have they done so? What has been helpful and what unhelpful?

3. How, if at all, has your view of God changed over the years? What brought about the change? Are there ways of talking about God, or depicting God, which you once found helpful but no longer? If so, what are they? What ways of thinking or talking about God do you now find helpful?

Some Bible passages relevant to the theme

Exodus 20:4-6
The Israelites were forbidden from making images of God. The character, life and mystery of God could not be captured in a picture or carving. In Genesis 1:26 humanity is created in the image of God.

Isaiah 40:12-31
The prophet Isaiah argues that no carved image can adequately express the greatness and energy of the living God.

Luke 7:36-50
Jesus commends for her faith a woman who knows that she is forgiven.

John 1:1-18
This gospel begins with a poem in which God's expression of himself, God's Word, is made flesh in the person of Jesus. Jesus shows what God is like. He makes God known.

Colossians 1:15-20
Quoting what is probably a very early Christian hymn, Paul declares that Jesus is 'the image of the invisible God'. He makes God known and by his death brings into one the whole creation.

Action

1. Make a collection of pictures or postcards which you find helpful in thinking about God; and another collection of favourite prayers, poems or other pieces of writing.

2. Choose a Bible story involving Jesus. Read it through twice and then sit still and take your time to imagine yourself in the story. You are in the place where it happened, and can feel the air and smell the scents. Then run through the story in your mind either as one of the main characters, or as a person in a crowd watching. Then, in your imagination, talk with one of the characters, including possibly Jesus, about what happened. Ask your own questions, and see what answers you get. After a while come out of your imagining into the real world, and think over what you found in the meditation. It might help to write it down. You may have found this a rich experience, or it may have done nothing for you at all. A lot will depend on your personality, and also on what you think and feel about the Bible, Jesus and God at this point in your life. You are who you are, and not every kind of prayer suits every person.

3. Pray to God about things that concern you. There are many ways of doing this. You might like to choose one of the three ways described below:

(i) Talk to God in your mind, or out loud, as if God were there listening to you. Do not worry about the way you are speaking, or the words you are using. Just talk in the way that seems natural to you.

(ii) Turn over in your mind different issues that concern you, and put them into words. Many people find that using words tends to stop worries going round in circles and helps them, when they have described one concern, to move on to the next. Think of yourself first, and then people close to you, your local community, and the world as a whole. Then read a general prayer such as this:

God, you know our needs, our fears and our hopes.
You love us, suffer with us, rejoice with us
and lift us to new life.
We pray for ourselves, our friends, our communities,
those distant from us,
and your whole creation.
Work in us what is good.
Make through us what is just.
And draw us into your ways, towards your kingdom. Amen.

(iii) Use a framework for prayer such as one of those from the Wild Goose Worship Group's *A Wee Worship Book* (Glasgow: Wild Goose Publications, 4th Edition 1999), for example on page 22, or a church's service book, and put in your own concerns.

Further reading

David Osborne, *The Owl and the Stereo: An introduction to radical Christianity* (Glasgow: Wild Goose Publications, 1997)
Looking at the world from two angles: our current scientific and historical understanding and the biblical and Christian tradition.

John V. Taylor, *The Christlike God* (London: SCM, 1992)
How we acquire and develop our ideas of God, and how they need to be continually discarded in order that we can encounter the reality that the ideas point to.

Paul Tillich, *The Shaking of the Foundations* (Harmondsworth: Penguin, 1962)
The building collapses and then God is encountered in the rubble. Sermons by one of the twentieth century's most influential Christian thinkers.

Tom Gordon, *A Need for Living: Signposts on the journey of life and beyond* (Glasgow: Wild Goose Publications, 2001)
Stories, poems and reflections by a hospice chaplain that provide images for meaningful life.

Rowan Williams, *Tokens of Trust: An introduction to Christian belief* (Norwich: Canterbury Press, 2007)
Talks on the basics by a poet, academic theologian and archbishop.

Books of prayers, liturgies or songs. Try to find ones with words that engage your imagination and connect with your life.

Nine

Fellow Travellers

From Edinburgh I went westwards, first pushing into a strong headwind to the small town of South Queensferry. I had lived there for a while in the '60s, when working in the construction industry before going off to university in Birmingham. It was an inspiring place for a prospective civil engineer with its two great bridges spanning the Firth of Forth. My work was rather more mundane. We were building flats for a local housing association. But now, here they were again, those two big and very different bridges – both of them impressive. It was good to see them as I walked into South Queensferry under the rail bridge, with the road bridge up ahead at the far end of the town.

I had lived back then on the hill above the old town centre, not far from the road bridge. On a clear day it was possible to see for a long way up the Firth of Forth and on a very clear day there was a mountain peak in the far distance. It intrigued me. From a map I guessed that it might be Ben Lomond, but without using a compass I could not be sure, and that I never did. But Ben Lomond has almost mythical status in Scottish romance. It is not the highest of the Scottish mountains but was once thought to be, mainly because it rises in the south of the Highland range and so can be seen from far away. It also features in what is probably the best known of Scottish romantic songs. I had been taught 'The Bonnie Banks of Loch Lomond' by one of my primary school teachers in Surrey. When I was living in Queensferry and was very occasionally able to see this mountain which I knew had Loch Lomond below it, I had thought it would be good to walk there. I never did, but now I would. Four days or so, I reckoned, from Edinburgh. And at its foot there was a youth hostel called Rowardennan. I would stay there and work out the next part of my route.

Basically, there were two possibilities. One was to continue westwards, finding a way through Argyll to Oban, and from there crossing to Mull and on to Iona. The other was to follow the West Highland Way northwards and then either follow a route southwestwards to Oban, or continue all the way up this long-distance path to Fort William, and come round to Mull through Morvern.

Going through Fort William would be a lot further but by all accounts the West Highland Way was a good path and it might be that by the time I got to Loch Lomond I would feel like walking it, at least part of the way.

There are very few long-distance footpaths in Scotland. At the time I walked to Iona there was just the West Highland Way and another route that followed the Southern Uplands from south-west to north-east. Since then one or two others have been opened. The main reason that there are fewer paths is that Scotland has a very long tradition of open access to uncultivated land. People have been free to walk across moorland and climb mountains. There might be fences, grouse shooters with shotguns, deer stalkers with rifles, and in earlier times rival clans, but there was no law which said you could not go there unless you had specific permission from the landowner or kept to a narrow footpath. A hundred years ago in England the situation was very different.

The Pennine Way was England's first long-distance footpath and was opened in 1965 after many years of campaigning, lobbying and negotiation. Its opening was a dream come true for many walkers at the time. Some had been involved years earlier in the campaigns to have open access to the great fells and moors around the industrial cities of northern England. Many people who were stuck working in the cities loved to get out into the open countryside but much of the land was closed to them. It was owned by people who kept it for breeding grouse and for shooting. The fells were patrolled by gamekeepers and trespassers could be charged with a civil offence. The law upheld the right of a few wealthy people to deny those who lived in crowded cities access to vast areas of open space.

The campaign for open access reached a peak in the so-called Mass Trespass on Kinder Scout in 1932. A small army of gamekeepers confronted a group of ramblers deliberately walking together in this open but private place as a demonstration against their exclusion from so many open spaces. There were arrests and five of the walkers received prison sentences, but slowly changes were made to the law. And when in 1965 the final section of the Pennine Way opened it completed a path from Edale in Derbyshire to Kirk Yetholm in the Cheviot Hills, taking in Kinder Scout. Other long routes were set up shortly afterwards and continue to be mapped out and registered with the national Long Distance Walkers' Association so that now the country is criss-crossed by a network of long paths. In 2000 an Act of Parliament gave the right of access to a considerable amount of privately owned open space, designated as Access Land.

By the 1970s the Pennine Way was being used so much that it was already showing signs of serious erosion. One person who was aware of this was Alfred Wainwright. For years Wainwright had spent his leisure time setting out onto the fells of the Lake District with his mack, sandwiches and notebooks, and had produced a stream of small books which served as guides for thousands of other people who wished to walk in the Lakes.

Then in 1973 he published another book called *A Coast to Coast Walk*.[1] What he had done was to look at the Ordnance Survey maps and work out a route from St Bees Head in Cumbria to Whitby in Yorkshire, and then walk it and write it up. The route took him from the Irish Sea to the North Sea through some wild country: the south of the Cumbrian Mountains, Shap Fell, the Pennines and the North York Moors. But his aim was to show walkers that they did not need to follow a path that someone else had worked out for them and signposted all the way, like the Pennine Way, but could work out their own routes linking up bridleways and public footpaths. They could then set off alone or in small groups walking their own paths rather than following a flood of other walkers along the ridge of the Pennines. What actually happened was that very quickly people also began to walk 'Wainwright's Coast to Coast Path' and it became one of the most popular of the long-distance paths in Britain.

But Alfred Wainwright was happiest when he was out on the fells on his own, walking where he chose, stopping when he wanted to, and travelling at his own pace. I can identify with that. If I had not liked walking that way I would never have considered walking alone to Iona. But on the way I also enjoyed meeting up with other people. Sometimes they were a great help, like the group of airmen I met at Kirkby Stephen who were walking Wainwright's route as a fundraiser.

A few days later I was joined at Carlisle by Rob Bianchi. It was the only part of the walk that I did not do alone. Rob was a friend from theological college who had managed to develop a job where he was an ordained minister but also ran outdoor activities, particularly for young people. His idea was to help people worship God in what he called 'the cathedral of the great outdoors'. He heard of my walk and wanted to join me for part of it.

As it happened, the only time he could get off work was a morning, and it turned out to be the day I was walking out of Carlisle. So he joined me and it was rather different from the walking he was used to. I had decided early on that I wanted to go through Carlisle and walk into Scotland at Gretna. It was a route I had travelled more times than I could remember, and seemed the appropriate direction for my personal walk. The problem was that there was a stretch of several miles where, after following back roads out of Carlisle, we had little choice – other than making a long detour inland – but to walk beside the main A6. This was a far cry from the fells and mountains where Rob would take his groups of young walkers.

It was also not an ideal day. There was a steady, strong wind blowing from the west, off the Solway Firth and across the road. And the visibility was poor. There were no views of the Scottish or Cumbrian Hills, just the road and surrounding fields disappearing into greyness. And the traffic was heavy. Cars and lorries were pounding north and south and the noise made conversation difficult as we pushed our way northwards along the grass verge. But we made it, and I was grateful for Rob's company. If I had walked alone I imagine I would still have made it, but it was easier walking it with someone else.

On this walk and on many others I have also appreciated being able to travel along routes that someone else has marked out clearly. Coming up through Yorkshire I had for many miles followed the Dales Way. All I had to do was look for the signposts. I would still sometimes consult my map because, not being committed to walking that path, I would on occasions take short cuts. But not needing to navigate carefully made for relaxing walking. It was noticeably different when I walked out of the Yorkshire Dales National Park into the Eden Valley and found that footpaths sometimes led into fields and disappeared, and overgrown signposts pointed through impenetrable hedges. I ended up in a farmyard way off where the path was meant to be. At times like that I wished there were other walkers, if not actually walking with me then at least at some time using these paths and making them clearer.

So while my preferred way of walking was to go alone I still relied on other people. As we all do. Some people prefer to have other folk constantly nearby. Others prefer to be alone much of the time. That is a matter of personality. The world probably needs both. The opening of the Pennine Way and the improvement of access to open land in England came about through people of different personalities working together. It needed the mass trespass to highlight the issues in public debate and to generate a momentum for change. It needed organisations like the Ramblers to keep the issues on the boil. But it also needed people to work away quietly, often on their own, reading laws, developing arguments, making proposals, crafting legislation, and feeding this into the legislative system, turning the energy of protest and frustration into legal change.

One of the things I like about solitary walking is the silence, moving at my own pace with the freedom to stop and go as I choose, and the challenge of possible loneliness. But others prefer to chat, to have others decide where they will go and when they will set off and stop, or to decide as a group. And some like the challenges that come from being with a group of people in demanding circumstances.

For some people a long-distance walk is simply not an option. They might be physically unable to do it, or even to walk at all. They may never have the opportunity. I was privileged in having the strength, the stamina, the skills and the opportunities I did. There are fortunately no prizes for doing the longest walk, or the toughest. And if there were, what would they mean?

In the years after my journey to Iona I walked through the Midlands and the south-west of England to Land's End. I then continued the trail northwards in a series of short holidays, finally to John O'Groats. I walked the Pilgrim's Way to Canterbury and Dover. Then to Paris. And eventually, in another sabbatical, on to Italy. But the hardest walk I ever did was not to Iona or to Italy, it was to the end of the road. I had been seriously ill for several weeks and was now improving. I could walk slowly about the house for a few minutes at a time. But I wanted to get outside and so I walked to the end of the road. It was only a hundred yards or so but walking back was like climbing a mountain. I got into the house and collapsed into a chair. When I walked to John O'Groats I could have bought a tee shirt to say I'd walked from Land's End. But no one gave me a tee shirt for walking to the end of the road that time so I didn't buy one at John O'Groats.

Later, when I was walking through France, people often assumed I was on my way to Santiago de Compostela.

'Ah, le Pèlerinage de St Jacques!' said the man at the cafe just outside Paris.

'Non,' I said. 'Je vais a l'Italie.'

It took him a moment to catch this. 'Ah,' he said, 'Rome!'

I didn't try to explain that I was not actually going to Rome either, but to a place called Bobbio where there had been a monastery founded by an Irish monk called Columbanus back in the seventh century. My French was not good enough to handle this explanation and any conversation that might follow.

But it happened many times. And often my explanation that I

was not going to Compostela was met with smile and a shrug. That was OK. A stupid Englishman wants to walk to Italy. OK. If I chose, I was quite free to do my crazy walk instead of what everyone else with a pair of boots and a rucksack seemed to be doing. They seemed happy with that.

I arrived at Loch Lomond four days after leaving Edinburgh and joined the queue to check in at Rowardennan Youth Hostel. Many of the other people checking in were walking the West Highland Way which I had joined a few miles earlier. And some of them seemed very unhappy with people who deviated from the norm.

I had seen quite a few walkers as I followed the designated route beside the loch. They had been in small groups or spread a hundred yards or so apart. At one point I had sat for a while enjoying the view of the loch when a walker had come up behind me, pulled out his camera, taken a photo and then moved on, all in the space of about ten seconds. He seemed to have taken a photo of a view he had not looked at.

Now the stream of walkers was arriving at the hostel and many of them were discussing the route. Had they started at the beginning, at Milngavie, or a few miles further on? Had they gone over Conic Hill or taken the short cut round it? How long had it taken them so far? It seemed that some of them were determined that everyone should do the walk properly. And that it was important to do it as quickly as possible.

Then, having established that, they moved on to talking of other feats they had achieved. It seemed there was a cross-Scotland route that someone, a kind of Scottish Wainwright, had set up some years ago, and those who had done this one were in the premier league of long-distance walkers. I had not heard of it, and I had no patience with this checking and competitiveness.

I booked in for two nights. My legs and feet had been hurting badly during the previous couple of days so I thought a rest would do them good and I could think about which way I would go from Rowardennan. As it was, by the next morning I did not feel like hanging around so, leaving my big rucksack at the hostel, I walked up Ben Lomond.

The view from the top was magnificent. South was a haze towards Glasgow, but north and west the mountains rolled away, range after range. To the east I was looking back down the way that I had come – from Queensferry to Linlithgow, then along beside the Union Canal with a clear view towards Grangemouth with its flares in the oil refinery and vapours rising from outlets at the chemical works. Past Falkirk I had camped near Denny and on a third night below the Campsie Fells. The next day I had limped into Drymen, and then joined the West Highland Way just before it came to the banks of Loch Lomond.

I could not see all that way. I had hoped to be able to look back to the Forth Bridges and know whether this was the hill that I had been able to see from Queensferry years before, but it was not clear enough. The view disappeared into a haze. But I could imagine my trail winding back to Edinburgh, and then southwards into England. The sense that I had now, looking back along this route, was one that I had a number of times on this walk. It was not a sense of achievement but of completion, of disparate things coming together. I did not feel that I was ticking off a success but that I was making something. And it was personal. This was my journey. My pilgrimage. My songline. No prizes. Simply pleasure overriding the pain, and a sense of satisfaction. I did not want to cheer but to smile. And to carry on.

The next morning I set off westwards towards Inverary. I did not want to be meeting up each night with people who were ticking off the miles and checking how others were matching up to their own achievements. I would go my own way, at my own pace, and not have to keep explaining that I was not trying to chalk up another footpath done.

These walkers on the West Highland Way reminded me of some Christians I had known – and of myself at one time – who had been very concerned that people should do things the right way, and believe the right things. Differences were seen as deviations, and generated anxiety. Like the folk at my church in Edinburgh years before who were very concerned that I no longer shared their enthusiasm for evangelism or read the Bible in the same way as they did and was even reluctant to talk about God because I had come to find the language empty. For them there was simply one way to live, one way of seeing things, and one true faith, as if faith were a package of beliefs and practices that one had to spend one's life unpacking. I too had thought like this, but now I saw it as a journey, a continual exploration. The outcome would be not achievement but completion. Or 'fulfilment' as the old Bible translations put it.

Having moved into that way of seeing things I soon found that many other people also saw faith as an exploration. People I met on courses, and in groups, in conversations and at other churches, for whom faith involved questions that had no answers, and debates that could not be resolved simply by finding a reference in the scriptures. I went to services where I was welcomed and no one tried to bring me into their way of seeing things. I read books by Christians from many ages for whom theology was, as Anselm put it, 'faith seeking understanding'. And as time went on things came together for me. Prayer. Church. The Bible. The faith journey was not just through open moorland; there were also green valleys, buzzing cities, friendly hostels and warm pubs.

To be fair to them, there were probably people in that Edinburgh church who saw faith that way too, but they were not the ones I knew well. And it was perhaps time for me to move on anyway. Much as it was not the time for me to walk the West Highland Way. I came back to it some years later, picking up the trail at Rowardennan and walking to Fort William. It was a magnificent walk, up through the green southern Highlands, across the stunningly bleak Rannoch Moor, and coming over the Devil's Staircase to see Binnein Mor and Ben Nevis at the end of the Way. And there was no one then checking that folk had done the walk correctly.

On my way north through England I had stayed in Appleby with another friend from theological college. Peter Norton was now the

Vicar of Appleby and had offered me a bed for the night on my pilgrimage. Appleby in Westmorland was a small market town, and the site of a famous annual horse fair. This fair was a gathering for Romanies from all over Britain and beyond, and was controversial. There were people who did not like having hundreds of Romanies turning up in the town. All over the world and down the centuries there have been tensions between settled communities and those who move from place to place. Appleby's tensions were not unique.

Peter Norton was inevitably caught up in this local argument because when they arrived for the fair, for family gatherings, horse trading and other dealing, some of the Romanies wanted their babies baptised. It seemed that while the Romanies had their own particular kind of church, with pastors having a significant role within the itinerant communities, they liked to have their children baptised in the Anglican parish church in Appleby. The names were there in the parish baptism registers going back for centuries. It was as if, while in so many ways they kept their mobile way of living and their independence from settled society, they also wanted to have this one significant point of contact and connection. And Peter conducted the baptisms.

For this he would have been criticised by various people, quietly if not to his face. There were those in the town who did not want to encourage the Romany visits. Some clergy and lay Christians would have argued that people should only be baptised if they were regular worshipping members of a congregation. Others would have said that baptism was for Christians and the Romany way of life was not Christian. And some would be concerned that the Romanies were not really Anglicans.

Part of Peter's argument to those who criticised him was that baptism is not admission into a particular church or organisation but into the whole Christian movement. And this is recognised by many denominations. If someone has been baptised in an Anglican or Methodist church and becomes a Roman Catholic, or vice versa, they are not baptised again. As for the suggestion that you should only be baptised in the parish in which you live, or in the congregation where you belong, here were people who lived in no particular parish. And as for the question of whether the Romany lifestyle was a Christian one, how was it less Christian than living in a house in one place for a long time? In fact Jesus had said of himself, 'The foxes have holes and the birds of the air their nests but the Son of Man has nowhere to lay his head.'[2]

Baptism is not simply a rite of initiation conducted by a priest or minister. It involves a commitment on the part of the person to be baptised, or in the case of a child their parents or guardians. But the commitment is not to a church or a lifestyle, it is to God as God is known in Jesus. That commitment may mean that a person moves from one church to another or from one place to another, or changes their way of living or how they see things. God is beyond definitions and in no particular place. Faith is often described as being like a journey.

But it is a journey that involves commitment. It is not just a matter of drifting from experience to experience or idea to idea. Commitment means giving yourself over to something, or someone. Putting yourself into a relationship with a clear view that you are going to stay with it. Commitment is not just sampling something, or giving it a try; it is saying, 'Yes, I will stay with this.' This person, this community, or God. And you never know how that will work out. Like a journey, however extensively you plan, and however much you try to find out beforehand, there comes a point where you set off, and you have then to deal with what arises.

Sometimes, certainly, you have to give up the journey that you thought you would make. You realise you are going the wrong way and need to change direction. Sometimes you do not have the energy, or the resources, or the mental strength to continue in the same way. But you only get into that situation if you are willing to take the risk of setting off in the first place. Until then it is all speculation and dreams.

John Hillaby tells of meeting a man on one of his long walks who admired what he was doing. 'I wish I could set off like that,' he says, 'on a long journey, not knowing what I was going to come across.' But he would not do it. He would not leave his work and home. John asked him what he did and the man said he was a travel agent.[3]

Faith is not a matter of reading books or watching programmes about religion, nor of simply developing ideas. It involves commitment. And so, too, responding to the ecological crisis means not only gathering information, expressing concern, and wishing things were different. It requires commitment. Changing how one lives. Joining a campaign. Supporting others with more than simple good wishes. And joining in with others who are trying to change things for the better.

The two things go together. The commitment to God that faith involves leads to a commitment to work to care for the earth that is part of God's creation, and to developing a way of living that respects it as such. In this we are involved with other people. As on a journey, sometimes they are people with whom we travel for an extended period. Or we may just meet them in passing, and give each other support and encouragement. And, like some travellers, there are those who prefer to beaver away quietly at their own projects which are from time to time shared with others, while others travel in groups: meeting, campaigning, acting together.

Faith communities and the green movement need both kinds of people. There is a place for solitaries who will often work on their own and are willing to go out on a limb, asking awkward questions, developing new insights, and perhaps sometimes challenging the mainstream. There is also a need for people who will work, think and act together.

The fundamental commitment of faith is not to the church or an organisation but to God, who is beyond them all. But as part of that commitment to God there is a need from time to time to be committed to particular churches and organisations. They have an important place. Visitors often appreciate church buildings and joining with the congregations that meet there. But for those congregations and their buildings to exist, there need to be people who will not be just visitors but will get involved and live out the Christian life within local communities, with the worship, community action and care for the building that might involve. And sometimes that local community life is not comfortable. People do not always agree. They challenge each other and sometimes they rub each other up the wrong way. But, hopefully, they respect each other's faith and find a way to live and work with a common concern.

Similarly, the fundamental commitment required for the world is not to a particular organisation or campaign, but to the good of the earth. Working that out will involve at times a commitment to particular organisations, group or causes. There will not be complete agreement among those taking part. There will be argument, challenge and sometimes compromise. There will be clashes of personality and disagreements about objectives or strategies. That is inevitable, but people need to be able to act together as well as alone, and to do so not only when the going is good, but when it is hard.

The greater challenge is to live with respect for the world, with compassion for other people and other creatures, and to work for justice. We cannot do that alone. And we cannot do that without commitment.

We must become less dependent on fossil fuels, and that change needs to be happening now. Many people and organisations are reminding us that fossil fuels are a finite resource and are bound to run out in due course. Estimates vary as to when we will reach that so-called point of peak oil, because large reserves are being discovered at deep levels, and technology has been developed that is now extracting oil from shale. In the past this has always been considered uneconomical. However, pushing the point where we start using less oil further into the future increases the amount of carbon in the atmosphere and contributes to climate change.

New communication technology enables us to keep in touch cheaply and quickly over long distances. Communities can develop or be maintained with the individuals involved only meeting rarely, if at all. But the need for physical encounters will never become completely redundant. People can keep in touch with friends and family members very easily with e-mails and Skype but they are still keen to fly across the globe to meet up when possible. What this means is that despite the new technology it will be increasingly important to develop local as well as disparate communities. Neighbourhoods, towns and villages will need to play a greater part in the future than they have in recent decades.

Resilience has become a keyword in the face of this. Some local communities now aim to self-produce more of what they require, going for locally grown food, installing combined heat and power systems, using local water sources and harvesting rainwater. Countries are beginning to think about their food security in ways that they have not done for decades.

At the same time, and almost inevitably, many governments are under pressure from those who are concerned about immigration, seeing this not as bringing additional skills but as putting pressure on resources. In this situation there is a danger that people will not only work for local resilience but, particularly as the world situation deteriorates, will want to pull up their drawbridges. There will be greater tensions between settled people and those who want to come into their communities. As between the Romanies and the locals in Appleby, such tensions are not new and have existed for years. In some parts of the world they are ancient.

In northern Nigeria, where I lived for several years, the tension between the nomadic Fulani people and the settled Nupe and Gwarri tribes was keenly felt. Slave-trading over the centuries had fuelled tensions in the past and led to longstanding resentment, but the issues now were about resources, and particularly land. When the Fulanis' cattle damaged the Nupes' crops, violence could break out. Similar ancient rivalries are found in many parts of the world and can be seen in various places in the Bible, including the myth of the arable farmer Cain who kills his herdsman brother Abel.

But what is equally ancient is the virtue of hospitality. In many cultures it was considered essential to offer shelter, food and drink to travelling people who needed it. This too is reflected in the Bible, and even commanded in the Hebrew laws. The basis of this was simple. Everything the people had was a gift from God who created all things and had led the people from their slavery into a place of freedom. As it was a gift from a generous God it was not to be hoarded but to be shared with those who needed help. This was one aspect of practising justice. Similarly, a concern for justice should lead us to challenge moves to turn resilience into self-protection and to make communities exclusive.

On my journey to Iona I benefited on many occasions from the hospitality of others. The community at Scargill existed for that purpose. In Appleby I stayed with Peter Norton and in Edinburgh with my sister. Others offered me hospitality at a chance meeting. There was the lady at Dunadd who offered me tea and cake and chatted about gardens, history and Iona. In Rochdale I was offered a bed for the night by Stanley and Kathleen Hope following a conversation with Stanley some weeks before. They were extending to me the hospitality that Stanley had for decades argued the people of Rochdale needed to extend to those who moved into the town looking for work. Samye Ling was a Buddhist centre and I was a Christian but I was welcomed as a fellow traveller.

In Wrockwardine, where I began my walk to Iona, there was an attitude among many of the inhabitants that real people were those who stayed in one place. It is a powerful idea. Those who have been in a place a long time are the 'locals'. Others simply come and go. And I was someone who had come from elsewhere and would in time move on. So while as the local vicar I had a clear role, I could not be, and never could be, a 'local'.

Reading Bruce Chatwin's *The Songlines* opened my mind to another idea. In writing about songlines Chatwin also argues that humans were nomadic for thousands of years before any of them settled for long in the same place.[4] The desire to be on the move, whether it be simply going for a walk to clear the mind or taking a longer journey to a distant place, he suggests, is very deep-seated in the human psyche. It was an interesting thought, and would seem to have the evidence of history behind it.

Around the same time I read Rowland Parker's book *The Common Stream*, about the history of the village of Foxton in Cambridgeshire.[5] He points out that the village records going back centuries show that surnames rarely continued within the same village for more than three generations. This was partly because people moved around. After the enclosures, when the common lands in England were taken from the majority and given to the few who were already wealthy, people had to travel to where there was work. And in Wrockwardine I discovered after a while that those families who felt themselves truly local were all descended from people who had moved into the village only a generation or two earlier.

In order to hold together the need for resilient local communities and the inevitable need of people to travel to where there is work, food or safety, four things are required. One is a recognition that what we have is a gift: we did not make our lives and much of what we have has been received from others, whether it be material goods or skills or mental abilities. The second is compassion so that we are able to see from their side the situations that other people are in and to feel for them. The third is justice: to act in ways that are for the good of those who are disadvantaged. The fourth is to recognise that we are all fellow travellers. Even when we stay in one place for a long while, it is still where we happen to be just for that time. We come and we go, and we meet up with others on the way.

References

1. Alfred Wainwright, *A Coast to Coast Walk – St Bees Head to Robin Hood's Bay* (Kendal: Westmorland Gazette, 1973)
2. Matthew 8:20
3. John Hillaby, *Journey Through Europe* (St Albans: Paladin, 1974)
4. Bruce Chatwin, *The Songlines* (London: Picador, 1988)
5. Rowland Parker, *The Common Stream* (St Albans: Paladin, 1976)

Resources 9: Fellowship

Elizabeth Fry

In the early 1500s William Tyndale translated part of the Bible into English and the authorities got frightened. If people could read the Bible for themselves they might misunderstand it. To which Tyndale and his friends would have replied, 'Or understand it too well.'

But in time translations into English were authorised and many of them, including the famous King James Version, depended very heavily on Tyndale's work. However, in one way they were consistently different from Tyndale's.

Tyndale had translated the Greek word 'ecclesia' as 'congregation'. In the Greek translation of the Hebrew scriptures, made many years before the New Testament was written, 'ecclesia' had been used for the Hebrew word meaning a gathering of the people. So, if there was a Christian 'ecclesia', Tyndale reckoned it should be translated as 'congregation'. In other words, a gathering of people.

The authorised versions preferred the word 'church', as it would remind Christian readers that they were part of something much bigger than their local meeting. However, it also came to signify the institution with its bishops and ceremonies, its power, its clergy, its courts and its councils.

In many ways it was congregations who resisted the overweening power of the established churches that gave individual Christians the freedom and encouragement to develop their gifts and apply themselves to new ways of working for justice. The Quakers were one such group.

Members of the Society of Friends, as they preferred to call themselves, had begun the movement to abolish the slave trade. Quakers went against the stream of society by arguing that war was never acceptable, and they refused to join the armed forces. And they recognised both men and women as their ministers.

One such minister was Elizabeth Fry who in the early 1800s

worked for the improvement of prisons. This work involved not only campaigning among politicians but also visiting prisoners. It is reckoned that between 1818 and 1843 she visited every convict ship that carried women prisoners to the colonies.

Of course, she did not do this alone. She was a member of a meeting – part of a congregation that was more than just a gathering of people in one place but a group that supported each other in prayer and in practice. A fellowship.

For reflection or discussion

1. Can you think of a group that you belonged to in the past that was particularly helpful to you? What was good about it? What can you do to create something of that now?

2. Who is helpful or supportive to you now? What can you do to affirm that, or encourage it? For example, by having more contact, meeting more often, talking on the phone, texting.

3. Who finds you helpful or supportive? How can you be more helpful and supportive for them?

Some Bible passages relevant to the theme

Exodus 23:10-13; Leviticus 25:1-28; Deuteronomy 15:1-18
In the Hebrew Law every seventh day was to be a day of rest for everyone, and for working animals. Every seventh year debts were to be written off and slaves released. The fiftieth year was to be a Jubilee when each portion of the land was to be returned to its original holders so that no family could get continually richer and richer.

Matthew 18:1-35
A collection of Jesus' teaching on community life.

Acts 2:37-47; Acts 4:32-35
The earliest Christian church was characterised by a strong and mutually supportive common life.

Romans 12:1-13; 1 Corinthians 12:4-30
Paul sees the different members of a church as having different gifts so that they can work together to continue what Jesus did.

James 2:1-9
The common life is to be characterised by respect and concern for all members without distinction.

Action

1. Which people have helpfully influenced your life journey so far? Write a list of 'acknowledgements'.

2. What matters deeply to you at the moment? Try to find a group of other people who share that passion? It might involve environmental action, a social issue, politics, or church. Meet them and see whether it might be good to join the group or organisation.

3. Find a group that is working together on a project that interests you. It may be developing a nature reserve, fundraising, setting up a playgroup, amateur drama, a band, orchestra or choir, or any number of things. Meet them and decide whether to join in.

Further reading

John V. Taylor, *The Go-Between God: The Holy Spirit and the Christian mission* (London: SCM, 1972)
A prize-winning classic on travelling with God, responding to God, and discovering God who is always beyond the definitions.

Jürgen Moltmann, *The Open Church: Invitation to a messianic lifestyle* (London: SCM, 1978)

Moltmann describes the kind of church that forms in the process of living for God's justice and which expresses God's welcome.

Elisabeth Moltmann-Wendel, *Rediscovering Friendship* (London: SCM, 2000)
The transition from acquaintance to friendship can be seen as both a gift from God and a process in which God is discovered.

Kathy Galloway, *A Story to Live By* (London: SPCK, 1999)
Seeing Christian faith not as belonging to an organisation but as being part of a movement.

Elaine Storkey, *The Search for Intimacy* (London: Hodder, 1995)
A Christian perspective on how our society and our past influence our ability to make close relationships, and how these need not be a barrier.

Ten

Songs and Stories

From Rowardennan I phoned Ardgartan Youth Hostel to book a bed for the next night. I was well into Scottish tourist country now, and though it was May it might be half-term, or the hostel might be filling fast with people viewing the southern Highlands. My call was answered by an Australian woman.

'I can book you a bed,' she said, 'but I'd better warn you …' I wondered for a moment what dangers might lie ahead. '… we have a group of children in at the moment.'

At least the hostel had some space among the children, unlike Haworth. 'That's OK,' I said. 'I'm used to children. I have some of my own.'

So I booked a bed and she told me she might be able to put me in a dormitory on my own. They had a group of children, but obviously not a school-load, and whatever tourists would be hitting the area for a spring break, they weren't there yet.

I would go westwards rather than north up the West Highland Way, and decide at Ardgartan which route I would follow through Argyll. I had only a rough idea, from a small-scale map, of how the land and the sea lay. I had a detailed map for a route north but now I had decided against going that way I would have to buy some others.

There was a thunderstorm during the night. By morning the rain had stopped but the air above was full of clouds and vapours. The day before I had been up on the top of Ben Lomond and able to see for miles. Now the mountain was in cloud above a hundred metres, and the lower slopes were appearing and fading through twisting mists. And everything dripped, including another walker who joined me at the jetty to get the boat across Loch Lomond. He had camped for the night. I was glad I had not. With few words we waited until a small boat arrived and we crossed the grey water under a grey duvet. On the western side of the loch I set off northwards. He disappeared somewhere. And slowly, as the morning wore on, the cloud thinned, lifted and moved hesitantly away. By the afternoon the sun was out.

I bought more maps at a tourist office and followed a road from Loch Lomond to the head of Loch Long. I realised that going this way I might have to follow roads for quite a lot of the walk, or take to the high ground which would be very rough with few paths. They each had their own risks.

Between the two lochs there was a straggling settlement and a footpath. It was a well used route: low land between the lochs with hills either side, with a main road and the railway from Glasgow to Fort William. In other places there was less likely to be a footpath, which meant there was danger from passing traffic. But up on the hilltops it would be hard going, and if there were no paths there would be no people. Although I liked walking on my own I still liked to know there were other people around from time to time. A fall, a fracture, a serious sprain even, and I could be in trouble. I decided to keep to the low ground and follow the main roads, and what I found was that there was often a track or path following the route, perhaps an older road or a farm or estate track. These sometimes took me into farmyards or even gardens, but I had been walking for several weeks now and was undeterred by the thought of irate farmers or householders. And I did not have the energy to spend days finding a way through the rough high ground.

As it was, over the next days in a few places I was walking at the roadside, but not often. When I was, it was sometimes noisy and at times dangerous. The verges were rough and occasionally there was no verge at all. Approaching traffic was no problem. I could see that. The problem was people overtaking, coming up behind me and passing very close and fast. I did my best to be visible. My blue and orchid rucksack helped and I put on my bright red waterproof, regardless of the weather. And I survived.

What I also did was think a lot about the way that so many roads were built, or had become, solely for cars, vans and trucks. They were unsuitable not only for walkers but also for horses or bikes. The assumption was that whoever travelled would be burning oil. And they all were, except me. Whether more people would have walked, cycled or ridden if there had been a safe path beside the road was hard to tell.

Slowly, since then, there have been changes in Britain. More designated cycle routes have been created, partly as a result of the work of Sustrans, a sustainable transport organisation. There is also now a National Byway which winds its way around Britain with signs directing cyclists onto quiet routes. The main A9 to the north of Scotland now has a cycle track beside it for a large part of the route.

I did not know then that there was in fact a network of byways across Scotland which were catalogued by the Scottish Rights of Way Society. This cataloguing of rights of way was a controversial activity in that many walkers reckoned that it undermined the Scottish right to roam. Suggesting that there were routes that one had a right to walk implied that there were other routes that one did not. But the organisation has described and mapped many old drove roads that can be used by people wanting to walk tracks through the hills away from the main roads but not wishing to discover them for themselves.

However, even if I had known about them, their value for the way I was going would have been limited, and I could possibly have found the routes on my maps anyway without knowing what they were. But, of course, the best ancient footways across the country had now become the tarmacked motor roads that followed the glens and passes. What remained were rougher, harder routes that, in this part of the country, simply crossed from one glen to another.

Until a couple hundred years ago much of the travel in Scotland was done by boat. It was a lot easier and quicker. The sea lochs winding into the country gave access to much of the land. If herds of cattle were being taken from one place to another they would go by land, along the drove roads, and be swum across the lochs in places. But people would more often go by boat if they could. Even in the 1930s when George MacLeod began to take people from Glasgow to Iona to work on the rebuilding of the

Abbey they went by boat. It would have been possible to go the way many people do now, by train to Oban, ferry to Mull, bus across Mull and then another ferry to Iona, but it was not the preferred route.

Back in the 500s when Columba travelled from Ireland and established his monastery on Iona it was not an out-of-the-way place. It was a hub for travelling the western side of Scotland. From there he and his companions could go east to what is now Argyll, which was at that time being settled by Scots from Ireland. To the north they could travel up the Great Glen into the kingdom of the Picts. To the west they could sail to the Outer Hebrides. South was the British kingdom of Strathclyde and the north coast of Ireland.

There are some treacherous waters off the west coast of Scotland but the Celtic monks travelled widely, often by sea. As did various tribes looking for new land, or raiding other peoples. Later, Norse raiders travelled round the north of Scotland to attack and then settle in these areas, and for centuries what is now thought of as the west of Scotland was in fact the almost independent territory of the Lords of the Isles who were descended from Norse leaders.

Although a sailor might see a chart of western Scotland as giving ready access to many parts of the mainland and islands, a walker, cyclist or motorist would possibly miss this. They would look at their map another way. They would not see the place as a myriad waterways stretching into the country but as a winding and ragged coastline with roads that hug the coasts, weave their way up the valleys and climb over passes. A network of twisting routes through a rough and rugged land. It is, of course, both.

On the short pass that I walked between Loch Lomond and Loch Long is a village called Tarbert. There are a number of Tarberts or Tarbets in Scotland. In Gaelic the word means 'across carrying'. Such places would be narrow necks of land where goods could be carried from a boat on one side to a boat on the other. Or even boats themselves might be carried.

On at least one occasion a Norse raiding party travelled up Loch Long and dragged their boat over the short pass to Loch Lomond, then sailed south to carry out a raid in the rich lands to the south of the Loch. War was part of the way of life. In the Orkneyinga Saga a Viking leader coolly talks about his 'summer campaign'. It was part of his way of life to take a group of men and go off raiding, down the west coast of Scotland and to Ireland. We would now call it murder and theft.

Such a change in attitude came very slowly, and it was largely the result of Christian faith and teaching. To the pagan Norse, warriors were the top rank in society, and warriors who died in battle were rewarded with Valhalla, where they could spend each day engaged in fighting, and each night in drinking. Although over time they adopted Christianity as their religion, accepting 'The White Christ' as their ultimate leader, these ideas and values did not disappear immediately. By 1100 many of the feudal lords of Western Europe were descended from Norse settlers and when the Pope called for a crusade to oust the Muslims from Jerusalem they answered the call in their droves. Kings like Richard I of England were much happier out killing people in foreign lands than they were trying to create peace and justice in their own. The thought that they might go to heaven as well, rewarded for their efforts, was the icing on the cake. The concept bore more resemblance to Valhalla than it did to the Kingdom of God that Jesus and his first followers spoke about.

Theft and murder are no longer generally acceptable. The United Nations and the International Court of Human Rights exist to try to settle disputes between nations and to bring to justice those who commit such crimes on an international scale. National police forces exist to do the same within nations – in most cases with some success. But war as such is not outlawed. Nations still have their armies, and their weapons, and will use them.

Life for most people in the world, and certainly in Western Europe, has become much more settled and peaceful since the days of the Viking raids and the subsequent feudal struggles. But the weapons have become much more terrible. A man with a sword or an axe could kill one other person at a time. After a short walk from Loch Lomond under a grey sky I arrived at the edge of Loch Long and sat on the rocks to eat my lunch. The water lapped on the seaweed, strewn with plastic bottles and other waste. Further down the loch, I knew, was the base for the British nuclear submarines, each one carrying weapons which could destroy cities, kill millions, and damage the land for generations. And unlike a Viking raider the people who ordered their use or who pressed the buttons would not see the people who would die. They would not even know what they looked like. And no one would even count the dead.

Ardgartan Youth Hostel was just above the shore of Loch Long, beneath the slopes of Ben Arthur. By the time I arrived the day had lightened. I approached along a footpath under sweeping beech trees. There was grass stretching down to the water. Children were practising archery. Others were out on the loch in canoes.

'I did warn you about the children, didn't I?' said the warden. 'There's a group up from Glasgow.'

If they kept me awake all night I would happily forgo a night's sleep so these children could enjoy the views of mountains and water, and experience play and action outdoors in this way. As it was, I was put in a separate dormitory and I slept soundly.

I met the children at the evening meal. Their places were set out on long tables. Their teachers or youth leaders were at another one. I had a place set for me on a table apart, and moved over to join the teachers. The children, I was told, were there as part of a scheme run by Strathclyde Regional Council to give city children a chance to take part in outdoor activities in a rural part of the region. Partly it was to give them self-confidence and new skills. Partly it was to help them learn to work together in a new environment. But the staff also saw it as a chance to help them become more in touch with the world, getting the wind, the rain and the seawater in their faces, feeling the pine needles and rock under their feet, and seeing the changing colours and solid shapes of the hills and forest.

Some of the adults were teachers. Others were from an outdoor activity centre at nearby Arrochar. The leader of the programme was a professional photographer called Derek Prescott who clearly did this because he enjoyed it and believed it was worthwhile. His specialism was photographing wildlife. He loved the colour, shape, movement and teeming life that was all around him and wanted other people to love it too. His photos would perhaps help adults see things in new ways, and appreciate them. Weeks like this would help children.

That evening there was to be a bonfire on the beach, and I was invited. I do not know who the children thought I was. Perhaps they did not even think about it. But they chatted to me like they chatted to Derek and the other leaders. They were from Glasgow, which in my experience is one of the friendliest cities in Britain. Sit in a cafe in Glasgow and if there is someone else there the chances are you will have a conversation. You'll find out who they are, why they are at that cafe and what they are doing later in the day, and they will find out about you. And for these children life went on in a continual flow of movement and chat.

Some of the children liked the archery. Others preferred the canoeing. Some liked being off on a walk, and others just messing about. But it was a good place. They agreed on that. There was no cinema or chip shop and they slept in dormitories. But it was worth coming. They did tug-o-war with a great rope and then marshmallows were produced, and toasted on sticks in the fire. Some dripped into the embers. Others ended up black. But whatever was left on their sticks the children ate. Until the midges came. Then we migrated indoors to look at more interesting wildlife.

Derek set up a slide show of some of his photos. These were the days before digital photography and data projectors. For its time it was a sophisticated sequence. The slides were synchronised with music from a tape player, and the pictures were stunning. One image faded into another producing a pattern of shapes, colours and sounds, giving a sense of the intricacy, delicacy, ruggedness and beauty of the world the children were part of. There were forest flowers, seals, osprey and deer, and moorland swept by wind and cloud. There were birches, oaks, burns and flickering lochs, and dragonflies hovering among reed beds. There were puffins and gulls, a soaring eagle and the sea swirling below a granite stack. The children loved it.

Another sequence was of the history of this part of Scotland. There were pictures of standing stones, mysterious rings and lines carved onto rocks, and the strange carvings of a boar and a footprint at Dunadd. This was art from the early Celtic era and much earlier. To the west, Derek told me, there were some fascinating remains – it was worth a visit; so I decided to go that way. I might have gone inland, perhaps crossing Loch Awe if I could get a boat, but decided to follow the coast to take in Lochgilphead, Kilmartin and Dunadd. I would then come to Oban and the Mull ferry from the south. I was now on the final leg of my journey to Iona. And there was no hurry.

The children finished off the evening with a song. At their school they had produced a musical about the South American rainforest, about how it was under threat and how the creatures within it needed our protection. They sang with energy. South America might be a long way away but it was not another world. They had been in the forest at Ardgartan, and paddled canoes on the loch. They had watched birds in the trees and on the water, and like the tribespeople of the forest they had shot arrows. They were not just thinking about these things. They had spent the last couple of days engaged with them. Now they sang their song about them. And I listened, encouraged by their enthusiasm.

As I left Ardgartan the next morning I still had the children's song in my mind. There were high white clouds and the sun was shining. Through birch leaves beside my path I could see the craggy peak of Ben Arthur and there was the sound of water flowing below me, and the song of a robin and a blackbird, and the calls of tits. The path took me into a conifer plantation and the sound died down. A few tits moved through the upper branches but conifer plantations are quiet places. The introduced species of tree that are grown commercially are not good for indigenous insect and bird life, and the trees and their carpet of needles deaden what little sound there is. I thought what a contrast this must be to the indigenous forest that had once existed here. On higher ground there would have been pine but in the valleys there would have been birch, rowan and oak, alive with the birds that now find sanctuary in gardens, and no doubt the woods would be bursting with songs and calls.

Coming round a bend I entered an area which had been cleared, or harvested as they say. The ground was churned up and scattered with dead branches. A few trees were still standing, their tops broken. It was a formless swathe of broken wood and turned soil, and even though the plantation had not been beautiful, this was desolate. I wondered what it must be like in the places in the world where virgin forest is destroyed, where trees which had been growing for generations over thousands of years, forming part of a rich ecosystem with other plants, insects, birds and animals, were now cut and removed to pave the way for arable farmland. That is what the children had sung about. This was a small picture of what it must be like.

This valley, this glen, had once been a forest of deciduous trees and they had been cleared a thousand years ago. But it had been done slowly and piecemeal, the wood being used for building houses and boats and as fuel for domestic fires. Many of the species of insect, plant and bird had found refuge in the fringes of fields and in the woodland that remained in steep valleys. Some had adjusted to a life of cohabitation with people. Some of the animals had been wiped out. Boar, wolves and elk had long ago disappeared from this land. The tropical forests of today's world are being removed on an industrial scale. At the time that I walked through this part of Scotland the main motive for removing the forests of South America was to create grazing land for cattle or to produce grains that could be used to feed animals. Now the forests of South America and South-East Asia are being removed to grow palm oil for food and for so-called eco-fuels. In a drive to reduce the amount of fossil fuel being burnt, vast areas of land are being turned over to produce oil-rich crops which can yield fuel for vehicles and heating systems. And numerous species are on the verge of extinction as a result, or have already gone.

It was a sunny day as I walked through this Scottish forest and not too hot. I climbed slowly up a mountain pass to a summit called Rest-and-Be-Thankful, with the idea that I would be able to buy a drink at whatever inn or cafe there was at the top which gave the pass its name. But there was no inn. I sat beside the road and ate my bread and cheese and drank from my water bottle. It was a disappointment but I would not go hungry. Down the other side I came to Loch Fyne and in the late afternoon I found a bed and breakfast beside the loch. The next night I was in Inveraray, then Minard, and four days from Ardgartan I walked into Lochgilphead. I was now going quite slowly: no longer at the pace of my early days in Cheshire. No doubt it was partly from fatigue but also I was now more confident that I would reach Iona. There was still plenty of walking to do, but I was no longer feeling the sense of urgency that accompanies uncertainty. Another week perhaps. Maybe less. I had been walking for about five weeks, but I had lost track of time long ago. Each day was another day, and another walk.

The sign at the edge of the small town of Lochgilphead had the town's motto: *Dochas*, which would translate into English as 'hope'. The town was founded at the time of the Clearances as a place for people turned off their land. While some were shipped to North America, others went to the growing towns and cities in the south, and some took crofts which were deliberately kept too small to support a family so that the occupants had to supplement their income with seasonal work for the local landlord. A few small towns were established with a view to helping people survive by fishing and gathering seaweed for fertiliser and soap. Lochgilphead was one such town. I do not know if the motto was thought of by the first settlers there or by the landowner trying to persuade them to accept their lot.

The children singing their song, and maybe their teachers, were optimistic. The rainforest could be saved. The children's lives could be improved. And the weapons of mass destruction twenty miles down the loch at Faslane would not be used. It is often said that optimism and hope are not the same thing. Optimism comes from looking at what is happening and believing that things will get better, while pessimism is believing that they will get worse. But hope is something else.

Much of the time we can see evidence for believing that things will improve. The weapons of mass destruction have not yet been used and seem less likely to be used now than they did thirty or forty years ago. There is a greater awareness of the damage that human activity is causing to the ecosystems of the planet. Many of the things that only dedicated friends of the earth were aware of and concerned about twenty years ago have become a part of the consciousness of many more people. Reducing fuel consumption, producing energy from renewable sources, using fewer plastic bags, and reducing, reusing and recycling have become watchwords. The major supermarkets now stock fair-trade coffee. Organic food is not only available in small shops on street corners.

But many people will point out that this is only scratching the surface of a deep-seated problem. Western society is still dedicated to increasing consumption, and now China, India, Brazil and other countries are in a headlong rush to industrialise, with little thought to the environmental impact they are having. The population of the world continues to increase exponentially. New sources of oil are being exploited, while in some parts of the world the climate is noticeably changing and only a few diehards believe that the burning of fossil fuels is not the cause.

Many of us swing from one view to the other. It almost depends on the weather. The landscape in Argyll might be a pattern of colour and shade, the mountains standing above the sea in exhilarating views. The sound of the birds is a chorus of song. The lambs running and tripping on the moors are a picture of natural comedy. But at another time it is a bleak and grey place. The moors are desolate. The mountains barren. The sea is a place of cold danger. The birds establish their territories and ward off rivals. And the sheep are all that now remain of a once-thriving agriculture. We can see it either way, depending on our mood or perhaps depending on what we want to see. Hope is neither of these things.

Time and again on my walk I had come across carved stones or inscriptions which consisted of a cross and a circle together. I noticed them, I suppose, because I was particularly alert to this Celtic cross design, and carried a small wooden one round my neck. It originated in the first centuries of Christianity's arrival in Britain. No one knows how it evolved. One theory is that it derived from the chi-rho symbol of the Mediterranean world which consisted of the first two letters of the Greek word 'Christos' fused together. Another idea is that it came from the cancellation of the pre-Christian symbol of the circle. But however it developed, once it had been invented it remained, and can be seen throughout Britain in both early medieval and modern sculpture and art. For fifteen hundred years people have valued this symbol.

Symbols cannot be translated like the words of a foreign language. Symbols do not speak clearly. They evoke other designs, or ideas, or things. They are pointers rather than representations, and the Celtic cross points towards many things. The cross is a reminder of the suffering and death of Christ, and of the suffering of so many people, and so much of the world. The circle is like a globe. The round world and all that dwells within it, as the Psalms put it. It is like the fire at the centre of a house, or the bread that might be baked on it. Like a rising sun, or full moon. A breast. A place of birth. The stone rolled away from the tomb of Christ. In the Celtic cross they are fused together. They are one. A whole. And usually a Celtic cross will be carved from one stone, or is drawn with the cross and the circle forming a balanced design as if they belong together.

Walking north from Lochgilphead the next day I came to a number of ancient standing stones. The Celtic monks who erected their stone crosses were following an ancient tradition of putting up tall stones in open places. I came to the carvings I had seen in Derek Prescott's photos, which pre-date Christianity by many centuries and remain a mystery. Lines and circles, obviously deliberately done but with no meaning that is obvious to us. Then at Kilmartin I came to an ancient church. In the churchyard were a number of medieval carved stone crosses in the Celtic design. One was explicit. On one side was a depiction of Christ hanging on a cross. Below him were twisting plants or snakes. Above him an angel playing a harp. On the other side of the cross was the glorified Christ, risen from the dead and ascended to heaven, with arms outstretched in greeting or blessing.

To me the artist was suggesting that these were two sides of the same story. They were back to back. Part and parcel of the same reality, as if to say that in the life of the world is the suffering of God, and the suffering of the world is taken into the glory of the Creator. And this is hope.

The story that the artist knew and depicted was of Jesus Christ. A healer and teacher, the messiah, he was killed by crucifixion on the orders of the Roman Governor. As he hung dying on the cross he cried out, 'My God, why have you forsaken me?' This man who seemed to show the character of God and spoke of his healing work as demonstrating the reign of God now feels abandoned by God, and he despairs and dies. But on the third day afterwards he is raised from the dead. He is alive in a new way: no longer confined by space or time, but alive in the life of God. As he meets his disciples they see that he still has the wounds of crucifixion in his hands and feet. It is not as if it had never happened. It had happened, but now it is taken into the greater life of God.[1]

Hope is a conviction that the pain, the grief, the struggle and suffering of the world is taken into a greater reality where the wounds are not removed but are healed. Out of loss comes new possibility. Out of death life, in time and in eternity. In the energy and new growth of the spring, in the passions and dreams of children, in the beauty that we can sometimes glimpse even in a scene of destruction, we have continual reminders of this. At times it is obscured. The light is hidden. Hope is the conviction that it is still there. That out of even the worst that can happen, God can and does create new life and possibilities. Even out of death.

Living with hope is not a matter of ignoring the bad and just looking at the good: watching the water lapping on the beach and not seeing the litter; seeing children round a barbecue on the shore and refusing to think about the nuclear missiles that are stored across the water; enjoying easy travel through a rugged landscape and not considering the price we are paying in climate change. Hope involves recognising the pain amidst the pleasure and the bad within the good. Recalling our human story as one of war, violence and exploitation as well as courage, justice and technological progress. It means recognising that there is death as well as life, but doing so with the conviction that goodness, creativity, life and joy ultimately overcome the destruction.

To me the Celtic cross is a symbol of hope that is beyond optimism. It suggests not that things will necessarily get better, although they might, but that out of even the worst that can happen God can bring new life and possibilities. What that might mean in practice, with regard to the ecological crisis, I do not know. In thinking about that we enter into cosmological questions about the nature of time and eternity, and the nature of creation. But the resurrection of Jesus provides a pointer for hope.

In the same way that wonder, compassion and a thirst for justice are not restricted to people who believe in God, so too hope is not confined to those who are able to believe in the resurrection of Christ. People live by hope. Since time immemorial people's songs, poems, stories and images have implied a conviction that what they experience has some kind of meaning. Or that what happens has a structure: a beginning, a middle and an end. That life can somehow be seen as a whole with some kind of value. In telling stories and singing songs people are expressing their faith in the value of life and their hope that this value will not be negated. The resurrection of Jesus is an affirmation of that.

References

1. Mark 15:21-16.8; John 19:17-20:29

Resources 10: Hope

Jürgen Moltmann

Jürgen Moltmann grew up in Germany in the 1930s. When he was 16, during the latter days of the Nazi regime, he was conscripted into the army. He was on anti-aircraft guns when the Allies bombed his home city of Hamburg and all his closest friends were killed in the firestorm. Somehow Moltmann survived.

He was then deployed to the front line and surrendered. He was sent to a prisoner-of-war camp in Britain and there more of his colleagues died, this time not from wounds or ill-treatment but because, as he saw it, they simply gave up. All that they had believed in had gone.

Moltmann was lent a Bible by a chaplain and through the course of many discussions and a lot of reading he came to have a different way of seeing things. He experienced hope and developed faith in God.

God, as he saw it, was in the ruins. As he put it in a book published in the '60s, the God of whom the Bible speaks is a crucified God. Crucified, but also risen. God was in the past, but is also in the future and the present – and in the present is continually creating new possibilities.

'God,' he said, 'comes to meet men and women out of his future, and in their history reveals to them new, open horizons, which entice them to set forth into the unknown and invite them to the beginning of the new.'[1] For him, the resurrection of Jesus Christ stands like a pointer in history to what many people have suspected: that there is hope for each person, each life, and for the world as a whole.

The question for us is how we can catch glimpses of these possibilities. How can we renew our sense that our present efforts are not futile, or that the end of all things is not death but life?

This is not a new task. Since the beginning of humanity people have developed ways of renewing their hope. We can appreciate their stories, songs, art and music. We can catch something of their hope and make it ours.

We can also tell new stories, make new songs, compose, paint, carve, weave and dance, using our senses and skills. In so doing we affirm that each moment and each life is not simply part of a meaningless flow of being but is something precious in itself, and always will be. And that all that grinds us down to despair will be overcome by God within God's time and eternity.

Reference

1. Jürgen Moltmann, *In the End – the Beginning* (London: SCM, 2004) p86

For reflection or discussion

1. Can you identify a time when things fell apart for you? Can you identify any good things that came out of that? If good came out of it, does it mean that what happened was not bad? Is this an example of new life coming out of death?

2. Do you sometimes feel that things in your life or in the world are going badly wrong? If so, what helps you to keep going?

3. Have you ever known or met a person or group of people who have remained hopeful in very difficult circumstances? If so, what helped them to stay hopeful?

Some Bible passages relevant to the theme

Isaiah 9:2-7; Isaiah 11:1-9; Micah 4:1-4
Three of many passages in the books of the prophets that have a message of hope.

Ezekiel 37:1-14
A vision of hope for people in exile who believe they have no more

hope in life than a pile of dry bones.

Mark 15:1-39
As Jesus is crucified he asks why he has been forsaken by God.

Mark 15:40-16:8; Luke 24:13-53
Jesus is raised from the dead.

Romans 8:14-39
Paul is convinced that not even death separates God's children from God, and that there is hope not only for them but for the whole creation.

Action

1. Music can sustain or renew a sense of hope. Not just singing songs but listening to instrumental music that weaves various strands into a satisfying pattern. Find a kind of music that does this for you and make a point of listening to it regularly.

2. The Celtic cross has been described as an icon of hope, incorporating symbols of suffering with symbols of new life. Find symbols or pictures which for you represent hope, and display them.

3. For a fortnight, at some point towards the end of each day count on your fingers ten things that have happened that day for which you are thankful. It is helpful to count on fingers as it makes you think hard to make up the number. At the end of the fortnight consider whether this has influenced how you feel about the world.

Further reading

Jürgen Moltmann, *In the End – the Beginning* (London: SCM, 2004)
A theologian who has explored the theme of hope throughout his life faces the issues of catastrophe, grief and death.

Richard Bauckham and Trevor Hart, *Hope Against Hope: Christian eschatology in contemporary context* (London: DLT, 1999)
A study of different theological approaches to the future and hope.

John Polkinghorne, *The God of Hope and the End of the World* (London: SPCK, 2002)
A theoretical physicist and theologian distils in a very readable way the results of an international interdisciplinary study of the nature of Christian hope.

Rowan Williams, *Resurrection: Interpreting the Easter Gospel* (London: DLT, 2002)
An exploration of the significance of the resurrection of Jesus for life in the present time.

Tom Wright, *Surprised by Hope* (London: SPCK, 2007)
An exploration of what the New Testament says about the nature and basis of hope.

Eleven

The Whole Way

I arrived in Oban early on a Friday afternoon. It was May and the weather was warm. The water was blue. The houses and shops along the front were bright in the sunshine. And it felt very busy.

I had walked up from Lochgilphead, following the Argyll coast. In places I had walked beside the main road but often I had been able to follow tracks and smaller roads which wove along the coastline. I had taken my time at first and stopped two nights near Kilmartin to look at the great standing stones, and the Celtic crosses in the churchyard. I had walked to a small piece of forest which I had been told was primeval. This was not some recent plantation but old forest which had somehow survived when most of the rest had been cleared centuries ago. It was light and alive with birdsong. Then I had increased my pace, not wishing to spend an idle afternoon at a campsite but wanting to press on, and after camping at Glen Euchar for a rainy night I was able to walk into Oban the next day.

Oban is not a big town by anybody's reckoning. A sea front, a quay, shops, hotels, a small spread of housing, and a railway station. But it is significant for the local area and for travellers from further afield. The likelihood is that if you want to go to Mull or Iona you will come to Oban. And it is the biggest shopping centre for many miles. For me, it was the largest place I had been in since Edinburgh. And though I had been in Edinburgh only a fortnight earlier it felt longer.

Early on in my walk my sense of time had changed. After only a few days it had seemed like weeks since I had left Wrockwardine. Now it felt like months. And yet it did not feel as if it was far away. I could recall the route, back south to Lochgilphead, then to the east to Loch Lomond and Edinburgh, south to Carlisle, and Scargill and Manchester, and then across Cheshire to my home. I could remember it in detail. If I had chosen to do so I could have followed the route back without maps. In fact, it all felt like one place.

That was the significant thing, and what had altered my sense of time. It was the continuity. I had not left one place and arrived in another. They were all part of the one whole. And the significant places like Edinburgh and Scargill, where I had spent time at crucial points in my life, were one with a caravan site at Tushielaw and a cafe in Hebden Bridge which had simply been places where I had stopped briefly on my way. Each day I had begun a new journey, leaving my campsite or hostel, and each day had had its own emotions, surprises and slog. But it was also a part of a whole journey.

I had stayed in Oban a number of times, first in the '60s when I had hitch-hiked here and then travelled on to Mull. Since then I had come on the train to catch the Mull ferry to travel across that island to Iona in the west. The ferry terminal and the sea front were familiar, but what for me, like most people, was distinctive about Oban was the great circular wall on the top of a hill overlooking the town. At a glance perhaps Oban could be any of a number of Scottish coastal towns, but nowhere else has anything like McCaig's Tower.

John Stuart McCaig, the son of a farmer, was born on the isle of Lismore in 1823. In 1851 he was working as a draper's assistant, and in 1861 as an Inspector of the Poor. By 1871 he had become a merchant and in the 1881 census he featured as a banker. He designed the great tower and work began in 1897. One of his concerns was to provide work in the winter months for local stonemasons. If they had no work they had no money and this was not a time when unemployed or poor people were given handouts. If they were to be helped they were to be given work. For that, at least, McCaig must be given credit.

But rather than employ them in building better houses for the poor McCaig employed them in building a great monument to himself and his family. His plan was for a tower, a museum and an art gallery with statues of himself and his family surrounded by a circular structure that recalled the Colosseum in Rome. In 1902 McCaig died and the work stopped. Only the outside wall had been built. And so it remains. McCaig's Tower, or – as it is more commonly known – McCaig's Folly.

Today it provides a good viewpoint for the harbour, the sea, and the islands of Mull and Lismore, and a place for picnics in good weather. It is, of course, a unique landmark, and a monument to human folly. But it was not the worst such monument that I had seen. I had been walking through one for days.

There were plenty of small signs of large-scale present-day foolishness. Wherever there was a beach there was plastic washed up on the shore. Much of it had been jettisoned from boats or discarded by people on land, and had then washed around in the water till it ended up on the shoreline. During this process small granules would break off to remain in the water for months, and often for years – granules of inert matter that caused damage to marine life. On the way into Oban I had passed a landfill site with a wire fence festooned with plastic bags blown from the waste deposits. These were the ones that had been caught. Others would make their way into the surrounding land or nearby water. Plastic revolutionised human life in the 1950s and it is hard to conceive of Western society today without it. But its cost in terms of pollution is enormous.

I had also passed by or through a number of conifer plantations. At the beginning of the twentieth century Britain did not produce enough of its own timber, and there was a particular need for pit props for the many coal mines. As a result the Forestry Commission was established and over the years landowners were encouraged to set aside land and plant conifers. And so it was that through that century acres and acres of trees were planted. However, more often than not economics overruled aesthetics, resulting in a landscape unlike the naturally sown conifer forests in Switzerland, Scandinavia and elsewhere, where wooded hillsides rise towards barer heights. Instead sharp, geometric patterns of forest appear willy-nilly across the hills, looking like giant doormats dropped from a great height.

Some of these trees were planted in remote areas with little thought to how the timber would be transported away when it was cut. Then, in the late twentieth century, the demand for pit props in Britain declined. By 1990 there were very few operational mines. And while the timber might have other uses, the increased costs of oil and labour mean that today there are great areas of conifer plantation in remote parts of Britain which are not economical to harvest, either financially or in terms of carbon footprint. The view of many ecologists is that even though they provide a poor habitat for wildlife they should simply be left.

In Argyll, as in much of the Scottish Highlands, the landscape as a whole bears witness to human greed, folly and injustice. As I walked north I passed Kilmichael Glassary. In the late 1700s this had been the site of a great cattle fair. The people in the valleys of Argyll and the isles grew various crops and raised cattle. Surplus cattle were moved down the drove roads to sites like this one where trading took place and then large herds were driven off to the population centres in the south. It was not a comfortable life, but in addition to what people had been able to grow for themselves the income from the sale of cattle provided a few extra essentials and paid the rent.

However, following the suppression of the Jacobite rising in 1745 many of the landowners became assimilated into city society and no longer lived in their Highland estates. There they had been clan chiefs and the people had paid dues not only in rent, which was low, but, more importantly, in allegiance. The local farming populace could, when called upon, become a small private army. But such armies were now forbidden. The clan chiefs became landlords, often absent, leaving the management of their land in the hands of a factor, and the people became their tenants. Then the landlords began to think about how they might improve their incomes.

Living the life of a wealthy aristocrat, whether in Scotland or England, was an expensive business. Fashion was competitive, and one had to keep up. Entertaining and the social round of balls did not come cheap. And amongst the most popular pastimes was gambling. Many of the landlords needed more money in order to be able to maintain their standing. And the way they believed they could do that was with sheep.

So began the Highland Clearances when thousands of people were removed from land that their families had worked for centuries in order to make room for sheep farming. There are stories of violent evictions and the burning of homes, of people packed into ships leaving for North America, of others scratching a living on small coastal crofts, or moving to small settlements like Lochgilphead, gathering seaweed or fishing the dangerous waters off the Scottish coast. And the signs of the evictions are still there.

In numerous glens there are the remains of former dwellings, now simple circles or rectangles of stone. On the ground there are the marks of land that was once cultivated with 'lazy beds', strips of seaweed and sand built up to make a richer growing environment on the naturally thin soil. The routes of drove roads are still sometimes visible across the landscape. And trees like holly give a clue to earlier human habitation.

But land on which, once, thousands of cattle were raised will now only support a few sheep. The effect of sheep on soil is not the same as that of cattle. They do not return the nutrients in the same way. And because the farming method involved large flocks looked after by only a few people, the land was not tended with the same care as when a family looked after their own patch.

It is easy with hindsight and with a later understanding of human geography and ecology to condemn the actions of people in the past. While at the time of the industrial revolution there was a lot of exploitation and injustice, the early industrialists cannot be condemned for the climate change that has come about as a result of the burning of fossil fuels. There was no way that they could know about that in the eighteenth century. But the impact of human activity on the landscape has been visible and documented for centuries and the landowners could have taken those facts into consideration. From Western Europe people had travelled to the Holy Land in the Middle Ages and seen few of the great cedars of Lebanon which had been mentioned in the Bible. The land was poorer for their loss. In parts of Spain vast flocks of sheep had overgrazed the land and fuelled the Spanish desire to find wealth overseas. Educated gentlemen read their classics but if they visited Greece on their Grand Tour they saw few of the woodlands referred to in the ancient literature. England had grown wealthy in the Middle Ages through sheep farming but it was not without its toll on the soil. While the Cotswolds survived, Cannock Chase became a sandy heath.

The Highland Clearances were a time of great injustice. Compassion was overridden by the desire for wealth, and human community was destroyed by those with power who valued the opinion of their peers more than the needs of their dependants. Many were made homeless and even died so that a few could become richer. It was a dark time on that basis alone. It was also a time of ecological folly. If the agents and factors had listened to people, had researched more carefully, and looked beyond their immediate concern to increase income, that might have been avoided. But they did not. It was a drive for quick wealth, and people, land and other life suffered as a result.

It would be good to think this was a thing of the past. But it is not. In the forests of South America and South-East Asia similar changes are happening but on a bigger scale. People are being removed from land they have lived on for centuries to create palm oil plantations that will make a few people rich. Oil pollution which would not be tolerated in North America or Europe continues in the Niger Delta, wrecking the livelihoods of local people. Industrial fishing by companies in wealthy nations destroys the livelihoods of those who live on the coasts of Africa. Great trawlers create havoc on the seabed and sweep up everything in their path, leaving those who have fished for generations from small boats with depleted stocks, unable to survive. Lives are wrecked and the land and sea are spoiled for future generations. The Highland Clearances are simply one episode of human and environmental injustice, and grave human folly. What we need is wisdom.

The first time I came to Scotland I was sixteen and travelled north from the south of England with a Scout group in a convoy of minibuses. Our Scout leaders had been to the north-west earlier in the year and found us a beautiful campsite on the edge of Loch Maree. There was a small wood and we were to camp among the trees, sheltered from any breezes that might disturb our campfires. This was in the days when tents were made from heavy canvas and closed with strings, and what the leaders had not reckoned with were midges.

We had no name for these tiny biting insects, but they came in clouds. Some of the campers suffered worse than others. I was not bitten too badly but some other Scouts had swollen faces for days. Our normal clothing for camps was shorts and a tee shirt. On some days it was warm enough for the tee shirt but we kept ourselves wrapped up. It made for a memorable summer camp.

Nearly thirty years later I was in the fray again. This time I had the advantage of a lightweight tent with a mesh inner door which kept most of the midges out. I lay in relative comfort in my tent at Lochgilphead, listening to the shouting and swearing of a couple of other campers who had gone to the pub and left their tent open to return fairly drunk to find that midges had taken it over. As I left in the morning their tent door was still open and I doubted if they would wake bright-eyed for the day ahead.

Then at Glen Euchar, after a night of rain, the morning was still and the midges were out by the million. I forewent breakfast and broke my camp by packing the rucksack as well as I could inside the tent and then hastily rolling it up and making a run for it. Even so, by the time I was off the campsite I could hardly see out of my left eye and for a couple of hours my hands, face and neck were stinging and itching.

Later, crossing Mull, I decided that if I possibly could I would take a bed and breakfast but at Kinloch I found that the only place with accommodation that I might be able to afford was full. However, in the bar I got good advice.

'Camp down by the water,' said another walker. 'Go for the

place which is as exposed as possible. They don't like the wind.'

So instead of camping up by the trees I found myself a perch on the rocks just above the shoreline. It was a still evening and I had to move several times while I ate my supper, but the tent was insect-free and in the morning I left without attack.

Our Scout leaders years before had not sought out local advice but had simply acted as we would have in our local campsite in Surrey. But it was not good practice in this different place. In the same way, and much more seriously, if the landowners and their agents had listened to the local people at the time of the Clearances instead of just moving them away, they might have been able to introduce a better quality of farming in keeping with the needs of the land that the locals knew so well. But it is a pattern that has been repeated across the world and down the centuries. Colonisers and developers have so often failed to listen to those who have engaged for years with the soil or the wildlife. They think they know best. And the result has been failure and long-term damage to the land.

In Zambia there is a church project that teaches the local farmers how to grow crops using homemade compost. The bishop remembers in his childhood the rich crops that were grown on his family's farm by traditional methods. But then there was a drive for 'improvement'. Development workers and salesmen encouraged the farmers to use imported chemical fertilisers, and at first the results were good. But then prices went down, the crops deteriorated and the farmers did not have the money they needed to buy more fertilisers. The way out, for them, was to return to more traditional and sustainable organic farming methods. The story is the same in many different parts of the world.

Traditionally one source of wisdom has been the elders of society. Particularly in societies with mainly oral traditions, those who had lived for a long time had a wealth of experience on which to draw. They had learnt lessons, either from those before them or from their own lives, which could benefit others. And many skills essential to survival could only be acquired from working alongside someone else: the making of lazy beds in the Scottish Highlands, the care of cattle, how to navigate a small boat through the treacherous currents of the sounds and sea lochs, where and how to catch different fish and at what times of year.

But wisdom is not just about learning skills. It is also about knowing how to live together and work alongside others. So one of the basic questions for people was: How are we to live? Wisdom was seen as answering that question. It was highly prized and was passed on in stories, songs, poems and proverbs. It was not just about getting on with other people but also about our relationship with the world as a whole, or at least the part with which we have dealings.

In the cities of ancient Greece, where the skills of rhetoric and analysis were highly prized, the search for wisdom also included debate and argument. The discipline of philosophy – the love of wisdom – flourished but it was regarded as something apart from the development of practical skills. Wisdom came from speculation, logical thought and debate.

Aristotle's writings on natural history were based on reflection but not on experiment. However, through the Middle Ages much of what he wrote was treated as authoritative, and many errors were perpetuated until the development of experimental science in the seventeenth century. It was only later that the Western intellectual tradition included experimentation in the search for understanding and knowledge.

In ancient Greece drama, sport and games also had their part, as too did music, which some philosophers suggested echoed the ultimate harmony of the cosmos. To be wise one should recognise the harmony of all things, attain a balance between body and soul, and understand not only how the world worked but also oneself. 'Know yourself' was the slogan above the entrance to the Academy at Athens.

The Hebrews, in their pursuit of wisdom, passed on proverbs, songs, poetry and stories from one generation to another. In the

Hebrew scriptures the so-called 'wisdom writings' take various forms: the Psalms are songs and poems, Job is a drama, Ecclesiastes is a poetic reflection on life, the Song of Songs is a love poem, Proverbs is what it says. Later books such as Ecclesiasticus and The Wisdom of Solomon contain similar kinds of writing, as well as stories.

Hebrew wisdom is not confined to these books. The Book of Proverbs and the Psalms state that the fear of the Lord is the beginning of wisdom. The Lord is to be known from his instruction, in the Torah or Law, and those who ignore it are fools. The epic narrative in the books of Samuel and Kings tells of how the ways of God are ignored and the people suffer as a result. The prophets time and again tried to recall people to the ways of God, and warned them of the dire consequences of continuing on their present path. 'Seek the Lord while he may be found. Return to him while he is near,' says Isaiah.[1]

The instruction in the Torah, the first books of the Hebrew scriptures, is not just what we would recognise as law. Also included are poetry and stories, such as the tale of the liberation of the people from slavery in Egypt and the stories of the beginning of all things. Here the world is described as being called into existence by God. The world is not God, but neither is it some malevolent power or valueless resource. It is created. It is good. And humanity has a place within it. Humanity is described as created 'in the image of God', to show to the rest of creation the character of God.[2] And that character is not fundamentally power, and certainly not a despotic or oppressive power. It is creative love.

This comes clearly to the fore in the Christian scriptures, the New Testament, where in Paul's letter to the Colossians, Jesus Christ is described as the image of the invisible God.[3] The answer to the question 'How are we to live?' is, 'To be like God.' And the answer to the question 'What is God like?' is 'Like Jesus.' So in Christian theology God is as he is in Jesus, and we are to be like that.

So if the basis of wisdom is 'the fear of the Lord',[4] that 'fear' is not a lurking terror. It will be more akin to awe. Contemplation of the world can lead to a sense of awe. So too can meditation on the images we have of the compassion of God. Fear is an appropriate word if it reminds us that neither the world nor the compassion of God are to be taken lightly. They call for respect. The fear of the Lord also calls for us to exercise compassion, and to work for justice.

Perhaps it also calls for us to take a long view. What has been billions of years in the making will, we presume, last for billions more. Humanity has existed for a few hundred thousand years. Western civilisation has lasted for only a couple of thousand so far, and we do not know how much longer it will continue. Clearly, though, attending only to what is profitable today will not help it survive. The destruction of good land and the pollution of water and air are so often the result of a desire for short-term gain. In the Western economy so many companies now no longer plan far ahead but struggle to produce immediate profits in order to avoid a destructive run on their shares.

The situation is urgent. For the people of Pacific islands threatened with rising sea levels, the people of Bangladesh faced with continually worse flooding, the animals, birds, plants and insects of the rainforests threatened with extinction by logging and plantations, the life in the Sahel in danger from expanding deserts and increasing droughts, there is no time for a leisurely response. Change is needed now – change that looks beyond the immediate problems to long-term survival.

For this, what we need is not a technical fix, but wisdom. Each day of this walk I made a new journey. Each step was a choice. But for it to be a journey to the place I wanted to go I had to see each of those steps as part of the whole. I had to have a goal for each particular day, but I also needed to plan out that day's journey with an eye to my ultimate destination. Wisdom is like that. And it may be that in reflecting on that journey I have been describing a path to wisdom. Wonder, humility, simplicity, compassion, active justice, repentance, faith and hope are perhaps all aspects of wisdom.

In order to make my journey I needed maps. I could have managed without but it would have been harder. I would have had to ask directions time and again, and to have consulted someone who had done the journey before about the general route to take. The maps simply made that easier. They are, after all, other people's knowledge set out on paper. And maps gave me both the big picture so I could work out my general direction and the detail which I used to navigate my route each day.

We have no map for the future. It is not set out like a pathway or a landscape. The future does not yet exist, but when it comes the form it will take will depend to some extent on the choices we make now. We can think about how we want the future to be, both for us and for the world as a whole, but in the same way that builders need an understanding of their materials and farmers an understanding of their land, so we too need to understand the world. Good intentions and hopeful visions have to relate to real possibilities.

As people together we must comprehend both the big picture and the detail. In our knowledge-rich society we have become increasingly specialised. In ancient Greek or Hebrew society, or even during the European Renaissance, one individual could hope to have both a broad and a deep understanding of many different disciplines. That time has long since gone. We are a society of specialists. But to generate wisdom we need to be able to talk to and listen to each other. That surely is possible. It simply requires us to develop a broad and general knowledge of other fields as well as our own, and to respect the insights of others and the bigger picture, accepting that our own perspective is only one of many. Of course, there is a danger that those who look at the big picture and stridently campaign for a greener world pay little attention to the detail. As a consequence those who attend to the detail, in the offices, committee rooms and laboratories of the world, write them off as impractical dreamers.

On my walk I was continually aware of the wildlife of the places I was passing through. Most noticeable to me were the birds, simply because I find them interesting. On the first day of my journey seeing my first swallow of the season was quite moving. It was not only the movement and the colour but the knowledge that this bird had just flown several thousand miles from Africa in less time than it would take me to walk a few hundred miles to Scotland.

Sometimes it was facts about the birds which were notable, but at other times they had a symbolic significance. Also on the first day I saw wild geese down by the River Tern. They were nothing exceptional, simply Canada geese, which are now common in Britain, although I had not seen them in that place before. But there was an idea circulating in the Iona Community at that time that the wild goose was an ancient Celtic symbol of the Holy Spirit. So as I set off on my journey to Iona the sight of the geese was for me a reminder that this was a pilgrimage, an encouraging pointer to the continual creative activity of God.

Wrens hopping around in hedges were always fun. *Troglodytes troglodytes* is their scientific name, and they are indeed like tiny cave dwellers. Lapwings, however, are like acrobats, and I was entertained by flocks of them tumbling above the moors in Yorkshire. Crows were always present. William Horwood in his fantasy novel *The Stonor Eagles* has a creature called the Raven of Storr who lives on Skye and knows all things because the crows and rooks pass on the knowledge they glean from observing everything.[5] But my favourites were always the buzzards. Unlike the crows they were not always present but I saw them often enough to lift my spirits. They are like small eagles. Riding on a thermal or wind current they will glide and circle for a long time, watching the land below for movement. And they remind me of words from the book of Isaiah:

> *'Those who wait on the Lord shall renew their strength, they shall rise up on wings like eagles; they shall run and not be weary, they shall walk and not faint.'*[6]

Seeing a buzzard would remind me that to accomplish this pilgrimage I needed to go at God's pace, which was the appropriate pace for me. There was no gain in rushing on if I then ended up too tired or injured. Nor was there any point worrying about where I would stay for the night, nor where I would buy food. Having made my preparations I could do no more than take what I found.

In much European folklore the owl is a symbol of wisdom but I wonder if the eagle is not a better icon. The eagle flies high and so has a broad picture of the land below. It also has the sight to attend to particular places and will dive to investigate further, or to hunt. Wisdom surely requires both a broad vision of what is happening – the possible consequences of particular courses of action and a sense of what really matters – and attention to detail.

I would have liked to have seen an eagle on my pilgrimage but I did not. I have seen both golden and white-tailed eagles in the West of Scotland, but not on that journey. Then there were only buzzards, but they reminded me of what I needed to recall, and that was enough.

References

1. Isaiah 55:6
2. Genesis 1:24-27
3. Colossians 1:15
4. Psalm 111:10; Proverbs 9:10
5. William Horwood, *The Stonor Eagles* (London: Country Life, 1982)
6. Isaiah 40:28-31

Resources 11: Wisdom

Fritz Schumacher

'Fools think their own way is right,' says the book of Proverbs, 'but the wise listen to advice.'[1] Fritz Schumacher was good at giving advice, and, especially when he was young, was often very sure about how good his advice was. But he was also willing to listen. And to change.

He was born in Bonn in 1911. His father was an economist and Fritz also studied economics. Unlike many others he was willing and able to see economics within a wider frame. He studied and worked in Britain, and was appreciated by Keynes and other leading economists. When war broke out he was interned for a while, then worked for the British government.

He was vigorously opposed to the Nazis. For a while he saw himself as a socialist and had some sympathy with Marx's views, but all the time he felt there was something missing from both the Marxist analysis and the capitalist approach to life. After the war he spent some time in Burma and came to appreciate the Buddhist way of seeing the world.

His own views continued to develop, and came to the notice of the world when his book *Small is Beautiful* was published in 1973. Its subtitle shows the angle that Schumacher was coming from: *A study of economics as if people mattered*. Within that book he developed a 'Buddhist economics' as a demonstration that there are other ways of looking at economic life apart from the polarised capitalist and socialist views.

In fact, Schumacher was attracted by Catholic teaching about the common good, and had, in 1971, been received into the Catholic Church. Shortly before he died, in 1977, he published a small book called *A Guide for the Perplexed*. Following Thomas Aquinas and Aristotle he wrote, 'If I limit myself to knowledge that I consider true beyond doubt, I minimise the risk of error but I maximise, at the same time, the risk of missing out on what may be the subtlest, most important and most rewarding things in life.'[2]

A way of seeing the world that ignores what cannot be measured may be simple. It may also be sterile, and it may be deadly.

References

1. Proverbs 12:15
2. E.F. Schumacher, *A Guide for the Perplexed* (London: Jonathan Cape, 1977) p13

For reflection or discussion

1. Whom can you think of that you could describe as a wise person? You may know them personally, or know about them, or know their films, music or books. What is it about them that means you would call them 'wise'?

2. Can you think of anything that you have done which, with hindsight, turned out to be foolish? In what way was it foolish? What difference is there, if any, between doing something foolish and making a mistake? What have you learnt from your experience?

3. We are all very limited in what we know and what we are able to do, so we rely on other people. Whom do you trust? In the media? In politics? In your personal life? Or when you are buying things or doing something else with your money? Why do you trust them?

Some Bible passages relevant to the theme

Psalm 111
Wisdom begins with contemplation of and reflection on God's creation and what God does.

Proverbs 3:1-35
Wisdom is seen not only as a matter of how we think but of how

we live.

Proverbs 8:12-9:6
A poem in which Wisdom is involved in the creation of all things and invites people to come to her and live.

Luke 2:40-52
Jesus is described as growing in wisdom as a child, and as doing this by asking questions.

James 3:13-18
In this letter by one of the leaders of the early church, the author is clear that wisdom is not simply a matter of thinking well but that it will lead to a compassionate life that builds good relationships.

Action

1. Do you have books, poems or songs that seem to you to contain wisdom? Make a list or gather them together in one place to browse or listen to from time to time.

2. Make a point of reading or listening to news you can trust which is very focused on particular events and stories, and also web or printed articles which give a bigger picture.

3. If a person or group is asking you to support them or vote for them, consider how wise they are, and how wise you would be to support them.

Further reading

John Eaton, *The Contemplative Face of Old Testament Wisdom* (London: SCM, 1989)
Within the context of world religions a biblical scholar looks at the wisdom writings of the Old Testament as a source for meditation and reflection rather than analysis.

E.F. Schumacher, *Small is Beautiful: A study of economics as if people mattered* (London: Bond and Briggs, 1973)
A challenge to the prevailing attitudes of the time by an economist who was able to see the big picture and the important detail, and willing to think outside his own discipline.

Alastair McIntosh, *Soil and Soul: People versus corporate power* (London: Aurum Press, 2001)
Drawing on a range of disciplines a human ecologist tells the story of two campaigns for justice in the Western Isles of Scotland and suggests their wider significance.

Colin Tudge, *Good Food for Everyone for Ever: A people's takeover of the world's food supply* (Pari, Italy: Pari Publishing, 2011)
With attention to the broad picture and to detail a scientist argues that the support of 'real farming' is the way to feed the world.

Celia Deane-Drummond, *Wonder and Wisdom: Conversations in science, spirituality and theology* (London: DLT, 2006)
An exploration of wonder as the interface of science and theology, and wisdom as the possible outcome of the journey.

Twelve

The End and the Beginning

Loch Scridain reaches into the Isle of Mull like a finger of sea. To the north of the loch are Ben More and Ardmeanach, a great block of ancient rock with high cliffs and raised beaches at its western end. To the south is the Ross of Mull, a fifteen-mile peninsula, beyond the end of which lies the island of Iona. I arrived at the loch shore late on a Saturday afternoon having walked across Mull from Craignure.

The ferry from Oban to Craignure had been crowded. It was a hot sunny morning and the beginning of a holiday weekend. The upper deck was full of people drinking the sunshine like thirsty cave dwellers. With a hot walk ahead of me, I kept to the shade.

I followed the road across Mull. A determined hillwalker might have found another route. I toyed with following the south side of the Ross of Mull where my map showed occasional paths, but not for long. I was now in no rush to reach Iona but I did not want to spend days trying to find paths through heather and bog miles from any roads or houses. The road it was, and the road was quiet.

Occasionally a small convoy of cars and coaches would pass – the deposit of a ferry at Craignure or from Iona – and sometimes a single car, but for long periods there was no traffic. And in places an older road was still walkable, following much the same route but rougher, and peaceful. My way took me inland up Glen More and then down in a long decline to Loch Scridain and there I camped for the night.

It was late May and the sky was light till after ten. Very occasionally there was the sound of a vehicle on the road but otherwise only the lapping of the sea and the calls of birds. A curlew, a gull, an oystercatcher, a sandpiper, a heron and, up towards a small wood just before dark, a blackbird sang for a few minutes. When I went out in the middle of the night there was a blaze of stars.

Lying in the darkness I turned over in my mind a short prayer I had come across some years before at Scargill. It was ascribed to the Iona Community although I had not yet found it in any of the Community's collections of services and prayers. Whether it is ancient or a modern composition it clearly belongs in the old Celtic tradition.

Deep peace of the running wave to you.
Deep peace of the flowing air to you.
Deep peace of the quiet earth to you.
Deep peace of the shining stars to you.
Deep peace of the Son of Peace to you.

This was a peaceful place. My pilgrimage was almost over and I felt at peace. Often, since then, when I have recited that prayer I have deliberately remembered that time and that place, the sound of the water and the sensation of the earth beneath me.

But I do not always feel at peace when I say that prayer. I think of waters polluted with oil and plastics, and stirred to turmoil by storm winds. I think of the air many people have to breathe that is laden with toxic fumes; of the earth's deeply wounded life-systems, its destroyed forests and eroded soils; of millions and billions of miles of space between innumerable stars, nebulae and galaxies; and of myself, one of seven billion humans on this tiny planet.

Sometimes the earth, the sea and the wind are calm and speak of peace. At other times they are terrifying. Sometimes they present a beauty before which we can only be silent and marvel. At other times they reduce us to a wry smile when we suddenly see our problems as of little consequence in the face of nature's magnitude and time span.

Whatever we do, the earth and life upon it will continue for many years. Tides will still run. Plants and maybe birds, fish and animals will survive and evolve in new ways. Stars will continue to burn for millions more years, and maybe, out there, there will be other beings looking at their own sky in wonder.

However, in the prayer quoted above the final basis of peace is not the world. We might be brought to a sense of peace by our surroundings. We might have a feeling of peace as we approach the completion of some personal project – and as I lay there in my tent beside Loch Scridain listening to the sound of water and the occasional call of birds my journey was almost accomplished. But the final basis of peace in that prayer is the Son of Peace. In Jesus the character of God, who is beyond time, space and matter, is made known. And that character is usually summed up in one word: 'love'.

Love is a rich word, but also, because of that, a tricky one. It can mean so many things. In ancient Greek writings there are four words that are often translated as 'love'. One is an affection for people or things. We may love a particular food or drink, in that we enjoy having them. We may love a place, in that we like to be there. We may love people in the sense of feeling good when they are around. For this sense the Greeks used the word *storge*.

One may also love people in the sense of being friends with them. There is something mutual about this. It involves trust and respect, and sometimes challenge. An adult may be fond of certain children, but friends with other adults. The Greek word for this friendship kind of love was *philia*.

The third word was *eros*. At its simplest it is the attraction that draws people towards each other, physically and sexually. Hence we have the English word 'erotic'. And an erotic attraction can be quite separate from friendship or affection. Someone can be attracted sexually to another person while there is little between them which could be called 'friendship', or is ever likely to be. And sometimes there can be little affection in sexual relationships. They can be violent, or abusive.

However, there are many relationships in which all three types of love are present, where people are fond of each other, friends with each other, and fancy each other. Most people hope for this – and many experience it – within a marriage or other committed partnership.

But in the New Testament the word that is used repeatedly for the love that God has for us, and that we are to have for each other, is neither *storge*, *philia* nor *eros*. It is another word again: *agape*. When Jesus in the gospels, repeating words from the Hebrew Torah, says to his listeners that they should love God and love their neighbour as themselves, the word is *agape*. When St Paul writes about love in his famous poem in 1 Corinthians 13 – 'Though I speak with the languages of people or of angels, if I do not have love, I am a sounding brass or a tinkling cymbal...' – the word is *agape*. When in John's Gospel Jesus says to his disciples, 'Love one another as I have loved you,' the word is *agape*.[1]

If we read the gospels and think about how Jesus got on with those around him, he clearly had friends. There were some people he was fond of. And he may have been sexually drawn towards others. There has been plenty of speculation about his relationship with Mary Magdalene, for example, although there is no suggestion in the gospels that their possible attraction ever developed physically. But Jesus did not relate to the perpetually critical Pharisees, or to the scheming High Priest, or to the Roman Governor Pilate in any of these three ways. And none of the writers suggest that in this he was failing to love. When Jesus says to his disciples that they should love their enemies, he is clearly talking about something else.

Its meaning can best be derived from reading or hearing about how Jesus treats other people and from the New Testament writers' reflections on Jesus' character and what he did. To try to capture it in a few words is hard but we might say that love, in Jesus' sense, is to look for what is good in a person and to do what is good for them. However, essentially in Christian faith we are not adhering to a form of words or following a set of rules but are engaging with, and trying to copy and learn from, a person: Jesus. Christian living is not fundamentally a matter of getting the words right, but of living with the kind of love that Jesus lived. Which is the kind of love that is characteristic of God.

The New Testament writers speak not only about the need for Jesus' followers to live with love, but of God's love for the world. The same word is used. John's gospel says: 'God so loved the world that he gave his only begotten Son so that whoever believes in him should not perish but should have eternal life.'[2] The word translated as 'love' is *agape*. And the word translated as 'world' is *cosmos*. And the word translated as 'believe in', *pisteo*, does not mean subscribing to certain statements about a person but trusting them.

In the first letter of John he writes, 'This is love, not that we love God but that God first loved us.'[3] *Agape* again. The initiative is God's. God reaches out, as we see in Jesus, concerned for the good of the world and of people within it. And we can respond to God with a faith that gives deep peace.

I could have walked from Kinloch to the Iona ferry in one day but chose not to. It was a Sunday and it would have meant arriving at Iona early on a Sunday evening. That would not have been helpful for the people running the Iona Community's centres. It would also have meant steady walking all day in order not to miss the last ferry and I wanted to take things easy. I also wanted to go to a church service if I could. I had not been to one since Rochdale four weeks earlier.

Again the day was warm. All I had to do was follow the road. I tried hard not to think about how far I had to go. It was not much of a distance compared to what I had done so far, nor compared to what I had walked on many other days, but it seemed a long way. The road along the Ross of Mull twists and rises and climbs over small hills. I was used to my rucksack but it was still heavy and to distract me from the tendency to count the miles and the discomfort of my load I tried to pay attention to where I was rather than think of where I wanted to be. There was rock and heather and occasional houses and clusters of small birch and alder trees. The great hills on Ardmeanach very, very slowly fell behind me. At one point I left the road to climb a small hill and thought I could see the sands at the north end of Iona, but mostly it was hidden.

My attempts to avoid thinking about the distance were hindered by the road markers. Just as I was forgetting about the road ahead and keeping my attention on what I was seeing I would pass another marker telling me it was fourteen or thirteen or twelve miles to the Iona ferry. These were dated 1897, which was presumably when the road was first built. And they were made of cast iron by Smith Pattison and Co of Blaydon. I could not understand why the road-builders did not simply employ a local mason to carve milestones out of blocks from the million tons of rock that were to hand but instead chose to bring iron markers all the way from Tyneside. But such foolishness is not a thing of the past. A large part of the world's energy consumption comes from moving things from one part of the world to another where they could equally well be made.

After ten miles I came to a monument at the roadside. This was made of local stone and was to a local poet, Mary MacDonald, who died in 1872. It carried an inscription of the opening lines of her best known poem.

Se leanagh an aigh
An leanagh Bh'aig Mairi.

Translated into English it is widely sung as the Christmas carol 'Child in the manger, infant of Mary', to a Hebridean tune named after the village of Bunessan which I was walking into, and which had been Mary MacDonald's home.

The festival of Christmas is a celebration of the love of God, not simply a distant love but one that involves God becoming engaged with the world. The opening of John's Gospel is a poem which tells of the Word of God – God's self-expression which brings everything into being – becoming human in Jesus. 'The Word was made flesh and dwelt among us.'[4] So, as John sees it, Jesus is on the one hand a man who teaches about God and shows God's attitudes and character in how he lives, while on the other hand God is, in Jesus, experiencing human life with all its limitations, frustrations, joy and pain. St Paul picks up the same theme in his letter to the Colossians where he says about Jesus that 'he is the image of the invisible God. In him the fullness of God was pleased to dwell.'[5]

The world is God's creation. As with a work of art, something of the character of the creator can be seen within it. But the creator, of course, is beyond it. The artist is not seen in the painting, nor the sculptor in the carving. Still, something of the creator can be known from looking at the creation. This is the idea conveyed at the beginning of the book of Genesis, in other places in the Hebrew scriptures, and in the beginning of the Gospel of John.

But on its own the creation is ambiguous. In the verges of the road to Bunessan there were flowers. I could marvel at the depth of their colour, the survival of such seemingly fragile plants in a hard environment, and the force of growth as they made their way into the sunlight. I would enjoy watching a buzzard gliding and soaring, catching the currents of air with immaculate skill. And as I stood beside the road to make way for another coach on its way to the ferry I might recognise the centuries of discovery and technical development which had gone into making such a machine.

At the same time I could also see the flowers as the latest development in the never-ending struggle of their genes to continue into the next generation. I could see the buzzard's superior flying skills and ability to kill small animals for food as having developed over many generations, so that it was well placed to support its offspring. And the technical skill of humans has enabled us to reproduce prolifically and dominate the earth in a manner that now endangers not only our own survival but that of many other species as well.

Looking at the world this second way does not necessarily deny the first. Understanding the world does not negate the possibility of wonder, any more than knowing how a painter used his materials inevitably reduces our appreciation of the painting. Or knowing how a composer works with harmonies and modulations lessens our appreciation of their music. It can often enhance it. But there is no logical step from one to the other. It means a change of gear, from analysis to contemplation and from understanding to wonder.

We have seen how both understanding and wonder are important if we are to respond to the crises of our society and ecology. Wisdom is vital, as is an understanding of detail as well as an appreciation of the big picture. We need to see how the world really is and not base our judgements on fantasy and wishful thinking. And the real world includes a struggle for life. In a woodland the plants compete for sunlight and minerals. The flowering plants that survive are those that best attract the limited number of pollinating insects. Robins and thrushes kill and eat insects. Young eagles will kill their siblings in the nest in order to get the food they need. This is how the world is.

Over the centuries many poets and prophets have put forward the idea that the creator God is not simply a spectator but is involved within creation. As mentioned earlier, in John's gospel and in Paul's letters the writers declare that God is distinctly and definitively involved in the life of the world in the man Jesus. In Jesus we see God's character, which can be described as love, but also in Jesus God is caught up in the injustice of human society and the pain of life. He is accused of blasphemy and corrupting society, is beaten up and painfully killed. As Mary MacDonald put it, the child in the manger is an outcast, and a stranger, but he is also the 'Lord of all'. God is not some feudal lord, secure in his castle and dominating his serfs, nor an absentee chief who clears aside his tenants for his own advantage, but one who shares the life of the poorest and those on the edge of society. In so doing he enables people to have a new kind of relationship with God. A relationship that is characterised by trust, and in which that trust, or faith, works out in hope and love.

The love of God that Jesus demonstrates means that while individual lives may appear insignificant within the whole scale of the creation and the years of history, they matter to the Creator. People who are pushed aside by the powerful are the very ones that Jesus gives time to. The crippled, blind and deaf beggars who could normally only hope to be given small change by the rich and powerful are brought centre stage by Jesus, and, in their healing, restored to human community. Women, who in Jesus' society were relegated to domestic tasks and debarred from political and religious discussion, were welcome to accompany Jesus and his other disciples and were supported in their decision to listen to him instead of keeping to their socially allotted role of housework. Children, who were seen as being valuable to society as the next generation, were considered of value to God as the children they are, and as people who demonstrate the way that God's new order, the Kingdom, is entered.

A billion years of evolution and half a million years of social development mean that we have it within our genes, our psyches and many of our social expectations to join the struggle for domination. Domination by one person of another, and domination as a species of all others. That, we believe, is how we have survived so far. But if we look where it is leading us it is clear we need to live differently. The enormous technological power that human societies now have means that conflict could easily end in the annihilation of all. The impoverishment of many by the wealthy, who often act only to their own advantage, leads to resentment, ill health, violence, and overpopulation by those whose only future security lies in having more children. The continual drive to consume more and more leads towards ecological disaster.

But we can live differently. The way of life that Jesus taught and lived was different. He and his followers had a lot to say about how it should work out, but it was characterised in the one word 'love'. Love for God the Creator, for other people, and for oneself.

At Bunessan I found a bed and breakfast and got myself a meal at the Argyll Tea Room. Then I joined the local church congregation for an evening service. Stranger that I was, I was welcome in this place. The next day was to be my last day walking.

I arrived at the Iona ferry in the late morning. The view is always impressive. You come over the hillcrest into the village of Fionnphort and there ahead, across a mile of water, is the island of Iona. Along the shore is a line of cottages. To the right is the

Abbey. The first one was founded in 563. It was destroyed by Vikings a few centuries later but another was built by Benedictine monks in the 1300s. That was ruined at the time of the Reformation, three centuries later, but then the Abbey church was restored in the nineteenth century and rededicated as a place of worship for Christians of all denominations. The residential part of the Abbey was then rebuilt over a period of thirty years from 1938 when George MacLeod arrived with a group of companions. Out of that rebuilding work came the Iona Community.

I was not due to stay in the Abbey itself but in a newer centre run by the Iona Community and named after George MacLeod. I had been there several times before, and now, having crossed to Iona on the small ferry, the walk from the jetty to the Abbey and MacLeod Centre was very familiar. But it was also very strange.

I was aware of a path stretching back across Mull and through Argyll, to Ben Lomond, to Edinburgh and south through England. It was my path. I could remember the detail, the rises and falls, the shapes of the hills, and people I had met on this walk. The path was my path, my songline, and now I had completed the journey. I was coming to the end of the song. And the end of the journey was one with the beginning. They were not separate places but one place. I had left home six weeks earlier. I was now arriving home. Both the beginning and the end were part of the whole.

It was very different from arriving by bus or car. Making the journey by train and bus, or by car, I would stop at points along the way but there was little sense of the beginning and the end and the places in between belonging together. But having walked them, I had a strong sense of their being part of one whole, together with some other places that were significant for me. Edinburgh. Carlisle. Scargill. And my feeling, walking up from the jetty, was as it had been when I arrived at the top of Ben Lomond, not one of achievement but of completion.

The Iona Community, which had begun in the 1930s with the

rebuilding of the Abbey, had about two hundred members by the time I walked there. Most of them were in Scotland, some were in England and a few in the United States. Within a few more years there would also be members in Germany, Switzerland, The Netherlands, Wales and Ireland.

Members had various occupations. Only a very few lived on Iona and were involved with running the centres there. There were also volunteers and some paid staff who together ran the Abbey and the MacLeod Centre as places of hospitality, worship and learning. All these formed a resident community. And one of the things that guests had to be ready for if they stayed at these centres was to give some time to helping with basic tasks of this common life. For the week they were there they too were to be part of a community.

Living and working on the island was not easy. Not everyone agreed with each other all the time. Not everyone got on easily. And it was a small island. There was nowhere to go to get away. On a day off one could walk across the island, or catch a bus along Mull and maybe spend an hour or so in Oban before coming back, but that was it. And the volunteers shared rooms, as did guests. It could be intense. It was a beautiful place, but it was not heaven. And no one pretended it was. But people there did say that in living and working together they were discovering new things about themselves, other people and community.

I called in at the office at the Abbey entrance to let them know I had arrived and then made my way up to the MacLeod Centre. It was quiet. Most people were out and about. But I was given a bed and at lunch I was welcomed, as new arrivals always are. Then from that afternoon I was a part of the community that had formed for that week. I had a place to sleep, a job to do each morning, meals with the staff, volunteers and other guests, and I joined in the worship at the Abbey each evening and morning.

Looking back over my journey I could identify a number of occasions when I had been a part of a community. Often it was short-lived, but no less important for that. This community I had now become a part of would last no more than a week or two. Others had lasted perhaps a few hours. But they had been significant. The evening spent with Stanley and Kathleen Hope in Rochdale, the group at Scargill, the evening talking and sharing stories with the walkers in Kirkby Lonsdale, and the conversations with the children and youth leaders at Ardgartan, these were important events in the journey. What made them communities, however short-lived, rather than simply meetings, was the mutual interest and concern. An interest in justice, or in journeys, in the environment, in God, or in each other. And not just an interest, but a concern. Within the conversations, the laughter, the listening and the advice, there was a concern for each other's welfare. They helped me. They did me good. Perhaps I helped them and did them some good too.

Throughout the Bible God is seen not only as the creator beyond all things, but as a creator within the creation. The image that is often used is that of the wind. In Hebrew and in Greek the word for breath is the same as that for wind. In the creation story in the first chapter of Genesis the wind of God moves over the waters of the primeval chaos.[6] It is God's breath that gives life to inert clay and makes a living being called Man.[7] In the Psalms it is God's breath that gives life to other beings.[8] In the gospels it is by the same power that Jesus carries out his work of healing and reconciliation, and then, after his resurrection, enables his disciples to continue his work.[9]

In English the word is often translated as 'spirit'. This is inevitable as the word 'spirit' was used when the Bible was first translated into English and, as the term features so much in prayers and hymns, it would be confusing now to use an alternative. However, in earlier times the word 'spirit' had echoes of life, power and mystery, some of which have been lost. Like many words used in religious talk it has come to be used rarely outside theological discussions and poetry and so has lost much of its association. The Spirit of God, or the Holy Spirit, can easily be spoken of as if it were some kind of entity, or thing.

But God's Spirit is God at work within the world, generating life, developing potential, giving skills, insight and wisdom. The Spirit cannot be contained, any more than the wind can be caught. The Spirit cannot be controlled, any more than God can be controlled. And like the wind that might at one time be still and calm, hardly noticeable, and at another become a hurricane, so too the Spirit of God is experienced in many different ways. And one way is in those interactions between people which are characterised by interest and concern for each other's good.

We call this 'community', although the word is sometimes used to refer to a number of people who have something in common but little concern for each other's welfare. Another word we could use for a community of shared concern and commitment is 'fellowship'. This is the most common translation of the Greek word *koinonia* which occurs in the short Christian prayer known as the Grace. It comes from one of St Paul's letters in the New Testament: 'May the grace of our Lord Jesus Christ, and the love of God, and the fellowship of the Holy Spirit be with us all evermore.'[10] J.R.R. Tolkien picked up this word and used it in *The Lord of the Rings* to describe the motley group of characters who set off on a long journey to destroy the ring of power. They were the Fellowship of the Ring. With all their differences they had a common purpose and a shared commitment to see it through.[11]

At the time I walked to Iona the Community was drawing deeply in its prayer and songs from the traditions of the Celtic strand of Christianity which had existed in earlier times in the West of Scotland, in Ireland and in Wales. Many of these ancient prayers invoked the Trinity. This is a concept that dates from the first few centuries of the church and can be seen within the New Testament, although it is not spelt out there.

When we speak of God as Trinity, we are saying that the different ways that we sense God are all of one God. What we sense behind the creation, and what we sense in Jesus, and what we sense within relationships and in the depths of our minds is all

God. Not three different powers, but one. And theologians of the past have often suggested that it is love that holds these three aspects of God together. So that when our relationships are characterised by the kind of love that Jesus lived we are caught up in the life of God. When our communities are characterised by love they are reflecting the love of God. In one of his letters St John said, 'God is love, and those who live in love live in God, and God lives in them.'[12]

While I was on Iona news was coming through about the Earth Summit in Rio. It was 1992. This was the first of these international conferences in Rio and many of us with concerns for the planet had great hopes for it, but the news was not good. With a few promises and some small agreements it was clearly going to be business as usual for the major industrialised nations, and the others would have to tag along.

Since then there have been many more such conferences in various places, and many more such disappointments. But there has been some change. The power balance within the world has altered. China and India have moved centre stage as industrialised powers and China has great wealth while Europe and the United States have great national debts. There has been considerable industrial development in South-East Asia and in South America.

In Europe and elsewhere there has been a lot of talk about the environment. Climate change is now recognised as a fact. In Britain matters like recycling, energy conservation, water harvesting and renewable energy were marginal interests in those days but are now spoken and written about widely, and encouraged by Government. But it is still small-scale. Talk of climate change now revolves around the possibility of limiting the temperature rise to two degrees, rather than maintaining temperatures at present levels, even though the effects of such a rise will be profound. Talks, conferences, books and papers continue, but there have not been the significant changes that twenty years ago many believed were necessary. We face a difficult future. A severe storm of environmental damage and social unrest is brewing. We need to be able to face it with love for the world and for other people. In doing so we will be sharing in the love of God.

The prayers in the Abbey church followed a similar form each morning, ending with worshippers going straight out to their work. Like Benedictines, for whom prayer is work and work is prayer, the Community was concerned not to draw a sharp distinction between work and worship. At midday there were prayers for justice and peace, often attended by day visitors to the island. In the evening the worship would follow a different theme each night around issues of peace, justice, respect for creation, healing and commitment. On the Friday evening, with many people due to leave the next morning, we sat at long tables and in a communion service recalled Jesus' last supper with his disciples. Bread was broken and shared. Wine was poured out and cups passed round so everyone could drink. All were welcome to join in. Everyone was challenged to commit themselves to living as Jesus' disciples wherever it was they were going to next.

I had walked there from Shropshire in England. Others had come by train, bus or car. Some had flown part of the way. There were people from the United States, South Africa, Sweden, Germany and the Czech Republic. They were all pilgrims, one way or another. They had come for a purpose, which was something to do with God. And they had travelled there knowing they would leave again. I stayed for a couple of weeks. Some might stay for six weeks, a year or even three. Most would be there for a week, and on the day they left this prayer would be said, with words from George MacLeod:

O Christ, you are within each one of us.
It is not just the interior of these walls:
it is our own inner being you have renewed.
We are your temple not made with hands.
We are your body.
If every wall should crumble, and every church decay,

we are your habitation.
Nearer are you than breathing, closer than hands and feet.
Ours are the eyes with which you, in the mystery,
look out with compassion on the world.
Yet we bless you for this place, for your directing of us,
your redeeming of us, and your indwelling.
Take us outside, O Christ, outside holiness,
out to where soldiers curse and nations clash
at the crossroads of the world.
So shall this building continue to be justified.
We ask it for your own name's sake.[13]

When the time came for me to leave I could say 'Amen' to those words.

References

1. 1 Corinthians 13; John 15:12-17
2. John 3:16
3. 1 John 4:10
4. John 1:1-14
5. Colossians 1:13-20
6. Genesis 1:2
7. Genesis 2:7
8. Psalm 104:24-30
9. Luke 4:14-18; Acts 2:1-21; etc
10. 2 Corinthians 13:14
11. J.R.R. Tolkien, *The Fellowship of the Ring* (London: Unwin, 1954)
12. 1 John 4:16
13. George F. MacLeod, *The Whole Earth Shall Cry Glory* (Glasgow: Wild Goose Publications, 1985) p45

Resources 12: Love

Martin Luther King

In 2008 Barack Obama was elected President of the United States. In 1958 it would have been inconceivable. Many thousands of people helped to bring about that change of attitude and political possibility. Among them was Martin Luther King – a leader, a prophet, a preacher, and a man who prayed. One of the iconic pictures from the '60s is of King kneeling in prayer with others in front of National Guardsmen.

It was not just prayer that brought about the changes, but for King prayer was essential because it was through prayer that one could receive the strength to engage in the struggle for civil rights and the overcoming of racial prejudice in the right way. That way was by creative non-violence.

King learnt the approach from Gandhi, and like Gandhi he saw it in the teaching of Jesus. Turning the other cheek and going the extra mile were not about letting yourself be bullied and humiliated but were a way to redirect the force of hatred so that love could overcome it. And it was not an easy option.

What you needed, King said, was a tough mind and a tender heart. A tough mind to overcome prejudice and resist platitudes, and a tender heart so that you could always see people as people, whoever they were and however they were treating you. For King, prayer and worship were the ways one could open oneself to God, who is both tough-minded and tender-hearted.

'When days grow dark and nights grow dreary, we can be thankful that our God combines in his nature a creative synthesis of love and justice which will lead us through life's dark valleys and into sunlit pathways of hope and fulfillment.'[1]

There is still racism in the world. There is still racism in the United States. But with the election of Barack Obama a significant point was passed in the struggle to overcome it. The struggle for justice for all life is bigger than that, and is urgent. But we can draw on the same resource that Martin Luther King and millions of others have drawn on down the years: the One to whom we open ourselves in prayer and worship.

Reference

1. Martin Luther King, *Strength to Love* (London: Hodder, 1964) p16

For reflection or discussion

1. What, if anything, is the difference between loving another person and doing what makes another person happy?

2. What can help you see the good in another person? What can help you do what is good for them? And, particularly, a person you find difficult or who makes life difficult for you?

3. What does it mean to forgive another person? Does it necessarily mean forgetting the harm they have done? What can help you to forgive?

4. What in your own praying or in your church life helps you to remember and think about God's love for you? For other people? And for the world?

Some Bible passages relevant to the theme

Deuteronomy 6:5; Leviticus 19:18; Luke 10:25-37
When asked which is the most important of the Hebrew laws Jesus quotes two statements which had long before been put together by rabbis as encapsulating the whole: loving God and loving one's neighbour. In reply to a further question he then argues that this love is to be extended to anyone who needs it.

Matthew 5:38-48
Jesus teaches his disciples that they are to live not by retaliation

but with creative non-violence, and that their concern for the good of others must extend even to their enemies.

John 15:9-12
Towards the end of John's Gospel Jesus tells his disciples that their life together is to be characterised by love, and that this is to be the kind of love that he has lived.

1 Corinthians 13:1-13
Paul's great poem on love.

1 John 4:7-5:4
John encourages his readers to live with the love that they believe God has towards them.

Action

1. Think of a few people and things that you 'love', and perhaps write a list. Which forms of love are coming into play here? Affection, friendship, attraction, or a concern for their good? It may be several or all of them.

2. On a large piece of plain paper draw a shape that represents you. It might be a neat circle, a human form, or a vague shape like a potato. Then in the shape write down what you think you are like: good things and bad, strengths and weaknesses, abilities and disabilities, and things that are simply facts, like your name. Then on the outside of the shape and around it write: Created, valued and loved by God.

3. Think back over the different reflections and discussions that you have had in following this book, and the things that you have done. Now that you are coming to the end, are there things you need to do again sometime? Are there things that you would do well to build into a daily or weekly routine? And how can you make time for them? If there are several of them, decide which is

the priority and work out how you will do that. Then return to the others some other time.

Further reading

C.S. Lewis, *The Four Loves* (London: Geoffrey Bles, 1960)
A brief study drawing on a wide range of classical and modern literature.

Henri Nouwen, *Seeds of Hope* (London: DLT, 1989)
A collection of extracts from the writings of a man who was continually exploring the character, meaning and significance of God's love and ours.

Erich Fromm, *The Art of Loving* (London: Unwin, 1957)
A short study of the theory and practice of love.

M. Scott Peck, *The Road Less Travelled: A new psychology of love, traditional values and spiritual growth* (London: Random House, 1983)
A best-selling description of the character of love and guidance on how to grow as a loving person.

Tom Gordon, *Welcoming Each Wonder*, *With An Open Eye* and *A Blessing to Follow* (Glasgow: Wild Goose Publications, 2010, 2011, 2012)
For each week, stories and poems that explore the mysterious and everyday love of people and God.

W.H. Vanstone, *Love's Endeavour, Love's Expense: The response of being to the love of God* (London: DLT, 1977)
A personal, philosophical and theological exploration of the nature of creative love.

Conclusion

Love for the Future

On my way back from Iona to Wrockwardine I called into Govan. This was where the Iona Community had begun in the 1930s. George MacLeod, the minister of Govan Parish Church, was concerned about the gulf that existed between the church and most of the people in his parish and believed that by getting people to work together on a project they could come to know and trust each other. In the 1990s, when I walked to Iona, the Iona Community's offices were still there.

I took a train into Glasgow and walked out beside the River Clyde. There were still clear signs of the great dock and ship-building centre that this had once been, and it was easy to imagine the desolation as this industry ground almost to a halt during the depression of the 1930s. The few cranes now on the skyline were but a shadow of what had once been a thriving industry.

It was a hot day and the traffic was stirring up dust. I found the Iona Community's office in the Pearce Institute and called in. Then I crossed the road and entered a cafe. Inside there was a woman serving at the counter and another standing talking to her. There was a younger man sitting a few feet away in a wheelchair. I said hello, asked for a coffee and went and sat near him. He was crumpled down in his chair, had a hearing aid in each ear and wore very thick glasses. We got talking.

I explained I'd never been to Govan before. He lived here, and always had done. Forty years he had lived in Govan.

He was the same age as me. And it turned out that his name was also David.

At one point he called over his shoulder that he wanted a burger. The woman standing at the counter said, 'You don't need a burger. You had your breakfast.'

'I want a burger,' he said again.

'All right,' she said. 'Have your burger.'

She was his mother. She had always lived in Govan as well.

I explained that I had come here to visit the Iona Community's office in the Pearce Institute, because I had just been to Iona and was interested to know where the Community had begun.

'I've never been to Iona,' said David. 'But I've been to Holy Island. It's beautiful. Really beautiful.'

'When did you go there?'

'A couple of years ago. I have some friends come and visit me. They're Christians. They took me there.' He paused for a moment, then said, ' Do you believe?'

That's not how I would normally put it but, 'Yes,' I said. 'In fact, I'm a church minister.'

David's burger appeared and was passed over to him.

'I don't believe,' said his mother. 'How can there be a God when there are so many people starving? And wars. And David here. He's in pain all the time.'

David looked at me over his burger. 'I believe,' he said.

I said something to his mother about how I didn't think of God as just outside all the suffering but as caught up in it as well. That I was convinced God also suffers.

She was not convinced. I did not expect her to be. Here she was with her son who had been in pain for forty years and who still could not look after himself. But her complaint was not about what she had to put up with but about what other people suffered, people that she did not know and her own son. I could only respect that. I was also aware that I was talking to someone who had gone through difficulties that I had been spared.

David chewed on his burger. A couple of other people came into the cafe. Traffic rumbled past outside.

'What keeps you in the chair, David?' I said after a while. 'What's up with you?'

'He's got soft bones,' said his mother.

David ignored her. 'I've got soft bones,' he said. 'They keep breaking. It's a disease.'

I had wondered if that might be the case.

'*Osteogenesis imperfecta*,' I said.

'That's right!' said David' How do you know about it?'

'It's in my family,' I said. 'I had a daughter who was born with it.'

'And how is she? How's she getting on?'

'She died, I'm afraid. She just lived a couple of weeks.'

'Oh. I'm sorry,' he said. 'I'm sorry.' And there were tears in his eyes.

'It's OK,' I said. 'It was ten years ago now.'

'I'm sorry,' he said again.

I was not upset about Miriam. Not any more. That had passed a long time ago. But I was overwhelmed by this man. I had spent my forty years moving from place to place, travelling, studying and working, and he had spent all that time in Govan. I had left my parents over twenty years before and he was still looked after by his mother and had to argue to get a burger. I had just walked six hundred miles through Britain and he spent his time in continual pain and confined to a wheelchair. But he could still affirm that life was worth living. It was sad, to him, that my daughter with the same disease had not survived. He was sorry, he said, and was visibly moved.

Then after a while he said, 'You're a minister. Bless me.'

I was reminded of the time in Matthew's gospel when Jesus goes to John the Baptist to be baptised and John says, 'I ought to be baptised by you.' David was the one who should bless me. He was the one with the strong faith. I had it easy. His life was like my fears. And still he believed.

By this time there were more people in the cafe and as burgers were passed behind us to people at other tables I prayed with him. He was quiet. I tried to find some words. People around us continued to chat and David's mother talked with her friend behind the counter.

A couple of years later I was back in Govan and decided to call in again at the same cafe. I did not expect to see them there, and if I did I knew they probably wouldn't recognise me. But the cafe had gone. I could not remember which shop in the row it had been, but none of them now was the place I had called into that day.

I do not know how David in the cafe managed to be so compassionate despite all that he had to deal with. Or to be so appreciative of his isolated visit to Holy Island. To value life so highly and to have faith in God. Maybe if I had met him again I could have found out. It might be that he did not know. Perhaps, to him, it just seemed to come naturally. I have no way of knowing now.

Some years later I was making a film on this theme of how we can develop the character we need to respond to the ecological crisis, and one of the people I interviewed was Margaret Armstrong. Margaret had been an athlete and had played hockey for England. But at some point in her life someone had driven into the back of her car. A moment of inattention, as she called it, and her life was radically changed. Now she could not walk and she moved around in a motorised wheelchair.

With her husband she lived in a house they had developed themselves which was as environmentally friendly as possible. Water was reused. There were pv cells on the roof, good insulation and solar panels for heating water. She was ordained in the Church of England and had recently been the minister in charge of several parishes while also working as an adviser on disability for her diocese. Her phrase was, 'You can't choose the cards you are dealt but you can choose how you play them.'

David in Govan lacked opportunities that I had taken for granted. His circumstances limited him in ways that to me were the stuff of bad dreams. He could do little for himself, but he could help others by his friendliness, compassion and faith. He helped me. He brought me up with a start simply by being himself. And he continually reminds me now of the millions of people in the world who struggle to get by against enormous odds and yet continue to be concerned about others. Who, despite the lack of what I so easily take for granted or consider essential, still affirm that life is good. Who, even though they are bypassed by society and sometimes even by those close to them, can still declare their own mind and value themselves.

Whether I could do the same in similar circumstances I cannot answer. None of us knows how we will respond in different circumstances. But there are two questions I can address. The first is: how can I become a person who will respond well to the challenges I face now? The second is: how will I use the opportunities that I have? Or, in Margaret Armstrong's words: how will I choose to play the cards I have been dealt?

Thinking back over my journey to Iona I have suggested a number of characteristics that I believe we need to develop for our journey into a difficult future. And I have suggested some methods by which we can possibly strengthen or develop those characteristics. They are kinds of meditation, or prayer or activity – what we might call forms of spirituality.

Some of these relate to us as individuals. Contemplation can enhance our respect for the world, and possibly give rise on occasions to a sense of wonder. Engaging with the world, getting our hands and faces wet and dirty, feeling the air, the water and the soil, we can let our senses help us remember that we are a part – and a small part – of the whole, and not simply disembodied minds. Understanding ourselves and getting to know ourselves through mindfulness helps us develop the simplicity that is essential if we are to resist the powers of persuasion that encourage us to be dissatisfied with what we have and urge us to consume ever more. With this awareness we will be able to learn to live lightly with the other life of the earth.

Some of these forms of spirituality concern our relationships with other people and the world. Using our imagination enables us to develop compassion or empathy for others. We can then act on this compassion, working towards justice for people whose lives are diminished and for creatures whose survival is threatened. In listening to others and reflecting on our lives as individuals and as societies we become open to change, and at times make those significant changes of lifestyle or attitude that are traditionally described as repentance.

Other practices more directly concern our relationship with God. Meditation and prayer perhaps help us to see our lives in relationship with God, and to develop that combination of insight and trust that is known as faith. Songs, stories, music and art encourage us to hope, restoring our sense that our struggles are neither meaningless nor without conclusion. Continually working to understand the world in both its detail and its wider relationships, and seeing these in the light of the world's significance as God's creation, will help us develop the wisdom we need.

To hold all these methods and approaches together and give them direction and energy we need love. This love may include affection for people, animals, plants and places. It will include friendships and sometimes an attraction towards certain people. But fundamentally it is a concern for the good of the world we are part of, and doing what is good for it. It is the kind of love we see lived out as well as taught by Jesus. It is the love which is God's, and which can be ours.

This love does not begin with our summoning up the strength do what is good or right. It begins with God's love for us. This is the love that lies behind creation, and gives us our skills, insight and energy as it calls all things into being. A love that reveals itself in the wisdom, creativity and lives of so many people, but supremely in Jesus. A love that continues to encourage, strengthen and challenge us, that reaches out to us even when we have failed badly, and that draws us into relationships with other people and other life so that we are not living and working alone but in communities.

Many writers have argued how this love is not something coldly purposeful but that the other forms of love are woven into it, not only among us but also in God. In the way that we are perhaps fond of other people, favourite animals and special places, so is God also fond of us. It is a fondness that values us, as we are. That hopes for the best for us. That takes us seriously, but can also, if we realise it, help us to like ourselves and perhaps stop taking ourselves too seriously.

There is an absurdity and a presumption in thinking about ourselves as God's friends. God is not a being like us. To think of ourselves as friends of the Creator could very easily make us lose our sense of being part of the matrix of life on the earth, with our weak bodies, physical needs and very limited understanding of ourselves, let alone of the cosmos. But in the gospels Jesus does call his disciples 'friends'. And where this has been recaptured in prayers and hymns people have often been set free from a sense that their lives are to be servile obedience to God and they have discovered ways of living joyfully as free, creative adults.

There is also a strand in Hebrew and Christian writing which sees *eros* as a characteristic of God, and a fundamental feature of our relationship with God: *eros* being fundamentally an attraction of one for another. The Hebrew scriptures contain a long erotic poem, The Song of Songs. It is a dialogue between a man and a woman deeply attracted to each other, which although perhaps included in the scriptures as a celebration of this beautiful aspect of our humanity, has often also been seen as symbolic of our human relationship with God. There is a deep attraction that leads people to explore different forms of spirituality, to take part in religious practices, to pray and to worship, to care for other people and other creatures at great cost to themselves, to explore endless questions of truth and meaning, and to continually try to understand better the world in which they live. This too is a part of being human, and might be seen as a response to God, who continually draws humanity and the whole of creation towards himself. Traditionally the imagery has been interpreted by both male and female writers in terms of a female humanity or church being drawn towards a male God. The interpretation could easily and creatively be reversed and we could think of God drawing us to herself.

But there is one significant characteristic of *agape* love that is not true of the others. When asked which was the greatest commandment Jesus famously repeated what other rabbis had said and was learnt by Hebrew children: 'You shall love the Lord your God with all your heart, soul, mind and strength; and love your neighbour as yourself.' This is a command, not a suggestion. And Jesus elaborated on this. 'Love your enemies,' he said, 'and pray for your persecutors.' And in John's Gospel, 'Love one another as

I have loved you.'

You cannot tell someone to be fond of another person. It is clearly helped by looking for the person's good features, and giving time to get to know them, but it cannot be made to happen. Similarly you cannot order people to be friends. To be friendly, yes. But friendship grows over time. It comes from shared experiences and interests. It can be encouraged but it cannot be made, and even given time it may not happen. And an attraction between two people can arise quite spontaneously, and even at unwanted moments. People sometimes talk about falling in love and there are ancient myths about how this is caused by an external agent. These stories developed from the sense that this kind of love was something unintentional, over which people sometimes felt they had little control. More recently people might talk about 'chemistry'.

Often these forms of love lead people to make commitments, the clearest of which is probably marriage. Two people who are fond of each other, attracted to each other, and also friends, not only declare their feelings but say that they will honour, protect and love one another. In the Church of England marriage service this is quite specific. The couple are asked whether they will love each other, and the answer is, 'I will.' This is not a matter of looking into the future and believing that their feelings will continue but of clearly stating that they are determined to do this. They *will* love. It is a decision and a determination.

Jesus and others tell people to love, in the fourth sense, as *agape*. Not only in a single one-to-one relationship but as a way of living. Looking for what is good in other people, the world and ourselves and doing what is good for them. Looking for the goodness of God and living in tune with God's concerns. This love is not something we switch on suddenly like a light. The drives, the genes, the history within us are too strong to simply adopt love as a way of living by a simple choice once and for all. But it does involve a decision – that this is how we will live, as far as possible, and that we will do what we can to help ourselves to love. And when we fail we will remind ourselves of God's love for us and do what we can to get back into the mode of living Jesus taught and demonstrated.

This fundamental decision to love provides our energy and direction as we look to develop respect, humility, simplicity and compassion. It motivates us to act for justice and to be willing to re-evaluate and change our way of living if necessary; to trust God, to hope for the future and to grow in wisdom. A decision and commitment to live with the love that Jesus demonstrated will work itself out in these characteristics, which are like the skills that come with the practice of a craft, or a piece of music that results from a composer's creativity and dedication.

Jesus' stories make clear that he was himself someone who looked at the world and the lives of the people around him with appreciation and respect. After years as a craftsman he turned to being an outdoors itinerant preacher, feeling the heat, caught up in storms, getting hungry and tired. He was clear in his sense of who he was and what he was to do but open to changing his approach when challenged by people in need. He was compassionate, working to bring in from the margins those who had been pushed out, and he taught and practised ways of living that overcame violence, possessiveness and greed. His teaching was wise. His faith in the One he called his Father gave him the courage to face up to opposition and not be swayed by his fears, and gave him hope even in the face of death.

Behind all this lay his love, his concern to see what was good as well as what was bad, and to act for the good of the people he had direct dealings with, and for the world as a whole. To live as his followers in our own very different time and place will involve developing these same personal characteristics. Because our societies and our challenges are different, following Jesus will not mean a simple transference of his lifestyle to our own situation. But it will mean developing a character like his. And that is what the world needs.

This is something we can do, not because we are capable of

summoning up the love that we see in Jesus, but because it is offered to us by God. God who calls all there is into being, who is continually at work within the world, and who shows himself in Jesus, invites us to join in his life. Jesus invited people to join in with what he was doing and be a part of the new community that he was forming. The invitation is there now. We do not meet up with Jesus of Nazareth walking along a beach in Galilee or pushing through the crowds of Jerusalem, but the invitation is still there, wherever we are, to join the movement, which is the life of God, a life of love.

My walk to Iona was a journey I chose to make. At some point I decided I was going to set out on that journey. Each day, in fact with every step, I had to continue that commitment. The journey did not just happen. I had to apply my various skills and stick with the decisions I had made, while also being open to reviewing what I was doing and making adjustments and changes when necessary. In other words, like any project, it required discipline.

In a similar way, to develop the character that we need to face up to and respond to the ecological crisis we need discipline. First, we have to make a fundamental decision that this is what we are going to do. That we are going to live with a concern not for our own immediate desires but for the world and for other people, and for their future. We are going to try to develop love for the future.

We then need to set out on the journey. This will mean making time, amidst the hundred tasks we have to do each day, for the kind of spiritual exercises that allow respect, humility and simplicity to grow within us. It will mean following the steps necessary to develop a compassionate life, and taking action, as and when we can, in pursuit of justice. It will mean being open to changing our way of living in response to the needs of others.

Because the source of love is God, and living with love is being involved in the life of God, it will also mean taking time for prayer, meditation and worship. And, particularly when the future looks bleak, making time for those things that can restore in us a sense of hope by helping us to trust God for the future as well as the present. It will mean trying to understand what is happening in the world and sometimes standing back from what we are immediately involved in to perceive the bigger picture, in order to develop something of the wisdom that is most desperately needed in the world.

But we do not have to do all this alone. Some of it we cannot do alone. There are other people with similar concerns. We need them and they need us. There are action groups, pressure groups and campaigning groups; there are meditation and walking groups, people who get together to encourage each other in their art, music, writing or reading; and there are churches and other communities which are quite explicit that God is the ultimate source of both hope and love for the future, and which are committed to living God's way.

Doing this may involve adjusting how we live: altering some of what we do and when we do it. It may mean giving up some things and taking up others. But it is like a journey. We cannot go on a journey and stay at home.

In fact, if we do stay at home things still change around us, and we change as time goes on. And what is around us, our environment, is changing fast. It will be better for us, for everyone else and for every thing if we set out to become people who are able to respond to what is happening in the world creatively and with love.

General Resource Books

David Runcorn, *Spirituality Workbook: a guide for explorers, pilgrims and seekers* (London: SPCK, 2006)
Draws on a broad range of Christian traditions and provides introductions, exercises and activities for readers wanting to grow in their personal prayer life.

Annie Heppenstall, *Wild Goose Chase: Exploring the spirituality of everyday life* (Glasgow: Wild Goose Publications, 2006)
For individuals and groups: stories, prayers, things to do, ways to be, at home, travelling, working, anywhere, which is where God is.

Chris Polhill, *A Heart for Creation: Worship resources and reflections on the environment* (Glasgow: Wild Goose Publications, 2010.
For individuals and groups: a range of stories, poems, songs, prayers and liturgies.

Mary Low, *Cherish the Earth* (Glasgow: Wild Goose Publications, 2003)
Reflections and quotes from a wide range of sources for individual meditation and group worship.

Neil Paynter & Helen Boothroyd, *Holy Ground: Liturgies and worship resources for an engaged spirituality* (Glasgow: Wild Goose Publications, 2005
Readings, songs and forms of worship on themes such as justice, community, peacemaking and care for the earth.

Catherine von Ruhland, *Living with the Planet: Making a difference in a time of climate change* (Oxford: Lion, 2008)
Information and insight, beautiful and evocative pictures, and serious and practical suggestions for taking action.

Marjorie J. Thompson, *Soul Feast: An invitation to the Christian spiritual life* (Louisville, Kentucky: Westminster John Knox Press, 1995)
Draws on writings and resources from various Christian traditions and all ages to provide practical guidance for developing different ways of praying.

Ruth Harvey, ed., *Wrestling and Resting: Exploring stories of spirituality from Britain and Ireland.* (London: CTBI, 1999)
Contributors from across the countries and a range of churches write on pilgrimage and journeying, pain and vulnerability, justice, peace and reconciliation, wild places and the city, community, hospitality, tradition and prayer.

Rob Hopkins, *The Transition Companion: Making your community more resilient in uncertain times* (Totnes: Green Books, 2011)
Drawing on the experience so far of the transition movement this guidebook is aimed to help communities become more resilient in the face of peak oil and climate change.

Julia Haynes, *The New Green Consumer Guide* (London: Simon and Schuster, 2007)
A directory and resource.

Wild Goose Publications is the publishing house of the Iona Community, which is:

- An ecumenical movement of men and women from different walks of life and different traditions in the Christian church
- Committed to the gospel of Jesus Christ, and to following where that leads, even into the unknown
- Engaged together, and with people of goodwill across the world, in acting, reflecting and praying for justice, peace and the integrity of creation
- Convinced that the inclusive community it seeks must be embodied in the community it practises

Together with its staff, the community is responsible for:

- The islands residential centres of Iona Abbey, the MacLeod Centre on Iona, and Camas Adventure Centre on the Ross of Mull

and in Glasgow:

- The administration of the Community
- Work with young people
- A publishing house, Wild Goose Publications
- Its association in the revitalising of worship with the Wild Goose Resource Group

The Iona Community was founded in Glasgow in 1938 by George MacLeod, minister, visionary and prophetic witness for peace, in the context of the poverty and despair of the Depression. Its original task of rebuilding the monastic ruins of Iona Abbey became a sign of hopeful rebuilding of community in Scotland and beyond. Today, it consists of about 280 Members, mostly in Britain, and 1500 Associate Members, with 1400 Friends worldwide. Together and apart, the community 'follows the light it has, and prays for more light'.

For information on the Iona Community contact:
The Iona Community, Fourth Floor, Savoy House,
140 Sauchiehall Street, Glasgow G2 3DH, UK.
Phone: 0141 332 6343
e-mail: admin@iona.org.uk; web: www.iona.org.uk

For enquiries about visiting Iona, please contact:
Iona Abbey, Isle of Iona, Argyll PA76 6SN, UK.
Phone: 01681 700404

For books, CDs & digital downloads published by Wild Goose Publications: www.ionabooks.com